AF869900

YEARNING TO BREATHE FREE

SEEKING ASYLUM IN AUSTRALIA

YEARNING TO BREATHE FREE

SEEKING ASYLUM IN AUSTRALIA

Give me your tired, your poor,
Your huddled masses yearning to breathe free.

Editors
Dean Lusher
Nick Haslam

Foreword by
Professor Glyn Davis

THE FEDERATION PRESS
2007

Published in Sydney by:

The Federation Press
PO Box 45, Annandale, NSW, 2038
71 John St, Leichhardt, NSW, 2040
Ph (02) 9552 2200 Fax (02) 9552 1681
E-mail: info@federationpress.com.au
Website: http://www.federationpress.com.au

National Library of Australia
Cataloguing-in-Publication entry

Yearning to breathe free: seeking asylum in Australia.

Bibliography.
Includes index.
ISBN 978 186287 656 9 (pbk).

1. Asylum, Right of – Australia – Government policy. 2. Asylum, Right of – Australia – History. 3. Asylum, Right of – Australia – Psychological aspects. 4. Human rights. I. Lusher, Dean. II. Haslam, Nick.

342.083

The verse on the title page is taken from *The New Colossus*, Emma Lazarus 1849-1887.

© The Federation Press

This publication is copyright. Other than for the purposes of and subject to the conditions prescribed under the Copyright Act, no part of it may in any form or by any means (electronic, mechanical, microcopying, photocopying, recording or otherwise) be reproduced, stored in a retrieval system or transmitted without prior written permission. Enquiries should be addressed to the publishers.

Text printed on
100% recycled paper

Typeset by The Federation Press, Leichhardt, NSW.
Printed by Ligare Pty Ltd, Riverwood, NSW.

Foreword

Australia's treatment of asylum seekers has been a contentious political issue for the past decade. Yet much analysis has focused on specific aspects of asylum seeker issues, without placing contemporary attitudes in a wider context.

The editors of this book, Dr Dean Lusher and Dr Nick Haslam, have set out to provide a comprehensive examination of the policies and their consequences for people seeking asylum in Australia. Dean Lusher and Nick Haslam are members of the University of Melbourne Psychology Department – Dean as a postdoctoral fellow in psychology with a long-standing involvement with asylum seeker issues as Coordinator of Researchers for Asylum Seekers (RAS), and Nick an Associate Professor in psychology who is a director of RAS. Together they have invited an eminent group of contributors to address these issues from a range of perspectives.

Yearning to Breathe Free has unusual breadth, representing academic, political, journalist and activist voices to similar degrees. Academic contributors come from a wide variety of disciplinary backgrounds, including psychology, social work, psychiatry, history, linguistics, and public health. Political contributors have backgrounds in three parties – Liberal, Labor and Democrats, each with a distinct policy about asylum seekers.

This work demonstrates the richness of thinking and analysis that can result from an exchange between academics, politicians, the media and other communities. With opinions based on scholarly analysis, the perspective of each contributor enriches the others.

Analysis begins with a historical background, laying out factual information about the international problem of refugees and asylum seekers, and detailing current Australian policy. While many readers would be aware of the Vietnamese 'boat people' of the 1970s, they may be surprised to learn that West Papuans sought refuge in Australia as early as the 1960s. Differences in political responses over time are discussed.

Social workers recount details of their research on the impact of deprivation on asylum seekers' physical and emotional wellbeing. Evidence is examined on both a psychological and neurological basis.

Recent policies and events are reviewed – the *Tampa* affair, SIEV-X, the 'Pacific Solution'; public reaction to each is analysed, the role of fear and its political manipulations discussed. Media experts and linguists engage in a systematic examination of how asylum seekers and refugees have been presented in the media and the consequent impact on public reaction. Social psychologists bring their expertise to bear in the study of prejudice, exploring public opinion of asylum seekers, considering the determinants of exclusionary responses to asylum seekers and discussing the social conditions that promote prejudice.

First-person stories from two asylum seekers are particularly moving, highlighting both the diversity of experience and the common difficulties faced. Volunteers recount the physical and mental health problems experienced by asylum seekers, while a refugee health researcher discusses ways in which social programs can assist successful settlement in Australia. Research is presented on the processes through which asylum seekers make sense of their experiences in Australia to find meaning in their encounters with our people and government, and develop a sense of connectedness to Australian society.

Finally, the book looks at changes to the workings of the Immigration Department in dealing with asylum seekers post-Palmer Report. There is an examination of the future of asylum seeker-related policies and practical and moral issues associated with the current policy regime. An eminent lawyer argues the case for the overhaul of current practices.

The University of Melbourne is pleased to support a work that explores difficult questions about our national response to the movement of people. A fundamental role for any University is to promote inquiry and open debate based on evidence and reason.

Yearning to Breathe Free exemplifies 'Knowledge Transfer' – the dynamic exchange of knowledge between researchers and the broader community, and the partnerships that result from such interaction. Knowledge transfer involves the development, exchange and application of knowledge and expertise for mutual benefit.

The University is proud that many of the contributors are Melbourne academics from a wide range of disciplines. Pieces from our linguists, social workers, psychologists and historians all add to the whole. Readers of *Yearning to Breathe Free* will come away with a more complete understanding of a complex issue and indeed of contemporary Australian society. For the character of a people is perhaps most comprehensively revealed – for better or worse – in how they tackle the most difficult and contentious issues. *Yearning to Breathe Free* is an important contribution to a vital process of self-examination.

Professor Glyn Davis
Vice-Chancellor
University of Melbourne

Contents

Contributors

Phillip Adams

Phillip Adams AO: writer, broadcaster, film-maker. Co-founder of 'A Just Australia', an organisation created to fight for the rights of the refugees the Australia government was putting behind the razor wire. Adams received the HREOC Human Rights Medal for 2006 for social justice activism stretching back to the 1960s.

Lyn Allison

Lyn Allison is a Senator for Victoria, elected in 1996 and now leader of the Australian Democrats. She tours the Maribyrnong Detention Centre regularly and was the first to raise the issue of detention of trafficked women. Lyn chaired the Senate inquiry into mental health, examining the plight of asylum seekers, taking the committee to Baxter at the height of the Cornelia Rau scandal. She and her Democrats colleagues vigorously opposed mandatory detention and 'Pacific Solution' legislation.

Patricia Austin

Patricia Austin is head of the psychology department at St Vincent's Hospital, conjoint lecturer UNSW, and senior clinical psychologist at Sacred Heart Palliative Care where she works with the bereaved and conducts research in palliative care. She also worked extensively in HIV/AIDS, and received a World AIDS Day Project Outstanding Contribution Award in 1998. Her interest in asylum seekers led to her investigation of the Immigration Detention Commissions of Inquiry.

Nikola Balvin

Nikola Balvin is a Doctorate candidate in psychology at the University of Melbourne. She has been a committee member of Researchers for Asylum Seekers since 2005. Her other research interests include attitudes towards Indigenous Australians and conflict resolution. Nikola's family came to Australia via the 'offshore' refugee program and her experience of integrating into the Australian society was very positive. She wishes this could be the case for all refugees.

Christopher Benjamin

Christopher Benjamin (BA, Hons) is completing a clinical neuropsychology Masters and research PhD at The University of Melbourne in Victoria. His research interests centre on the brain regions involved in complex thought, and his doctoral research, completed with the support of Monash Medical Centre (Australia), is examining the neurological basis of memory for space and time. He has also been involved with research in developmental neuropsychology and executive function.

Di Bretherton

Di Bretherton was the founding Director of the International Conflict Resolution Centre at the Department of Psychology at the University of Melbourne and is now an Honorary Professor at the Australian Centre for Peace and Conflict at the University of Queensland. On Australia Day 2007 she was made a Member of the Order of Australia for service to psychology and scholarship in the area of peace, mediation and conflict resolution.

Linda Briskman

Professor Linda Briskman holds the Dr Haruhisa Handa Chair of Human Rights Education at Curtin University. She conducts research and publishes extensively on human rights issues including Indigenous child and family policies and refugee rights. She actively opposes the policies of mandatory detention of asylum seekers through the People's Inquiry into Detention. Her most recent book, *Social Work with Indigenous Communities*, was published by The Federation Press in 2007.

Julian Burnside

Julian Burnside is a barrister specialising in commercial litigation and human rights. He acted for the Ok Tedi natives against BHP, for Alan Bond in fraud trials, for Rose Porteous in numerous actions against Gina Rinehart, and for the Maritime Union of Australia in the 1998 waterfront dispute against Patrick Stevedores. He was the Senior Counsel assisting the Australian Broadcasting Authority in the 'Cash for Comment' inquiry and was senior counsel for Liberty Victoria in the Tampa litigation. He is President of Liberty Victoria.

Christine Canty

Christine Canty (BBScHons, MAPS) is a Clinical Neuropsychologist, currently completing her PhD at the University of Melbourne. Her doctoral research is in the area of attention and cognitive control. Christine has a keen interest in the treatment of asylum seekers and refugees, and is currently secretary of the Researchers for Asylum Seekers group.

Michael Clyne

Michael Clyne, AM, PhD (Monash), Hon Dr Phil (Munich), FASSA, FAHA, is honorary Professorial Fellow, School of Languages and Linguistics, University of Melbourne and Emeritus Professor of Monash University, having held professorial appointments in Linguistics at both universities. His main fields of research are multilingualism, Australian and European sociolinguistics, inter-cultural communication and second language acquisition. It is in these fields that most of his 28 books and over 300 articles have appeared.

Pamela Curr

Pamela Curr has worked as Campaign Coordinator at the Asylum Seeker Resource Centre in Melbourne since 2004. This is the largest community agency providing advocacy and services to refugees and asylum seekers in Australia. Pamela previously coordinated the FairWear Campaign which worked for justice for outworkers in the clothing industry. She had an early career in nursing and midwifery before undertaking Welfare Studies and then a Bachelor of Arts – community development stream.

Malcolm Fraser

Rt Hon Malcolm Fraser AC CH was Prime Minister of Australia from 1975 to 1983. His humanitarian work includes prominent roles with the United Nations, the Commonwealth, CARE Australia and CARE International. His work has been recognised by numerous awards and honorary doctorates, including the 2000 Australian Human Rights Medal from the Human Rights and Equal Opportunity Commission. His book *Common Ground – Issues that should bind and not divide us* was published in 2002.

Chris Goddard

Professor Chris Goddard is Director of the National Research Centre for the Prevention of Child Abuse, a joint initiative between Monash University and the Australian Childhood Foundation. He has published extensively on child abuse, child protection and children's rights both in refereed journals and in the broader media. His latest book, with Dr Neerosh Mudaly, is *The Truth is Longer than a Lie: Children's experiences of abuse and professional interventions* (2006).

Michael Gordon

Michael Gordon is a senior editor at *The Age*. His books include the Paul Keating biography, *A Question of Leadership* (1993), later updated as *A True Believer* (1996); *Reconciliation, A Journey* (2001) and *Freeing Ali* (2005). He was the founding editor of *Backdoor Surfer Magazine* and is a former New York correspondent of *The Herald*, political editor of *The Australian* and national editor of *The Age*.

Nick Haslam

Nick Haslam is associate professor of psychology at the University of Melbourne, and Director of the Researchers for Asylum Seekers group. A social and clinical psychologist, he has published widely on prejudice, stereotyping, dehumanisation and refugee mental health, and has authored or edited three previous books.

Ida Kaplan

Dr Kaplan is Direct Services Manager at the Victorian Foundation for Survivors of Torture (VFST). In that role she oversees client services and is involved in the development of appropriate service models and policy relating to the mental and social health and wellbeing of refugees. She conducts research on psychosocial factors that promote mental health and well-being in adolescent refugees and has had extensive local and international experience training professionals in appropriate interventions for survivors of torture and trauma.

Carmen Lawrence

After training as a research psychologist and lecturing in a number of Australian universities, Dr Lawrence entered politics in 1986, serving at both State and Federal levels for 21 years. She was at various times WA Minister for Education and Aboriginal affairs, Premier and Treasurer and Federal Minister for Health and Human Services. She has held various portfolios in opposition and was elected national President of the Labor Party in 2004.

Dean Lusher

Dean Lusher is a Research Fellow in the Department of Psychology at the University of Melbourne and Coordinator of the Researchers for Asylum Seekers group. His research interests include a social network approach to social and justice issues, including gender, refugees and asylum seekers, violence and inter-group conflict.

David Manne

David Manne is a lawyer and migration agent and Co-ordinator of the Refugee & Immigration Legal Centre, the largest provider of free legal assistance to disadvantaged migrants, asylum seekers and refugees in Australia. He sits on the Boards of the Refugee Council of Australia and the Victorian Foundation for the Survivors of Torture Ethics Committee, and is a regular and prominent contributor to the public debate on Australia's refugee and immigration laws and policies

Peter Mares

Peter Mares is a journalist and broadcaster with a long-standing interest in issues of human movement and human rights. He is an adjunct researcher at the Institute for Social Research at Swinburne University of Technology and presents *The National Interest* on ABC Radio National. Peter is the author of *Borderline* (2002) a critical evaluation of Australia's treatment of refugees and asylum seekers and numerous articles and book chapters on migration related issues.

Stuart Macintyre

Stuart Macintyre is the Ernest Scott Professor of History at the University of Melbourne. He has written extensively on aspects of Australian history, and is currently the president of the Academy of the Social Sciences in Australia.

Grant Mitchell

Grant Mitchell began working with asylum seekers in 1993 at the Swedish Migration Board and completed a Master of Social Anthropology in International Migration from Stockholm University in 1998. Since 2000, Grant has managed the Hotham Mission Asylum Seeker Project in Melbourne, Australia's largest housing agency for asylum seekers. The agency won the Human Rights Award for Community (HREOC) in 2002 for its work with detainees with physical or mental illness. Grant is a Board member of the Refugee Council of Australia.

Amy Nethery

Amy Nethery is a PhD candidate in the School for International and Political Studies at Deakin University. She is conducting research into the social and political function of immigration detention in Australian society.

Klaus Neumann

Klaus Neumann is a research professor in the Institute for Social Research, Swinburne University of Technology. He is a historian who has written extensively about Australian, New Zealand, Pacific Island and German histories and cultures. He is the author of five books, including the award-winning *Refuge Australia: Australia's Humanitarian Record* (2004).

Sir Gustav Nossal

Sir Gustav Nossal, one of the world's leading medical scientists, was Director of the Walter and Eliza Hall Institute of Medical Research from 1965 to 1996 and Professor of Medical Biology at the University of Melbourne. He has received numerous scientific and general awards, including Australian of the Year 2000, and continues to work on global health with the Bill and Melinda Gates Foundation and the World Health Organization.

Anne Pedersen

Anne Pedersen is an applied social psychologist at Murdoch University, Western Australia. Her research interests involve prejudice against asylum seekers and refugees, Indigenous Australians, and Muslim Australians. On a personal level, she has worked with asylum seekers and asylum seeker issues since 2002, and has spent more time in Perth Detention Centre than she would care to remember.

Winsome Roberts

Dr Winsome Roberts is a lecturer at the University of Melbourne, where she teaches critical social policy. She is co-author of *Australians and Globalisation* (2001) and *Australian Citizenship* (2004) and co-editor of *The Oxford Companion to Australian Politics* (2007).

Chelsea Piper Rodd

Chelsea Piper Rodd holds degrees in History and Australian Studies and a graduate diploma in Education. This chapter is the product of research undertaken as part of a recently completed Masters thesis on Australia's response to refugees during the Fraser and Howard years. Chelsea currently teaches in the School of Social and Political Inquiry at Monash University and continues to explore her research interests in Australian nationalism and nation-states' denial of people's humanity.

Angela Romano

Dr Angela Romano is a Senior Lecturer and Postgraduate Coordinator in Journalism at the Queensland University of Technology. Angela produced and edited a three-part documentary-style series about asylum seekers and refugees, which won a United Nations Association of Australia 'Media Peace Award' for Best Radio programming in 2005. Angela conducts research on a wide range of issues relating to journalism, including media coverage of refugees and asylum seekers.

Derrick Silove

Derrick Silove, MD, FRANZCP, MB ChB is a Professor of Psychiatry at the Centre for Population Mental Health Research, University of NSW and Director of the Psychiatry Research and Teaching Unit at Liverpool Hospital. He is a Visiting Professor at the Karolinska Institute, Sweden and has worked as a collaborator in initiatives with the UNHCR, the Harvard Program in Refugee Trauma, the World Federation for Mental Health, the International Society for Traumatic Stress Studies, and the World Bank.

Zachary Steel

Zachary Steel is a clinical psychologist and senior lecturer at the Centre for Population Mental Health Research at Liverpool Hospital and the School of Psychiatry, University of NSW. He has worked as a clinician and researcher with refugee and asylum seeker populations since 1992 documenting the psychological impact of government policies of deterrence on asylum seekers, the long-term effects of trauma on refugees, and transcultural psychiatric epidemiology.

Lindsay Tanner

Lindsay Tanner, Shadow Minister for Finance, has represented the seat of Melbourne in the House of Representatives since March 1993. His previous portfolios include Finance, Consumer Affairs, Transport, Communications and Community Relationships. Before entering the Federal Parliament, Lindsay was State Secretary of the Federated Clerks Union (Victorian Branch). He has published widely on social, labour, transport and economic issues. His most recent book is *Crowded Lives* (2003), and has also published *Open Australia* (1999), *The Politics of Pollution* (1978) and *The Last Battle* (1996).

Erin Taylor

Erin Taylor is currently a PhD Candidate at the School of Historical Studies, University of Melbourne, where she is researching the history of Burmese migration to Australia. Erin is also the Knowledge Transfer Research Coordinator for Researchers for Asylum Seekers (RAS). Through this role she is jointly responsible for assisting RAS in its goal of forging stronger connections between refugee and asylum seeker advocacy, service provision and research groups.

Margaret Theologou

Margaret Theologou, BA, BSW, is a social worker who has worked in child protection and immigrant welfare organisations. She is undertaking postgraduate research investigating the impact of Bridging Visas on families and community agencies at the School of Social Work, The University of Melbourne. She has participated in community-based projects advocating for the protection of the human rights of children and people seeking asylum.

Susannah Tipping

Susannah Tipping is a registered Psychologist completing a MPsych (Clinical)/PhD at the University of Melbourne. Susannah has worked for the Victorian Foundation for Survivors of Torture Inc as a Counsellor/Advocate and is currently working part-time at the Australian Centre for Posttraumatic Health as a Research Fellow on the Promoting Recovery Study. She was also a member of the organising committee for the 2006 Australian Sudanese Youth Conference.

Joanne Tropea

Joanne Tropea has a clinical and research background in health and is currently working at the Royal Melbourne Hospital. She has been a committee member of Researchers for Asylum Seekers since early 2005 and is committed to working towards better health and social outcomes for asylum seekers and other minority groups in Australia.

Arnold Zable

Arnold Zable is a writer, educator, and human rights advocate. His books include *Jewels and Ashes* (1991), *The Fig Tree* (2002), *Café Scheherazade* (2001) and, most recently, *Scraps of Heaven* (2004), a novel set in the immigrant community of post-war Carlton. He has written extensively about the plight of refugees and been involved in campaigns on their behalf. He is a co-writer of the play *Kan Yama Kan,* in which asylum seekers tell their stories, president of Melbourne International PEN, and has a doctorate in the School of Creative Arts, Melbourne University.

Acknowledgments

Yearning to Breathe Free is an initiative of the Researchers for Asylum Seekers (RAS) group at the University of Melbourne. Officially affiliated with the School of Behavioural Science, RAS is a voluntary group of staff and students concerned with current policies towards people seeking asylum in Australia (<www.ras.unimelb.edu.au>). This book would not have been possible without the committed and generous work of RAS members. We wish to thank especially Jackie Bornstein for her role in laying the foundations for RAS and this book, Dr Anina Rich and Dr Mark Williams for their dedicated efforts, and Professor Jason Mattingley, who helped to establish RAS. The RAS Committee and Advisory Board have been wonderfully supportive, as has Professor Glyn Davis, University of Melbourne Vice-Chancellor. Finally, we thank Professor Henry Jackson who has been an unflinching and generous supporter of RAS in its attempts to improve the situation of asylum seekers.

Dean Lusher
Nick Haslam

September 2007

Introduction

Yearning to Breathe Free is an account of Australian government policies towards asylum seekers and their consequences. In putting this book together we were aware that emotions run high, both for those who support asylum seekers and for those who do not. Although such strong feelings can never be fully erased, we aimed to provide an objective, thoughtful and multi-faceted analysis of Australia's response to people seeking its protection. In doing so, we sought to present an alternative perspective on asylum seekers, making clear the disparity between Australia's policies and practices and those in many other parts of the world. Although Australia is very generous in its treatment of some who seek asylum here, our treatment of others has been extremely destructive. In examining these issues, the book is organised into six sections, which explore the predicament of asylum seekers from a variety of angles: historical, political, psychological and humanitarian. The sections are introduced by prominent Australians, who offer their personal perspectives on Australia's asylum seeker policies and their aftermath.

Part I of the book, *Historical Perspective and Background*, begins with Dean Lusher, Nikola Balvin, Joanne Tropea and Amy Nethery, who detail Australia's current policies towards asylum seekers. They describe Australia's two-tiered system for dealing with asylum seekers, in which some are officially recognised as 'refugees' on humanitarian grounds and allowed to resettle here permanently, but others are detained and denied basic security and services while they await decisions on their refugee status. Lusher and colleagues demonstrate how the treatment of asylum seekers in this second tier – the primary focus of the book – demonstrating how the second tier is confusing in its application and in breach of our international obligations. Klaus Neumann follows with a historical analysis of Australia's treatment of asylum seekers, particularly as it relates to West Papuans coming to Australia. Chelsea Piper Rodd adds to this historical dimension, comparing the treatment of asylum seekers at the time of the 1977 and 2001 Australian Federal elections.

In Part II, *Coming to Australia*, we explore issues facing asylum seekers on their journey to Australia. It is here that a detailed analysis of some of the most infamous components and consequences of Australia's policies is presented. Peter Mares explores the case of the *Tampa* in compelling detail. Arnold Zable gives a moving account of Amal Basry, who survived the SIEV-X sinking on her way to Australia by boat, and of other asylum seekers who have been touched by the tragedy. To conclude the section, Michael Gordon, one of the few journalists to visit Nauru, gives an account of the 'Pacific Solution' and the 'outsourcing' of our problem.

The *Treatment of Arrived Asylum Seekers* is examined in Part III. Linda Briskman and Chris Goddard demonstrate the determination of some Australians to find out more about the traumatising effects of detention on asylum seekers. Patricia Austin, Derrick Silove and Zachary Steel review the scientific evidence of adverse mental health consequences of immigration detention, while Christine Canty and Christopher Benjamin examine the neurological consequences of detention. Finally, Margaret Theologou and Winsome Roberts demonstrate the isolation and invisibility that engulfs people who have been granted protection through the bridging visa system, a system with extremely limited entitlements.

Part IV is concerned with *Resettlement in Australia*, and begins with two asylum seekers' personal stories, written by Erin Taylor. Pamela Curr gives an inspiring insight into the experience of those who find Australia's policies unjust and who have taken practical, personally costly but often transforming steps to assist asylum seekers. Finally, Susannah Tipping, Di Bretherton and Ida Kaplan demonstrate the difficulties, existential challenges and inner resources that refugees encounter in the continuing process of resettlement.

Australian Public Opinion about Asylum Seekers is presented in Part V. Carmen Lawrence examines the distorting effects of fear on the public perception of asylum seekers. Angela Romano analyses media representation of asylum seekers, while Michael Clyne shows how the language we use to describe asylum seekers can promote hostility and exclusion. Finally, Nick Haslam and Anne Pedersen explore the social psychology of prejudice towards asylum seekers and refugees, exploring the underlying dynamics of rejection, anger, neglect and dehumanisation.

Part VI concludes the book with discussions of *The Future of Asylum Seeker Policies*, pointing hopeful directions for positive change. David Manne examines how policy and practice have progressed since the Palmer Report's critical findings on policy implementation by the Immigration Department. Grant Mitchell outlines alternative responses that Australia could embrace towards asylum seekers, detailing how some other countries deal differently with the same issues. In a concluding chapter, Julian Burnside reviews the failings of recent policies and outlines a way forward that enables Australia to meet its international obligations while maintaining the integrity of its borders.

Ultimately, this book is for two groups of people. In the first instance, the book pays tribute to those people who have come to Australia seeking our protection, who have suffered further at the hands of our current asylum seeker policies, but who nonetheless push on to tell their stories, work for change, and strive to contribute as much as they can to Australian society. They inspire us with courage and hope. This book is also for those Australians who know relatively little about Australia's asylum seeker policies, or whose knowledge is limited to the official government perspective. We present here a different way of looking at the asylum seeker issue – one that is not tied to party politics but instead to a thorough and humane analysis of the facts of the matter.

Dean Lusher
Nick Haslam

September 2007

PART I

Historical perspectives and background

STUART MACINTYRE

Part I Introduction

Australia has a long history of accepting refugees, and also of turning them away. The ships that docked during the gold rush of the 1850s brought newcomers from all parts of the world. Some headed for the Victorian diggings but others clustered in Melbourne and a journalist wrote in 1857 that in the city streets 'you saw men who had fought in the streets of Paris, political refugees from Frankfort, Berlin, Vienna and Buda Pesth, and Carbonari from Italy'. They had fled their homelands following the suppression of popular movements that had briefly won power in many European countries in 1848, but were then put down brutally.

Fifty years later Australia provided a sanctuary for some of the men and women fleeing persecution in Russia, either because of their Jewish identity (the Tsarist regime whipped anti-Semitic pogroms to divert popular discontent), their nationality (the Russian empire extended over central Europe) or their radical politics. The failed revolution of 1905 swelled the numbers who came here.

These were refugees whose circumstances were understood sufficiently for the term to be used, but it had no formal meaning or consequences for their acceptance. Until the First World War the entry of Europeans to Australia was almost unrestricted so there was no reason to look into the motives of those who came to escape persecution. The United Kingdom had a tradition of offering sanctuary to liberal nationalists and radical internationalists from the European mainland, and sometimes defended the practice against criticism from illiberal foreign governments, but the government also reserved discretion to decide who would be given shelter.

International agreements to recognise refugees and codify practices for their resettlement arose only in the 20th century, after the fascist regimes elevated racial purity and political conformity into a binding ideology. Australia participated in the international scheme to provide refuge to Jewish victims of Nazi Germany in the late 1930s, albeit reluctantly and with limits on numbers.

Australia was also a participant in the negotiations worked out to deal with the much greater refugee problem created by the Second World War and postwar settlement. It was a signatory to the constitution of the International Refugee Organization in 1947, and took in 170,000 'Displaced Persons' from central and eastern Europe. It was also one of the first signatories of the Convention Relating to the Status of Refugees formulated by United Nations in 1951, and from 1952 to 1961 cooperated with the Office of the United Nations High Commissioner for Refugees to accept 70,000 refugees. As the contributors to Part I make clear, this was by no means a purely humanitarian program. The Australian government chose some refugees and rejected others on grounds of race or politics.

These were 'offshore' refugees, and that allowed the government to exercise choice. As Klaus Neumann explains, Australian refugee policy has always been determined as an aspect of its immigration policy. And while Australia had some experience with 'onshore' refugees – for example, Indonesian nationalists who were brought here when the Netherlands colonial officials retreated to Australia before the Japanese invasion and were understandably reluctant to return to colonial rule after 1945 – its geographical location meant that such 'onshore' refugees were uncommon in the postwar years.

Two of the chapters in this section explore the response to 'onshore' refugees as they began to appear and seek asylum. Klaus Neumann relates the refusal of residence permits to eight men from West Papua who landed on an island in the Torres Strait. He explains how the government's refusal to grant them residence permits was influenced by foreign policy considerations, especially the concern not to antagonise Indonesia, and facilitated by Australia's refusal to sign the 1967 Protocol to the 1951 Convention (removing the original restrictions to persecution that began before that year) precisely because it did not want to have to deal with West Papuan refugees.

Chelsea Piper Rodd reminds us of the 1977 controversy surrounding the arrival in Darwin of a boat carrying Vietnamese refugees, the first of many subsequent 'boat people'. Press coverage introduced many of the themes that would become familiar, denouncing the refugees as alien criminals and 'queuejumpers', except that the political division over the issue was strikingly different from the present alignment. Gough Whitlam as the Labor leader and Bob Hawke as head of the ACTU, led opposition, while a Coalition government defended the legitimacy of the refugees.

Both these chapters explore the continuities and discontinuities that link these early episodes to *Tampa* and the 'Pacific Solution', while Dean Lusher and his colleagues provide a succinct account of how Australia devised the policies that now operate. All three of these chapters are alert to the issues that arise from our treatment of refugees. All of them employ a historical perspective that makes clear the present procedures are more than a lapse from more generous previous standards. They resist the simplifications that are sometimes generated by an understandable indignation over the Howard government's cynical and inhumane treatment of the refugees. And for precisely that reason their accounts have both intellectual and moral force.

1

DEAN LUSHER • NIKOLA BALVIN •
AMY NETHERY • JOANNE TROPEA

Australia's response to asylum seekers

Introduction

Australia's asylum seeker policies are not widely understood. They are complex, and have changed many times, particularly since 2001. This chapter outlines Australia's policies towards asylum seekers and refugees. First, it highlights the fundamental tenets of the Refugee Convention, which forms the basis of Australia's obligations to refugees. It then explains the different categories of intake, and the different procedures asylum seekers and refugees encounter to start a new life in Australia. We demonstrate that Australia's policies are based on a distinction between two groups of people needing protection: 'offshore' refugees and 'onshore' asylum seekers. The different reception of these two groups by the Australian government could not be greater. The result is a system of two classes of refugees – a distinction that contravenes our international obligations.

The Refugee Convention

The 1948 Universal Declaration of Human Rights came about as a result of the events of World War II and the vast numbers of refugees throughout Europe that it created. Article 14(1) of the Universal Declaration states that 'everyone has the right to seek and to enjoy in other countries asylum from persecution'.[1] The 1951 United Nations Convention Relating to the Status of Refugees and the 1967 United Nations Protocol Relating to the Status of Refugees (usually referred to together as the Refugee Convention) form the international framework outlining the responsibility of nations towards refugees. Article 1A(2) of the Refugee Convention defines a refugee as any person who:

> owing to well-founded fear of being persecuted for reasons of race, religion, nationality, membership of a particular social group or political opinion, is outside the country of his nationality and is unable or, owing to such fear, is unwilling to avail himself of the protection of that country; or who, not having a nationality and being outside the country of his former fear, is unwilling to return to it.[2]

This definition forms the basic criterion, used by the United Nations High Commission for Refugees (UNHCR) and individual nations, for assessing who is a refugee and thus eligible for protection in another country. Some States apply additional criteria, often based on other international treaties, such as persecution based on gender or sexuality.

There are two important articles of the Refugee Convention. The first is the principle of non-refoulement, indicating that a nation must not return a refugee to a place where he or she may face further persecution. This principle means that not only does Australia have an obligation to provide protection to refugees who arrive on its shores, but those refugees are the only ones who Australia has an obligation to protect. Second is the principle that asylum seekers or refugees must not be punished or discriminated against for the way in which they have entered the country in which they wish to seek asylum. Article 31(1) states:

> The Contracting States shall not impose penalties, on account of their illegal entry or presence, on refugees who, coming directly from a territory where their life or freedom was threatened in the sense of article 1, enter or are present in their territory without authorisation, provided they present themselves without delay to the authorities and show good cause for their illegal entry or presence.[3]

Australia was one of the first signatories to the Refugee Convention, ratifying in 1954. This means that it is morally, and to a certain extent legally, obliged to respond to refugees in accordance with the Refugee Convention.

'Offshore' refugees

The vast majority of refugees who have been resettled in Australia fit under the category of 'offshore' refugees, or 'offshore' humanitarian entrants. These are people who have fled persecution and spent time in refugee camps run by the UNHCR, who process claims for asylum and grant refugee status to people using the Refugee Convention criteria. The government also offers resettlement to some people who do not meet the definition of refugee outlined in the Refugee Convention, but nevertheless have suffered discrimination amounting to gross violation of human rights, and who have strong support from an Australian citizen or community group. This program is called the Special Humanitarian Program (SHP). Australia has an annual refugee quota of around 13,000 a year. This intake is made up of three categories. The first two are 'offshore' applications: refugees, who make up 6000 of the total, and the SHP. The third category is 'onshore' asylum seekers, discussed more fully below.

'Offshore' refugees are assisted by the Australian government in all aspects of their resettlement. They are given permanent residence visas, with the opportunity to apply for citizenship after two years. They are supported with initial information and orientation assistance, accommodation support, household formation support, early health assessment and intervention, adult migrant English programs, translating and interpreting services, and migrant community services. They also have access to all services available to the Australian community, including Medicare, income support payments, and education.

'Onshore' asylum seekers

'Onshore' asylum seekers are people who make their own way to Australia and seek asylum once they arrive. This group is divided into those who arrive with a valid entry visa, and those who do not. Although the Refugee Convention clearly states in Article 31(1) that refugees should not be discriminated against based on their method of entry to a country, Australia's policy with regards to unauthorised arrivals is vastly different from its policy towards 'offshore' refugees. Generally speaking, those people who arrive in Australia with a valid entry visa (eg, student or tourist visa) and apply for asylum within 45 days after arrival can live in the community on a bridging visa while their applications for protection are processed. They are permitted to work and access public medical services while their application is before the Department of Immigration and the Refugee Review Tribunal, but at no time are they permitted Centrelink payments and education is restricted. Applying after the 45-day mark however results in the immediate loss of work rights and Medicare and little or no entitlement to services.

People who enter Australia without a valid entry visa have made an 'unauthorised' entry into Australia. This group is sometimes referred to as 'illegals', an incorrect term because they have not broken any domestic or international law. This group enters Australia either by boat or by plane. Australia has a comprehensive system of immigration checks at domestic and international airports, as well as heavy fines for carriers, to pick up those who attempt to enter Australia by plane without a valid entry visa. As a result, very few asylum seekers successfully make it to Australia by plane. The only other way to enter Australia without a valid entry visa is by boat, and it is towards this category of asylum seekers that many of Australia's radical and controversial asylum seeker policies are directed. These policies include mandatory detention, Temporary Protection Visas, the Pacific Strategy and excision of Australia's own territory from the Migration Zone, and Operation Relex (ie, sending boats back). Before outlining here the first three, it is worth noting that the number of asylum seekers arriving by boat in Australia is quite small. 'Unauthorised' boat arrivals in Australia have varied over the past decade, and at its peak from 1999 to 2001, numbers were about 4000 people per year, with most people from Afghanistan and Iraq. Before this time, the average was about 2000 people per year. There were no arrivals from July 2002 to June 2003, and July 2004 to June 2005, and fewer than 100 for 2005-2006. The peak figure is about one-third of the number of people Australia takes via the UN program, and 3% of the 130,000 to 140,000 migrants planned for Australia's immigration program for 2005-2006.[4]

Mandatory detention

In 1989, Cambodian asylum seekers arriving in Australia by boat were the first to be held in immigration detention centres. Then in

1992, the policy of mandatory detention was introduced, attracting bipartisan support and maintenance by successive governments.[5] This policy states that all people who arrive by boat without a valid entry visa must be detained in immigration detention centres until they are either granted permission to stay in Australia, or are removed from the country. Exceptions to this rule include the elderly, the sick, and, since 2005, children under the age of 18. Australia was the first country to introduce a policy of mandatory detention, and remains the only country in which the length of time spent in detention is indefinite.

According to the UNHCR Guidelines on Detention, the use of detention against asylum seekers is 'inherently undesirable'.[6] Yet the UNHCR guidelines do allow provision for countries to subject asylum seekers to health, identity and security checks, which it acknowledges may require some form of detention. Australia's policy of mandatory detention, however, extends beyond these UNHCR permitted checks to include the application process itself. Australia is the only country to do this, and as a result asylum seekers can remain in detention indefinitely. As of 30 June 2005, over 100 of asylum seekers in detention at that time had been there for over three years.[7]

The Australian government states that the policy of mandatory detention has five main aims. In reality, these aims are either not met or their success is questionable. First, the policy of mandatory detention aims to protect the community from the dangers posed by unlawful arrivals. As ASIO (The Australian Security Intelligence Organisation) reported to the Parliament in 2002, not one of the 6000 unauthorised arrivals they screened in the previous five years was deemed to be a security risk.[8] Secondly, mandatory detention aims to prevent unlawful arrivals disappearing into the community, yet there is little evidence to support the idea that asylum seekers would abscond. Thirdly, the policy aims to facilitate the speedy processing of asylum claims. However, administrative processes are slowed down and made more difficult by detaining asylum seekers in remote places like Port Augusta (Baxter), Port Hedland, or Christmas Island, due to a lack of access of legal support and a general lack of access to the asylum seekers. Fourthly, the policy aims to ensure failed asylum seekers are available for removal. Is it necessary to detain all asylum seekers for the whole length of their application process, so the few who are deported are available? Finally, the policy aims to deter potential unlawful migrants from coming to Australia. There is no evidence to argue that the policy has succeeded in deterring asylum seekers. The policy of mandatory detention has been in place since 1992, after which many more asylum seekers have come to Australia by boat than before the policy was introduced.

Aside from not meeting these explicit objectives, there are other objections to the policy of mandatory detention. Building, maintaining and running detention facilities is enormously costly. For instance, the construction of the Christmas Island detention centre, opening in 2007, is expected to reach $400 million. More fundamentally, the long-term detention of asylum seekers, many of whom have already experienced torture and trauma, is damaging to their mental and physical wellbeing. In May and June 2002, the UN Working Group on Arbitrary Detention was invited by the Australian government to compare Australian detention practices to international standards. The UN Working Group concluded that detention centre conditions were similar to those of prisons, with razor wire fences, permanent supervision, handcuffing of detainees escorted outside the centre, and the escape from detention constituting a criminal offence. They also reported high amounts of self-harm by detained adults and children.[9]

There is much evidence that suicidal behaviours are extraordinarily high among detained asylum seekers,[10] and that there are other severe impacts on mental health through detention. While there are many examples, the case of five-year-old Shayan Badraie, who spent over one year in immigration detention, is a telling illustration of the harm that can be caused by the policy and practice of mandatory detention. Shayan and his parents arrived in Australia by boat and were detained in Woomera and Villawood detention centres. In Woomera, Shayan witnessed 'hunger strikes, fires, riots … and saw an adult detainee slash his chest with a shard of glass and jump from a tree'.[11] While in detention, Shayan had nightmares and woke up during the night crying, he hid under his blanket, wet himself, would not eat and could not sleep. His drawings depicted his environment, as well as his anxiety, portraying himself and his family behind razor wire, with guards holding batons and detainees bleeding from self-harm. Shayan was admitted to the Villawood detention centre medical service 70 times and to Westmead Hospital specialists eight times. He was diagnosed with 'acute and chronic Posttraumatic Stress Disorder as a result of traumatic experiences' in detention.[12] In August 2002, Shayan's family were recognised as refugees and granted Temporary Protection Visas.

In 2005 Australia made changes to its immigration policy, most notably discretionary powers given to the Minister for Immigration to release children and their families into community care. While such changes have provided more humane conditions for refugee children on the Australian mainland, it is unclear whether 'offshore' detention facilities will follow the same protocol. The Christmas Island detention centre, due to be completed in 2007, includes a baby compound with eight cots and playrooms within the military-level security facility.

Temporary Protection Visas

'Unauthorised' arrivals who have been found to be refugees are released from detention on Temporary Protection Visas (TPVs), which are valid for only three years. After 30 months the refugees are eligible to apply for another TPV, but must again demonstrate why they require continued protection in Australia. The TPV was introduced in 1999 with the aim to deter 'unauthorised' arrivals from making their own way to Australia. As such, the conditions of the visa and the services available to people who hold it are limited and restrictive. TPV holders are denied access to settlement services including English language classes, housing assistance and migrant resource centre support schemes. They do have access to Medicare, and may receive 'Special Benefit' payments from Centrelink, but these are much less than those received by refugees with permanent residence visas. In short, TPV holders are 'specifically denied rights and services available to other refugees'.[13] The most distressing aspect is the lack of family reunion rights, as in many cases refugees on TPVs are fathers or sons who have travelled the dangerous journey by boat with the hope of bringing their families to Australia once they have been accepted as refugees. Further, while TPV holders have the right to travel overseas, once they have left the country they are not allowed to return to Australia. In effect, the TPV separates families.[14]

The Pacific Strategy

In 2001 the government introduced the Pacific Strategy – an agreement between Australia and Nauru, whereby all unauthorised asylum seekers who arrive in Australian territory that has been excised from the migration zone will be detained and have their applications for asylum processed in Nauru. Papua New Guinea was part of the 'Pacific Solution' from 2001 to 2004. In 2001 and 2002, the Australian government excised all Australian territory excluding the mainland from its migration zone. This means that unless a boat lands on the mainland, the asylum seekers will be detained and have their applications processed in Nauru – a country that is not a signatory to the Refugee Convention. As part of the agreement, Australia is not obliged to resettle those who are found to be refugees. The Pacific Strategy is problematic. The conditions of detention in Nauru are extremely poor, affecting the wellbeing of asylum seekers. In addition, applications for protection processed in Nauru, although conducted by Australian immigration officials, are outside the jurisdiction of Australia's domestic migration laws. As a result, the refugee recognition rates are much lower than those of mainland Australia. In the fashion of Australia's 'Pacific Solution', Italy recently opened a temporary holding centre on the Italian island of Lampedusa, where asylum seekers are imprisoned before being sent to processing facilities in Libya or released into the Italian community with instructions to leave the country within five days.[15] Australia with its relatively small influx of asylum seekers has led the way in the strictest, harshest and most deterring detention conditions in the industrialised world.

Refugees: an international perspective

To put these policies in context, it is important to understand how Australia shares the burden of responsibility for refugees compared with other countries in the world. Australia is one of ten countries that have annual resettlement quotas, currently around 13,000 per year. Australia is therefore a regular participant in the resettlement of refugees and this is something to be proud of. Yet many countries do not set annual quotas and accommodate much larger numbers of refugees that arrive within their borders. For instance, in 2005 there were over one million refugees hosted by

Pakistan and over 700,000 in Iran.[16] An examination of the asylum applications received by 50 industrialised countries between 2001 and 2005 gives a truer picture of how Australia compares to the rest of the industrialised world.[17] In this period, Australia received 28,940 applications for asylum (excluding persons who arrived offshore and were processed on Manus Island and Nauru).[18] This contrasts with large numbers received by the USA (396,838), the United Kingdom (339,720) and France (298,004) for the same period.[19] Australia receives 1.4 applications per 1000 inhabitants and this on a *per capita* basis ranks Australia 23rd in the industrialised world.[20]

The refugee queue?

Why do people travel directly to Australia to seek asylum, rather than wait to be processed by the UNHCR and arrive as an 'offshore' refugee? In answering this question we need to consider two things: the size of the refugee problem internationally, and the options available to people seeking asylum:

> At the beginning of 2006, the number of people of concern to UNHCR was 20.8 million. They included 8.4 million refugees (40%), 773,500 asylum seekers (4%), 1.6 million returned refugees and IDPs [internally displaced persons] (7%), 6.6 million internally displaced people (32%), 2.4 million stateless people (11%) and 960,400 'others of concern' to UNHCR.[21]

The 8.4 million refugees is an extraordinary number of people. Yet in 2005, only 80,800 people were resettled around the world as refugees.[22] While returning to one's own country is said to be the preference for many refugees, this resettlement to other countries represents less than 1% of the world's refugees. And this is ignoring the other 12.4 million 'people of concern' to the UNHCR. It is inconceivable that all of the remaining 99% of refugees wish to or can go home. Amnesty International Australia suggests that:

> contrary to the popular misconception, legal avenues available to asylum seekers to access protection under the Convention are limited. In some nations … the state has collapsed; there is no possibility of obtaining a passport, let alone a legal visa for entry into Australia. In other nations … it is the state that is the agent of persecution. Approaching the state or foreign embassies for

> travel documents or attempting to leave through official channels is liable to pose a danger to the asylum seeker and possibly their extended family. Even if an asylum seeker can flee their country of origin this does not guarantee safety. Neighbouring countries are not always signatories to the Convention, some states may instigate further persecution, and others are simply unable to provide protection from what the refugee fears. Australia does not have large numbers of foreign posts near major refugee producing regions … those it does have face overwhelming problems of under-staffing, under-resourcing and bribery.[23]

In many places, there is simply no queue to join. Given less than 1% of refugees are resettled annually, and the lack of access for many to this resettlement program anyway, it is little surprise that other means of seeking asylum must be sought for people fleeing persecution.

We know that 'authorised' arrivals to Australia are refugees as defined by the Refugee Convention. In contrast, it is widely assumed that 'unauthorised' arrivals are not genuine refugees. Yet the overwhelming majority of 'onshore' asylum seekers are eventually found to be genuine refugees. The Immigration Department's Annual Report for 2002-2003 states:

> In the three program years from July 1999 to June 2002 some 9160 unauthorised boat arrivals, principally from Afghanistan and Iraq, applied for Protection visas within Australia's migration zone. These applications were considered progressively over the period 1999 to 2003 with final primary decisions being made in early 2003. Of this group, to 30 June 2003 some 8260 were found to require Australia's protection.[24]

This means that, of this group of asylum seekers who have arrived in Australia by boat, over 90% were granted refugee status. Further, some of the remaining asylum seekers of this group were awaiting a review of their decisions, indicating that the percentage could be even higher. Amnesty International Australia also suggests that the strict definition of refugee can fail many people who would also qualify for protection because in other countries the meaning of 'political opinion' and 'social group' are interpreted differently, while others who may not fall within the strict refugee definition 'nevertheless face torture or death on return to their home country'.[25] Finally, regarding the more recent boat arrival of West Papuan asylum seekers in 2006, all 43, or 100%, were granted refugee status.

Conclusion

In signing the Refugee Convention, Australia has made a public commitment to refugees. Yet Australia treats one group of refugees with compassion and concern, and another with suspicion and contempt. This difference in approach contradicts international law and norms maintaining that asylum seekers should not be discriminated against depending on their mode of arrival to the country in which they seek protection. The logic behind the policy, followed through, would be the same as suggesting that hospitals should only treat people who arrive by ambulance, and that they should delay or deliver minimal treatment to anyone who walks in off the street because we cannot be sure that they are genuinely ill. If the overwhelming majority of asylum seekers arriving directly in Australia are awarded refugee status, as adjudged by Australia's own strict standards, then there is virtually no difference between these two groups of people seeking protection other than the way we treat them. Australia needs a single and humane policy for treating people seeking protection. There are other ways for Australia to maintain border protection that do not violate its international obligations to people seeking asylum.

Notes

1 United Nations, Universal Declaration of Human Rights, 1948.

2 Convention relating to the Status of Refugees, 1951.

3 Ibid.

4 Department of Immigration and Citizenship (DIAC), *Fact Sheet 2: Key Facts in Immigration*, 2007.

5 Department of Immigration and Citizenship (DIAC), *Fact Sheet 82: Immigration Detention*, 2007.

6 UNHCR, *UNHCR Revised Guidelines on Applicable Criteria and Standards Relating to the Detention of Asylum Seekers*, 1999.

7 Department of Immigration and Multicultural and Indigenous Affairs (DIMIA), 'Chapter 10, Detaining Unlawful Non-Citizens', *Managing the Border: Immigration Compliance 2004-2005 edition*, 2005.

8 Crock, M, Saul, B, and Dastyari, A, *Future Seekers II: Refugees and Irregular Migration in Australia*, Federation Press, Sydney, 2006.

9 UNHCR, *Report of the Working Group on Arbitrary Detention*, UNHCR, 2002.

10 Dudley, M, 'Contradictory Australian national policies on self-harm and suicide: the case of asylum seekers in mandatory detention', *Australian Psychiatry*, vol 11, 2003, pp S102-S108.

11 Human Rights and Equal Opportunity Commission (HREOC), *A Last Resort: National Inquiry into Children in Immigration Detention*, HREOC, 2004.

12 Ibid.

13 Leach, M and Mansouri, F, *Lives in Limbo: Voices of Refugees Under Temporary Protection*, UNSW Press, Sydney, 2004.

14 Ibid.

15 European United Left/Nordic Green Left (GUE/NGL), *Lampedusa and Mellila: Southern Frontier of Fortress Europe*, Arte Print, Brussels, 2005.

16 UNHCR, *Refugees by Numbers 2006 Edition,* UNHCR, Geneva, 2006.

17 UNHCR, *Asylum Levels and Trends in Industrialized Countries, 2005: Overview of asylum applications lodged in Europe and non-European industrialized countries in 2005*, UNHCR, Geneva, 2006.

18 Ibid.

19 Ibid; UNHCR, *Asylum Levels and Trends in Industrialized Countries, First Quarter, 2006: Comparative overview of asylum applications lodged in 31 European and five non-European countries*, UNHCR, Geneva, 2006; UNHCR, *Asylum Levels and Trends in Industrialized Countries, Second Quarter, 2006: Overview of asylum applications lodged in 31 European and five non-European countries,* UNHCR, Geneva, 2006.

20 UNHCR, above, n 17.

21 UNHCR, above, n 16.

22 Ibid.

23 Amnesty International Australia, *People Smuggling – Fact Sheet,* <http://203.147.147.39/refugees/ref-fact12.html>.

24 Department of Immigration and Multicultural and Indigenous Affairs (DIMIA), *2002-2003 Annual Report,* 2003.

25 Amnesty International Australia, *Australia's Refugee Determination Process – Fact Sheet,* <http://203.147.147.39/refugees/ref-fact06.html>.

2

KLAUS NEUMANN

Been there, done that?

On 16 February 1969 eight men landed on Moa (Banks) Island in the Torres Strait. They were West Papuans who had travelled by raft from a village near Merauke in what was then known as West Irian, the Indonesian part of the island of New Guinea. Merauke is less than 300 kilometres from Moa, but because of unfavourable winds, their journey had lasted more than a month. One of their party had died while they were drifting between the New Guinea mainland and Australia.

There are two written accounts of interviews held with the men in the days after their arrival in Australia. One was compiled by DJ O'Connor, a sub-collector of customs who on 18 February had spoken to the men on behalf of the Department of Immigration, and arranged for their transfer to Thursday Island. His report for the Commonwealth Director of Migration in Brisbane includes a description of their harrowing journey. He also noted that the men were members of the Organisasi Papua Merdeka (OPM, or Free Papua Movement), which had been fighting for independence for the Indonesian-controlled half of New Guinea since 1965.[1] He later added that the men had 'not specifically sought 'Political Asylum'' but when asked if they would return to West Irian they became depressed and said that 'this would mean the end'.[2]

The other account was provided by a Thursday Island resident, Roland ('Rolly') Cantley, who had interviewed the men a day after their arrival. He recorded a first person narrative from Alexander Toembay, the leader of the West Papuans. Toembay spoke of Indonesian persecution. He also shed light on the decision to head for Australia:

> I hope that Australian people give us political protection and allow us to live in peace. But I also hope that people of Australia help us to get independence that was promised in the United Nations for people of West Irian. Then we would like to go back and help make it a good country to live in.[3]

Since 1962, hundreds of West Papuans had crossed the border into Papua and New Guinea to seek Australia's protection,[4] but never before had they sought asylum in Australia itself. In his interview with Cantley, Toembay explained that it was:

> [n]o good crossing the Papuan border because Australian and Papuan patrols have orders to send all refugees back to West Irian and people sent back to West Irian after trying to escape are put in prison.[5]

While the first half of Toembay's reasoning was incorrect – by August 1969, Australia had granted permissive residence permits to 75 West Papuan refugees and their families[6] – there was evidence that some of those sent back had suffered at the hands of the Indonesian army or police.

Five days after the arrival of the eight West Papuans, representatives of the external affairs, external territories and immigration departments conferred in Canberra. The immigration department's representative favoured their removal to the Territory of Papua and New Guinea (TPNG), where their claims for protection could be assessed in line with the procedures in place for West Papuans seeking asylum in the Australian territory. He argued that 'it would be undesirable to encourage future refugees to make for Australia by allowing this group to settle there'.[7]

An external affairs official pointed out that 'if settled in Australia, refugees would be much more accessible to the press whereas it would be possible to isolate them to some extent in TPNG'. His department was mindful of the Prime Minister's policy directive 'that there is to be no trouble with the Indonesians over West Irian',[8] but he did not think that it extended to deporting the men to West Irian (although he did not want to rule out deportation as one possible option).

The Minister for External Territories, Charles Edward ('Ceb') Barnes believed that the eight West Papuans were 'not an External Territories problem'. A representative of his department therefore argued against sending them to TPNG. He said that a forcible removal to TPNG 'could lead to unfavourable comment' in the Port Moresby parliament 'to the effect that they were not good enough to be allowed to live in Australia'. But he, too, thought that their deportation to West Irian was an option, if only because it was guaranteed to please the Indonesian government.[9]

In the end, the arguments of the immigration and external affairs departments and their respective ministers, Billy Snedden and Gordon Freeth, prevailed, and it was decided that the West Papuans ought to be processed in Papua and New Guinea and, in case their asylum applications were successful, be resettled there. But the government also acknowledged the validity of a point made by Tim Besley of the Department of External Territories, namely 'that the refugees had indicated that they did not wish to go to TPNG and ... that they should not be moved against their will'.[10] This argument was presumably given additional weight by the fact that, probably thanks to Rolly Cantley, the Australian news media knew about the West Papuans' arrival.[11]

As the government ruled out the enforced removal of the eight West Papuans from Thursday Island, it relied on their co-operation. The task to persuade them that their own interests were best served by their transfer to Papua and New Guinea fell to an immigration official. He was instructed to inform the men that 'the Australian government had decided they will not be allowed to remain in Australia', that the government offered to hear their cases in TPNG and that alternatively 'serious consideration will have to be given to their departure for West Irian'.[12] He reported that the men's response to the government's offer had been 'luke-warm', but that the implied threat of deporting them to Indonesia was eventually effective: 'After much deliberation the group decided to go to Papua New Guinea on my assurance that their cases would be properly heard on their arrival there'.[13]

On 24 February 1969, the day after their meeting with the immigration official, the men were flown to the Weam patrol post near the border between West Irian and Papua's Western District. In Parliament, Gordon Freeth was able to tell the ALP's Jim Cairns that the 'eight refugees' 'voluntarily went to Papua and New Guinea to have their request for permissive residence examined'.[14] He also commented more generally on those crossing the border into the Australian territory, suggesting that they also included people who came 'with the intention of carrying out aggressive tendencies against the Territory'.[15] Freeth later asked for his statement to be corrected in Hansard; in the edited version he refers to West Papuans entering Papua and New Guinea 'with the intention of carrying out aggressive or political activities against the area they have left'.[16]

Notwithstanding the headaches he was causing in 1969, Toembay was already known to members of the Territory administration as a 'genuine refugee' – the label officially used to describe those whose protection claims merited recognition by the Australian government.[17] He had first entered Papua and New Guinea in 1963, been granted permissive residence, and worked for Radio Daru. In April 1968, Toembay returned to West Irian of his own volition. He was accompanied by ten other West Papuan émigrés (including two who were to join him again on his 1969 trip to Australia). He claimed:

> that his decision to return to West Irian was influenced by a Radio Australia news broadcast in Bahasa Indonesia which stated that the United Nations was going to 'move back' into West Irian on 1st May 1968 in order to supervise and prepare the country for the 'plebiscite' in 1969.[18]

The TPNG administration moved quickly to assess the eight men's claims for political asylum. Two days after their transfer from Thursday Island, a special branch officer interviewed them at Weam. His findings were then evaluated by the administration in Port Moresby. On 17 April 1969, the Territory's Administrator, David Hay, found that:

> on political grounds it is not considered that the situation in West Irian has deteriorated since April, 1968 when [Toembay and two others] voluntarily elected to return. In fact, it is only because of their continued anti-Indonesian attitudes, unwillingness to adapt to the regime there, that their future may be compromised. In view of the Indonesian offer to West Irianese abroad it is not unlikely that if they returned to West Irian and settled down to make an honest attempt to work and live, they could do so without much hindrance …
>
> The circumstances do not clearly warrant the grant of permissive residency on humanitarian grounds. That is, we are not

> convinced that the eight persons would be in danger of loss of life or serious loss of liberty.[19]

The Administrator was mindful that 'largely resulting from the sympathy and widespread publicity following their raft trip, it could be politically embarrassing to return them'. But he cited another reason for not granting the men permissive residence permits. He pointed out that the behaviour of five of them, who had been living in Daru before returning to West Irian in 1968, had been 'most unsatisfactory':

> [T]hey are lazy, unwilling to work or assimilate, have an exaggerated opinion of their own importance and capabilities, and hold the Australian government responsible for much of what has happened to them. They regard it as a right to be fed, clothed and housed – without working.[20]

Following the line of argument provided by the Administrator, the Department of External Territories recommended that the eight applications for permissive residence in Papua and New Guinea be refused, that the men be removed to West Irian unless the Dutch government offered to take them within one month of the submission's ministerial approval, and that the Indonesian government be informed of the decision before their return to West Irian. The ministers responsible for the granting of residence to asylum seekers in the Australian territory, Freeth and Barnes, concurred with this recommendation.[21]

Two days after Ceb Barnes had approved of Toembay's deportation, the Indonesians came looking for him. A group of 10 soldiers crossed the border into Papua and New Guinea near the Weam patrol post, abducted three adults and six children, and questioned them about refugee movements, the number of West Papuans at Weam and Toembay's whereabouts.[22] I do not know whether or not he came to harm after his deportation. He reappeared in Papua and New Guinea a year later – not to stay, but with the intention of 'just passing through to go on to Thursday Island'.[23] But his second attempt at entering Australia via the Torres Strait Islands also failed: according to the files of the Department of External Territories, he briefly visited Boigu Island, but then returned to West Irian.

There are both striking parallels and evident differences between Australia's response to Toembay and his companions in 1969, on the one hand, and the more recent response to asylum seekers, on the other.

In 1969, Australia's response to West Papuan asylum seekers was not circumscribed by its international legal obligations under the 1951 United Nations Convention Relating to the Status of Refugees. Australia had acceded to the Convention in 1954, but had not signed its 1967 Protocol, which removed the Convention's temporal and geographical limitations; in the version signed by Australia, the Convention applied only to people who had become refugees on account of events taking place before 1 January 1951 in Europe. Australia's decision not to sign the Protocol was largely due to its reluctance to involve the High Commissioner for Refugees in its handling of the refugee situation in Papua and New Guinea and to commit itself to treating West Papuan refugees according to the 1951 Convention.[24] Australia acceded to the Protocol only after granting self-governing status to its colony and thereby divesting itself of any direct responsibility for West Papuan refugees in Papua New Guinea.

The asylum seeker policy that was in place in 1969 dated from 1956. Then, in anticipation of defections during the Melbourne Olympic Games, the government established a procedure for dealing with people who sought asylum in Australia. Their claims were to be assessed by the Department of External Affairs in consultation with ASIO and the Department of Immigration. In 1962, that policy was extended to Papua and New Guinea, with the difference that here the decision about asylum requests involved the Minister for Territories (later External Territories) as well as the Minister for External Affairs. Subsequently, Australia created a special visa, a five-year renewable permissive residence permit, for West Papuans whose requests for asylum had been successful.

When developing its policy in 1956, the government had envisaged instances in which asylum seekers would be of significant intelligence and propaganda value. But arguably the only asylum seeker ever to fit this description was Vladimir Petrov. In fact, officially, Australia granted political asylum only in the cases of defecting diplomats: that of the Petrovs in 1954, and that of Ryszard Stanislaw Zielinski, the Commercial Consul at the Polish

Consulate-General in Sydney who had defected in 1961. In many other cases, including those involving Hungarian athletes during and after the Melbourne Olympics, Eastern European seamen jumping ship, and three Portuguese naval ratings, asylum seekers were granted residence visas as if they had applied to migrate to Australia.[25]

The Petrovs aside, the Australian government has never welcomed asylum seekers *as asylum seekers*. Even in cases in which they were allowed to remain in Australia or its territories, the government's welcome to asylum seekers has always been lukewarm at best. That has been due to two main reasons:

First, successive governments have understood asylum seekers potentially to compromise Australia's immigration policy. Since 1938, Australia has regularly admitted refugees to Australia. Since 1947, these refugees have been carefully selected overseas by Australian immigration officials,[26] and refugees settling in Australia have been considered to comprise a proportion of Australia's migrant intake. The government determines the size of this intake largely in response to the demands for labour and Australia's ability to accommodate new arrivals. In the late 1940s and early 1950s, the government recruited hundreds of thousands of refugees because it would otherwise not have been able to meet its ambitious immigration targets, whereas in the early 1970s, Australia resettled comparatively few refugees because of a recession-induced reduction of the overall migrant intake. Asylum seekers have been seen to be trying to bypass Australia's stringent migrant selection procedures and, in cases where they arrived in large numbers, to compromise its population policy.

Second, by responding favourably to a request for asylum, Australia has acknowledged that the asylum seeker in question had good reason to fear a return to his or her own country. That is, Australia acknowledged that he or she had been or was likely to be persecuted and to suffer, in the words of David Hay, 'danger of loss of life or serious loss of liberty'. Many countries take such an acknowledgment as an affront. Potentially, the granting of asylum, even when disguised as the granting of permanent residence in response to a request to migrate to Australia, has always had diplomatic repercussions.

Both reasons would have influenced the government's thinking in 1969. By granting asylum to the eight West Papuans under its 1956 policy, the government would have both compromised a cornerstone of its immigration policy, the 'White Australia policy', and offended the government of Indonesia.

* * * * * * * * * * * * * *

In more recent times, the government has dubbed asylum seekers 'queuejumpers', thus again emphasising how they supposedly try to bypass an orderly migrant selection procedure and thereby compromise Australia's immigration policy. In relation to asylum seekers from Indonesia, be they East Timorese at various times after 1975, or West Papuans during 1985-1986 and in 2006, and to Cambodian 'boat people' in the early 1990s, the Australian government has been at pains to avoid giving the impression that it condoned their fleeing to Australia or intended to indict the country whence they came on account of the human rights abuses that presumably influenced its decision to resettle them, if only temporarily.

The key role Australia's diplomatic interests play in its response to asylum seekers has been obscured by the fact that in the 1970s the immigration department replaced the foreign affairs department as the government agency responsible for coordinating and publicly defending that response. The aborted attempt in 2006 to pass legislation which specifically targeted West Papuan asylum seekers may serve as a reminder that in cases where Australia's response to asylum seekers has a bearing on its relationship with other countries, the Department of Foreign Affairs and its minister still influence – and perhaps determine – the government's asylum seeker policy. In the case of Indonesian nationals, in particular, Australia's response to asylum seekers has always been an important foreign policy issue. Indonesia being a powerful neighbour, the Australian government sometimes makes Indonesia's interests its own. In 1969, responding to Jim Cairns's question in Parliament, Gordon Freeth confused opposition to Indonesian rule in the Western half of New Guinea with subversive activities in Papua and New Guinea. In 2006, then Immigration Minister Amanda Vanstone similarly identified West Papuan refugees as dangerous, when commenting that the clamouring for West Papuan independence would result in 'chaos, death and suffering on our doorstep'.[27]

Freeth and Vanstone had reason to be concerned, however. Toembay hoped that Australians would support West Papuans' quest for independence. It is likely that he would have tried to influence Australian public opinion if he had been given the opportunity to do so – much in the same way in which the West Papuan refugees who sought Australia's protection in January 2006 have tried to draw attention to the struggle of their people. Asylum seekers who are trying to mobilise public opinion in support of, say, the overthrow of the government of the countries they fled, exacerbate the problems faced by the governments of their host nations on account of recognising the validity of their asylum claims.

In 1969, the Australian government was concerned about possible public reactions in Australia and in Papua and New Guinea. It did not want to be seen to be burdening Papua and New Guinea with an Australian problem. In recent years, however, the government has evidenced little concern for how its response to asylum seekers might be perceived by its Pacific Island neighbours. Foreign policy considerations now seem to be reserved for issues affecting powerful countries.

The move of asylum seeker policy from the foreign affairs to the immigration portfolio has underscored the perception that asylum seekers ought to be thought of first and foremost as prospective immigrants. Immigration officials are more likely than diplomats to think of asylum seekers as people who are jeopardising Australia's carefully calibrated immigration program. Immigration minister Philip Ruddock's decision in 2001 to reduce the designated intake of 'offshore' humanitarian entrants by the number of protection visas granted to 'onshore' asylum seekers, which has been interpreted as evidence of the minister's vindictiveness, could also be seen as an attempt to regularise asylum seekers within the context of Australia's immigration policy.

* * * * * * * * * * * * *

Theoretically, Australia's response to prospective immigrants differs fundamentally from its response to asylum seekers: the former are selected on account of what they have to offer (their skills, their ability to adapt to life in Australia, their state of health, or their wealth), whereas the latter are selected on account of their needs. The ideal immigrant is a young, able-bodied, English-speaking person who possesses skills Australia urgently needs and qualifications Australia recognises. The 'ideal' asylum seeker, on the other hand, is somebody for whom the flight to Australia was a last resort – somebody who would be killed on account of his or her political beliefs, religion or ethnicity if returned to his or her own country.

In practice, however, asylum seekers are also considered prospective immigrants. Therefore the question of whether or not they have something to offer to Australia becomes an issue, and the argument that Australia should only admit those who are deserving becomes crucial. In 1969, David Hay's observation that Toembay was anything but a model resident during his time in Daru became admissible evidence, as it were, even though, strictly speaking, his conduct in Papua and New Guinea was not one of the criteria established to identify 'genuine refugees'.

In recent years, both the government and refugee advocates have relied heavily on the argument that asylum seekers need to be deserving to be resettled in Australia. The former have drawn attention to actions by asylum seekers which supposedly precluded them from having earned Australia's generosity (including the claim that asylum seekers risked the lives of their children, made most dramatically during the so-called children overboard affair). The latter have depicted asylum seekers as essentially good and as people who have the energy and the skills to make a valuable contribution to Australia.[28]

All Australian governments would have preferred not to have to deal with asylum seekers, and to limit their numbers. The idea that the granting of asylum or of refugee status to some would have a snowball effect resulting in vast numbers of asylum seekers heading for Australia was as alive in 1969 as it is in 2007. The argument put forward by the Immigration Department then that the eight West Papuans should not be processed and resettled in Australia because such action would trigger a flood of West Papuan refugees heading for Queensland implied that deterrence would be the best course of action for curbing the flow of asylum seekers. In more recent years, mandatory detention, extraterritorial processing and the introduction of the Temporary Protection Visa (TPV) have all been conceived as means to deter would-be asylum seekers by treating harshly those who succeeded in reaching Australia.

In 1969, the perils faced by Toembay and his companions on their journey to Australia featured prominently in the press coverage of their arrival, but had no bearing on the government's assessment of their asylum claim. The risks taken by asylum seekers to reach Australia have mattered even less in recent years, despite being a reflection of the degree of desperation that drives people to seek an alternative home.

In the late 1960s, the Australian news media's coverage of the situation in West Irian that was responsible for the exodus of refugees, was lacking. Generally, Australians knew very little about the Indonesian-controlled half of New Guinea. They know only marginally more in 2007. Neither in 1969 nor in 2006 was it in the Australian government's interest to raise the level of awareness about human rights violations in Indonesia. Both then and now, the government therefore tried to restrict access to West Papuan asylum seekers – in 1969 by processing their claims at a remote border post in Papua, rather than in Australia, and in 2006 by processing their claim on Christmas Island (and by introducing legislation that, if passed, would have ensured that in future West Papuan asylum claims would be processed on Nauru).

By isolating asylum seekers from the media and by being secretive about the refugee determination process, the government makes it more difficult for the Australian public to appreciate the complexities of the issues involved, and to reject overly simplistic claims such as 'Anybody claiming asylum is fleeing persecution', or 'All asylum seekers are economic refugees', in favour of informed analysis. These complexities are nowhere more pronounced than in the official adjudication of the question of whether or not and on which grounds an asylum seeker ought to be accorded protection.[29] They are compounded by hearsay and misinformation about the circumstances that compel people to flee their homes.[30]

The complexities of the issues involved are more easily apparent (and could perhaps be better understood) when viewed from a historical perspective. Such a perspective makes it possible to detect patterns, commonalities and genealogies, and to understand some of the structural constraints governing Australia's response to asylum seekers. A historical perspective also makes it possible to recognise the exceptionality of the present – to view the present as a state of affairs that does not need to be taken for granted.

* * * * * * * * * * * * *

Toembay and his companions are not representative of those who have sought asylum in Australia over the past 100 years. But then, neither is any other group – be they East Timorese, Vietnamese, Hazaras from Afghanistan or Tamils from Sri Lanka. I have chosen to write about a case involving West Papuans seeking Australia's protection because I believe it ought to be of particular interest to those trying to envisage a new policy approach to asylum seekers. Australia's geographical isolation will ensure that the number of people from faraway places such as Iraq who are trying to enter Australia as asylum seekers will always be comparatively small. Australia will, however, remain a country of first asylum for Indonesians, and it would become a country of first asylum should there be serious civil unrest in either East Timor or Papua New Guinea.

In either of those cases, the scenario of thousands of refugees landing on Australia's shores, which was conjured in the wake of the *Tampa*'s arrival in 2001 (and which was unfounded at the time) may yet prove to be realistic. A critical examination of how Australia has responded in cases in which it was a country of first asylum could facilitate a discussion about how to respond in such an eventuality.

Notes

1 Sub-Collector of Customs, Thursday Island, to Commonwealth Director of Migration, 19 February 1969, National Archives of Australia [hereafter: NAA]: A452, 1969/1177.

2 Quoted in: First Assistant Secretary Department of External Territories, minute, 21 February 1969, NAA: A452, 1969/1177.

3 Roland Cantley, notes, copied by DJ O'Connor, 17 February 1969, NAA: A452, 1969/1177.

4 See Neumann, K, 'Asylum seekers and "non-political native refugees" in Papua and New Guinea', *Australian Historical Studies,* vol 33(120), 2002, pp 359-372; Palmer, D, 'Between a rock and a hard place: the case of Papuan asylum-seekers', *Australian Journal of Politics and History,* vol 52(4), 2006, pp 576-603.

5 Cantley, above, n 3.

6 Department of External Affairs, 'Notes prepared as background information on the border between West Irian and the Territory of Papua and New Guinea', 30 September 1969, NAA: A1838, 932/5/14 part 3.

7 EL Charles, quoted in 'Summary record of interdepartmental meeting held at External Affairs – Friday, 21st February, 1969', NAA: A1838, 3036/14/1/6 part 12.

8 JR Rowland, quoted in 'Summary record of interdepartmental meeting held at External Affairs – Friday, 21st February, 1969', NAA: A1838, 3036/14/1/6 part 12; PJ Galvin, note for file, nd [21 February 1969], NAA: A452, 1969/1177.

9 A Besley, quoted in 'Summary record of interdepartmental meeting held at External Affairs – Friday, 21st February, 1969', NAA: A1838, 3036/14/1/6 part 12.

10 Ibid.

11 For example, 'A Kon Tiki voyage for 8 W. Irians', *The Courier-Mail*, 19 February 1969.

12 TA Byrnes to Commonwealth Director of Migration, Brisbane, 28 February 1969, NAA: A1838, 3036/10/2/2/6.

13 Ibid.

14 Commonwealth Parliamentary Debates (CPD), Representatives, vol 62, 6 March 1969, p 462.

15 Quoted in 'Aggressive tendencies in border crossers', *Canberra Times*, 7 March 1969, and in 'Some Irian border crossers sent back', *The Australian,* 7 March 1969.

16 CPD, Representatives, vol 62, 6 March 1969, p 462; see A Besley, file note, 7 March 1969, NAA: A452, 1969/1177.

17 For example, R Rose to Secretary, Department of External Affairs, 27 June 1966, NAA: A1838, 932/5/14 part 1.

18 Intelligence report Weam IR 11/69, 26 February 1969, p 2, NAA: A452, 1969/21.

19 DO Hay to Secretary, Department of External Territories, 17 April 1969, NAA: A452, 1969/1177.

20 Ibid.

21 A Besley to Minister, 19 May 1969, NAA: A452, 1969/1177.

22 DO Hay to Secretary, Department of External Territories, 21 May 1969, NAA: A452, 1969/21.

23 RP Kekedo to District Commissioner Western District, 7 April 1970, NAA: A452, 1969/1177.

24 Neumann, K, 'Hush-hushing the whole matter: The UNHCR, Australia, and West Papuan refugees', *Refuge*, vol 23(1), 2006, pp 69-80.

25 See Neumann, K, 'Seeking asylum in Australia: a historical perspective', in S Aykut and J Taylor (eds), *Seeking Asylum in Australia: 1995-2005: Experiences and Policies*, Institute for Public History, Monash University, Clayton, 2006, pp 73-84, <http://arts.monash.edu.au/public-history-institute/assets/asylum-forms/neumann.pdf>; specifically on the case of the Portuguese asylum seekers, see Neumann, K, '"Stayputs" and asylum seekers in Darwin, 1961-1962: or, How three Portuguese sailors helped to undermine the White Australia policy', *Journal of Northern Territory History*, vol 16, 2005, pp 1-25.

26 Neumann, K, *Refuge Australia: Australia's Humanitarian Record*, UNSW Press, Sydney, 2004, chapter 2.

27 Vanstone, A, 'Let's not support separatism', *The Australian*, 29 April 2006.

28 See Neumann, K, 'Refugee advocacy and the sound of good intentions', 2006, <www.latrobe.edu.au/rhrc/documents/Foundation%20House%20paper.pdf>.

29 This issue is brilliantly explored in Showler, P, *Refugee Sandwich: Stories of Exile and Asylum*, McGill/Queens University Press, Montreal, 2006.

30 An analysis of Australian intelligence reports about individual refugees suggests that those assessing protection claims often did not fully understand what drove West Papuans to cross the border into Papua and New Guinea, and that those who fled West Irian did so also because of fears based on rumours of Indonesian atrocities. Note that Toembay returned to West Irian in 1968 – probably because he misinterpreted a Radio Australia broadcast. On how rumour has 'informed' the decisions of West Papuans to flee, see Kirsch, S, 'Rumour and other narratives of political violence in West Papua', *Critique of Anthropology*, vol 22(1), 2002, pp 53-79.

3

CHELSEA PIPER RODD

Boats and borders: asylum seekers and elections, 1977 and 2001

Asylum seekers, boats and borders featured prominently in the federal election campaign of 2001. Australia was inundated with refugees fleeing from terror, having been forced to surrender the familiarity of homelands, homes and families in countries no-longer safe and liveable. People fled lives and loved ones in countries such as Afghanistan and Iraq and attempted to gain entry to Australia by boat. In 2001 this influx of so-called 'boat people' culminated in late August with the arrival of the *Tampa*. The extent of the impact and political controversy which surrounded this boat inspired some commentators to dub the political campaign under-way that year the '*Tampa* election'.[1]

Comparable to the extensive media attention, public emotion and political energies Australia invested in the *Tampa*, the lead-up to the federal election of 1977 saw a boat transporting almost 200 Vietnamese refugees to Australia which engendered similar reactions. This boat, the *Song Be*, and these 'boat people', like the *Tampa* refugees, were unsolicited and uninvited, and their arrival stirred deep divisions at a time of intense political and media scrutiny. Unlike the *Tampa* refugees, the Vietnamese people who sought asylum in Australia became what political analysts term a political 'non-issue' in the 1977 election.[2] But this is not to say that the press ignored these refugees. To the contrary, throughout November 1977, preceding the election, as boats arrived in quick succession, newspapers across the country filled their pages with stories announcing the arrival of the 'boat people'. Though the stories of these boats are, in many ways, remarkably similar, ultimately the outcomes for the people most significant to the tales –

the refugees themselves – were vastly different. Within these boats it is possible to glimpse where Australia has stood not just in relation to refugees. Australia's response to these boats and the people on them informs us of the moral, legal, cultural and political temperament of the nation on a much wider scale.

The *Song Be* – Fraser's *Tampa*?

The week before the 1977 election, a Vietnamese fishing boat sailed into Darwin with 181 refugees on board. *The Age* reported the incident on the front page of the paper on 1 December, describing for Melbourne readers the potential for Cold War diplomacy to heat up with the arrival of the boat.[3] For days leading up to the election, the *Song Be* became the centrepiece of press coverage relating to the issue of refugees arriving unsolicited on Australian shores. The very public controversy surrounding the boat symbolised for many the complexities that the Vietnamese refugees presented to Australia. The *Song Be* aroused diplomatic tensions between the Vietnamese and Australian governments. A spokesperson for the Vietnamese embassy said the *Song Be* belonged to the Vietnamese people and had been seized by 'pirates' who had then forced it to sail to Australia.[4] The Vietnamese government claimed that the *Song Be* and its human cargo belonged to the People of the Communist Republic and demanded the boat and the people on it all be returned to the country from which they had fled.

The Vietnamese government was correct when it claimed that the trawler had been hijacked by its occupants. But Liberal Prime Minister Malcolm Fraser and Immigration Minister Michael MacKellar refused to acquiesce to its demands. All the *Song Be* refugees, the Australian government maintained, would remain in Australia unless they requested to do otherwise. Headlines across the country sensationalised the *Song Be*'s arrival in Australia with attention-grabbing declarations from prominent Labor politicians. Foremost among those on the vocal Left was Bob Hawke, the head of the Australian Council of Trade Unions and national president of the Labor Party and future Prime Minister, who urged the government to 'Return Bogus Refugees' who were 'Jumping the Queue'.[5] *The Australian* made the *Song Be* front-page news, declaring 'Pirate Ship Boarded' by Australian police who discovered and confiscated 'weapons on Viet trawler'.[6] There were dramatic accusations that the boat was loaded with Soviet-made AK-47s. The boat, the media suggested, posed a serious threat to Australian security and sovereignty: Australia was being inundated with 'hordes' of invading foreigners, armed and prepared to storm Australia's peaceful shores. Fanning these anxieties, *The Australian* headed a page in its national news ominously, '"Let us in": plea by 90,000 refugees'.[7] The *Song Be* was fast becoming a trigger for Australia's invasion anxieties.

On 1 December the national broadsheet proclaimed that Australia's diplomatic ties, admittedly with an enemy, were under threat because the *Song Be* had been allowed to dock, as its refugee cargo had requested, on Australian shores.[8] On the same day, the front page of Melbourne's *Age* led with the story of the *Song Be*, headlining with the caption 'Viet Refugees to Stay: Peacock'.[9] Similarly, the *West Australian* made the foreign affairs tension front-page news with the headline, 'Send pirates back to us – Vietnam'.[10] *The Australian* sensationalised the potential for diplomatic discord, leading its daily news on the first day of summer with, 'We defy refugee demand by Hanoi: Diplomatic ties under threat'.[11] Fraser's rejection of the Vietnamese government's request for the boat and all the people onboard it to be returned to Vietnam, was undeniably a politically charged gesture. The Australian government made clear its intention not to recognise the legitimacy of the new Communist regime in Vietnam. Victory for democracy had been wrested from Australia. The protracted and costly Vietnam War in which Australia actively fought against the Communists, and which Fraser strongly supported, was, in 1977, still a vivid memory. The Cold War was still in full-swing.

The Left and Right of Human Rights

The politics of the issue was shaped by the fact that the refugees were not simply displaced people who had left a world behind them. They brought with them a history and attitudes. Australian politicians and members of the press attempted to discern the political sympathies and prejudices of these strangers. Many on the Left believed that the refugees were war profiteers or right-wingers who had collaborated with the Americans against the nationalist struggle of their own people. Why else would they be fleeing? The Communist Party of Australia denounced the refugees as 'criminals and queuejumpers'[12] – exactly the terms which the Liberal Howard government would use to vilify a later generation of refugees. As Whitlam's 'fucking Balts' outburst of 1975[13] had signified, these were not people who were welcome in a left-wing Australia. For the Left, Fraser was simply opening the doors to Asians who shared his own right-wing agenda. There were a number of commentators in the conservative press who supported the refugees. Writing in the nationalist journal the *Bulletin*, columnist Peter Samuel argued that the asylum seekers were part of the unfinished business of a war we had caused.[14]

The Liberal government, however, was not unanimous in its support of Fraser's approach. Or rather, it took some members a while to fall into line. In response to the public pressure emerging from his government's reaction to this incident, the Minister for Defence, Jim Killen, asserted that he would review Australia's surveillance capabilities in the north of the country. Killen claimed that he was acting at the behest of the Immigration and Health Departments as refugees were believed to pose a quarantine risk.[15] The issue of coastal surveillance ran hot in the press. Whitlam ridiculed Fraser for his choice of buying a frigate rather than pouring the money into the purchase of a number of small patrol boats. Days before the election, Whitlam asserted that more patrol boats were needed to control the influx of refugees from countries like Vietnam, and 'to counter widespread drug-running, and to prevent animal, plant and human diseases from entering Australia'.[16]

While those on the Left were most vocally opposed to the refugees entering Australia, rogue and radical members of both parties were outspoken in their opinions. Minister for Transport, Peter Nixon, warned that refugees who attempted to enter Australia by boat could well be refused entry. While Australia was prepared to accept refugees, it wanted to be seen to be discouraging unsolicited and dangerous journeys by boat. Nixon explained that those who made for Australia from South-East Asia in this manner, and without Australian immigration clearance, risked being turned away. Nixon reported that the Minister for Immigration, MacKellar, had instructed immigration teams in refugee camps in Thailand and Malaysia to make this clear.[17] Mac-

Kellar, however, denied he had issued such instructions. Instead, he simply emphasised the proper channels for refugees to go through, with Australian immigration teams processing claims in the camps. With officials assessing refugees' claims in such camps, there was no need for anyone to attempt a hazardous journey to Australia.[18]

Liberal Party policy was later to strengthen this position by increasing the intake quota, working with the international community to reach a cooperative solution to the problem, as well as deploying Australian immigration officials in refugee camps in South-East Asia to speed up refugee processing. Opposing the government's position, Labor's spokesman on immigration issues, Tony Mulvihill suggested that 'some of the refugees should be turned away from Australia', while Whitlam assumed a more moderate view, arguing that once the refugees neared Australian shores, they could not be turned back.[19] Countering the perspective of the Left, the *Bulletin* expressed continued support for the refugees' rightful claim to asylum, contending that Australia must usher them into the community with minimal fuss and provide them with access to the necessary support mechanisms. To do otherwise would be a gross miscarriage of justice and a contravention of humane principles. Condemning suggestions that the 'boat people' be disrupted or intercepted as 'some bigots' had suggested, Peter Samuel argued that such interference with ships on the high seas would be an act of piracy. Furthermore, he contended, 'they cannot be 'turned back' or 'flown back' because that would be sentencing heroes to deprivation and death, and destroying Australia's moral standing in the world'.[20] The overall tone of reporting on the issue suggested that the unauthorised arrival of refugees was indicative of a larger, international, humanitarian problem. The plight of these refugees who made it to Australian shores, therefore, should not be manipulated for domestic partisan political gain. Despite the extreme views expressed by some – 'the Mulvihills and Hawkes and Bjelke-Petersens' – the general consensus of both political parties endorsed the basic humanitarian insistence of supplying refuge to those who made it to Australian shores.[21] MacKellar stressed that the government had no intention of taking a tougher line against 'boat people' despite exaggerated rumours to the contrary by members of the opposition.

The *Tampa*: the most famous boat to (almost) reach Australia

By 2001, while boats still figured prominently as a symbol of the partisan political divisions surrounding refugees seeking Australia's asylum, the conditions into which the refugees arrived were dramatically altered. In the lead-up to the 2001 election, Labor complained about the Liberal government's use of the navy to police and repel boats of refugees attempting to enter the country. Reminiscent of the decades-old party politics, the opposition leader Kim Beazley argued that Australia needed a coastguard capable of repelling refugee boats from Australian waters. This, Beazley contended, would leave the navy free for military defence of the island nation.[22] Both parties agreed that there was a plethora of dangers floating around the periphery of Australia.

By the second half of 2001 the Howard government, nearing the end of its second term in office, was confronted with problems arising from the policy of mandatory detention. The incarceration of all unauthorised asylum seeker entrants arriving by boat had been compulsory in Australia since 1991,[23] under laws introduced by the Labor Keating government. Melbourne tabloid, the *Herald Sun* referred to the jail-like detention facilities euphemistically as 'reception centres'.[24] By the end of August 2001, Australia was holding 3600 asylum seekers, in so called 'detention'.[25] In short, they were in jail. And the jails were full beyond capacity.

The popular press in 2001 represented asylum seekers as an onerous and unjust burden, heavily taxing the Australian economy. *They* were enjoying a high standard of living at *our* expense and exploiting the intrinsic magnanimity of Australian society, bleeding us dry. The cost, the *Herald Sun*, declared, was exploding as increasing numbers of people attempted to enter Australia. To house each 'illegal' cost $115 per day, while on average, each 'illegal arrival' cost $50,000 from detention to release or deportation. Further compounding this expense, the paper thundered, was a '$12 million legal bill' set to swell to unprecedented heights as 'people from Syria, Iran, Pakistan and Afghanistan appeal against attempts to send them back home'.[26] Human life, in this instance, is accorded a monetary value, which attaches blame to the 'illegals' for the costly way in which the Australian government was choosing to receive them and process their claims to asylum. Refugees were viewed as costly transgressors against the Australian State.

While the media projected an image of expense and public indignation, inside the walls of the packed detention centres tensions ran high and the human price of compulsory, indefinite detention was exacting an even higher cost on those whom Australia chose to imprison. Detainees staged hunger strikes and some people began sewing their lips together in protest against their prolonged incarceration. Others slashed themselves with the barbed wire which encased them. As evidence of the cruelty of the government's policy, critics of mandatory detention cited the severe psychological and physical suffering of a young boy, Shayan Badraie, who, along with his family, had been detained for months.[27] While Shayan's suffering was extreme, it was not unique. This young boy's story came to public prominence only because a journalist had the tenacity to smuggle in a video camera.[28] Recording within the walls of the detention camps was officially banned.

Guards at the isolated Woomera detention centre clashed with asylum seekers who rioted, while other detainees tried to take their own lives.[29] Concern mounted over a 19-year-old boy on hunger strike on the other side of the country, at the Curtin Detention Centre in Western Australia.[30] Amidst the tensions precipitated by the unfolding events, the government strengthened its calls for more detention facilities. Commentators predicted that refugees would be a major issue in the upcoming federal election campaign. And the terms by which they were known – terms which had been employed two decades earlier by Labor politicians – were now set and used with bipartisan acceptance. These ranged from 'asylum seekers', 'boat people' and 'unauthorised arrivals' to 'illegal immigrants' or, simply, 'illegals'. Opinion polls began to suggest that a major public concern was that 'illegal immigrants' were 'queuejumpers' who didn't deserve Australia's refuge and were 'costing us millions'.[31] Empathy was becoming increasingly costly.

Australia's response to refugees became an issue of bipartisan political exploitation. The press, and politicians of both major parties, asserted publicly that Australia's lax security of its extensive borders was imperilling national sovereignty. The opposition attacked the government for failing to prevent the influx of boats. Calling for a special paramilitary coastguard to be established, Labor criticised the government for failing to make more use of the powers of coastal patrol boats to warn off vessels before they reached Australia.[32] While critics of government policy, such as Democrats Senator Andrew Bartlett, attacked mandatory detention for failing to deter people smugglers and asylum seekers from targeting Australia as a favoured destination,[33] the government continued to step up its hardline position against boatpeople. And as the federal election loomed, polls indicated that there was strong popular approval for the government's detention policy. More respondents called it 'too soft' rather than 'too tough'.[34] While accusations of racism featured within the public debate regarding refugee policy at this time, with a steady flow of refugees coming towards Australia, nobody, it seemed, was prepared to reject completely the practice of compulsory detention. The predominant view within the Australian community accepted that the imprisonment of refugees was necessary.

Minister for Immigration Philip Ruddock stood firmly by the policy of mandatory detention of all unauthorised boat arrivals. He denounced people smugglers, strategically directing his attack at these profiteers. By doing so, Ruddock avoided being seen as levelling blame at the asylum seekers themselves for their own plight. According to the Minister, the people smugglers were becoming wealthy at *Australia's* expense.[35] They were, Ruddock insisted, well-organised, ruthless and greedy and they were exploiting 'Australia's humanity and vulnerability'.[36] Australia was thus positioned as the victim. Ruddock's moral calculus had no place for the asylum seekers at this stage. The point was that people smugglers were evil – and that Australia refused to encourage their activities by allowing refugees to reach a place of sanctuary and achieve a situation of justice. Principle demanded that the asylum seekers suffer. And Ruddock was a man of principle. The Minister for Immigration declared that Australia was being 'very deliberately targeted' by the 'boat people' because of the reputed generosity of the country. 'Our humanity', Ruddock explained to the Australian public, 'is their incentive'.[37]

Sovereignty protected, compassion set adrift

The *Tampa* fiasco began as the straightforward story of a rescue at sea. The Norwegian freighter, the MV *Tampa*, rescued more than 400 refugees on their way to Australia. They had become stranded when the *Palapa*, the decrepit Indonesian fishing boat they had been travelling on, broke down in the middle of the ocean.[38] Like the *Song Be* before it, the story unfolded quickly in newspapers across the country, rapidly becoming a tale of international diplomatic tension as Prime Minister Howard took the 'unusual action' of refusing the asylum seekers entry to Australia.[39] As the *Tampa* dominated front-page news, Howard insisted that the rescued refugees were not Australia's responsibility. The boat and, importantly, the people on it, were a problem for Norway and Indonesia to resolve. The Prime Minister entrenched his denial of the *Tampa*, stating that 'on this particular vessel, we have decided to take a stand'.[40]

Howard's determination to disallow these refugees entrance to Australia reset the moral clock. Rhetoric of protecting 'shared values' and a pronounced hostility to people who were different replaced that of diversity and multiculturalism – not to mention a legal and moral responsibility as part of the international community and signatory to the United Nations Refugee Convention – which had characterised Fraser's acceptance of the Vietnamese refugees. The Howard government represented these people as foreign intruders with base, uncivilised ethics and criminal intentions. With Australia's mainland immigration detention centres full, the government had nowhere to readily imprison the latest asylum seekers. While the *Tampa* floated in the waters just off the Australian coast, a tense stand-off ensued, precipitating a scenario that gave the lie to a professed reputation for generosity and humanity. Howard announced that the 438 refuge seekers on board would not be permitted to land in Australia. It was a matter of 'defending the integrity of our borders'.[41] The message was clear: the *Tampa* refugees posed a real threat to Australia's wholeness, to its political and cultural coherence as a nation-state.

Howard assured his audience of the legality and, implicitly, the ethicalness of his actions against the border transgressors, valorising territorial sovereignty while neutralising or condemning talk of human rights and he promised Australians that 'genuine refugees' would be welcome. As criminologist Sharon Pickering has argued, the notion of sovereignty, closely bound to that of national integrity, contains within it the right to enforce borders and the right to treat humanitarian claims and international law as outside interference.[42] The government and the popular media represented the refugee as suspicious, deviant, criminal and abnormal. The sense that the *Tampa* represented an attack on Australia, rather than a compounded tragedy for those onboard, continued to escalate through the final days of August.

Despite a divided public opinion, the events surrounding the *Tampa* transformed the tone of the outrage expressed against refugees into a successful government policy. Views which a few years earlier would have seemed extreme were now commonplace: the government was being a 'soft-touch' if it allowed the entry of a few hundred refugees in rickety boats. The *Tampa* incident was popularly perceived to be an act of trespass against Australian territory and the sovereign authority of the government. As one impassioned letter-writer to the *West Australian* demanded to know, 'how long is our gutless government going to permit this passive invasion of our sovereignty by these people … of the dogmatic and inflexible Muslim religion'.[43] In the same newspaper another letter-writer warned that, 'the numbers of these illegals [will reach] uncontrollable proportions and overrun this country … our whole Australian way of life is being threatened by this insidious invasion'.[44] While the government was attentive to such forceful public opinion, both major political parties apparently agreed, falling into line with populist politics that were becoming increasingly riddled with fear. The Labor Party did little to actively oppose the government rhetoric, refusing to dispute such accusations. Labor leader, Kim Beazley, issued support for the government's hardline stance against refugees insisting that while Australia's sovereignty was under threat, the nation did not need a 'carping opposition'.[45] Far from opposing or condemning the increasingly harsh policy of indefinite mandatory detention, Beazley reminded the Australian public that it had been his party who had introduced compulsory incarceration in the first place.[46]

Just days into the *Tampa* crisis, which the Howard government had precipitated, popular support for his government's unyielding denial of the ship and its human cargo began to galvanise. The front page of the *Herald Sun* on the final day of August produced its latest 'Voteline' result, assuring readers that 94% of respondents had affirmed the government's action of storming the ship with Special Air Services (SAS) troops to ensure it did not reach Australia. The government was treating the *Tampa* as a 'hostile' ship.[47] Under increasing pressure from the refugees on board, the *Tampa* sailed into Australian waters. The government presented this departure from diplomatic limbo-land as a transgression against the Australian State. This defiance, the government insisted, justified the SAS usurpation of Captain Rinnan's control of the vessel. The Prime Minister explained that his government had been 'left with no alternative but to … board and secure the vessel'.[48] Howard asserted that his actions were the 'right thing to do … the legal thing to do' and insinuated that the United Nations was on side with Australia's hardline action, saying ambiguously that he had 'very good relations' with the international organisation.[49] However, contradicting Howard's vague claim to mutual goodwill, Mary Robinson, United Nations High Commissioner for Human Rights, declared that the *Tampa* should be allowed to dock and disembark the asylum seekers at Christmas Island.[50] Human rights and multicultural groups accused Howard of 'moral cowardice', callousness and inappropriate behaviour. But the Prime Minister withstood these attacks, the government's credibility remaining intact.[51] A public majority believed that Howard had demonstrated strong and uncompromising leadership in the face of unfair criticism.

By 2001 refugees who sought to enter Australia by boat aroused bipartisan and populist antagonism. In 1977, a time of nascent multiculturalism, and at the height of the Cold War, the 'boatpeople' raised the ire of those on the political and cultural left-wing of society. Only two decades later the left/right divide had dissolved into popular contempt and inhumanity meted out to all people who attempted to enter Australia by boat. The *Tampa* and the *Song Be* carried not only people who sought to engage their right to asylum, but these boats also serve to highlight a dramatically altered moral state, indeed an Australia in which human rights were denied universally. In 2001 Howard was correct when he argued that his government's response to the refugees onboard the *Tampa* was significant to Australia's sovereignty. By refusing people their internationally sanctioned right to seek Australia's asylum, Howard demonstrated that his nation was on shaky ground in terms of its legal, ethical and political character. This contrasts starkly with Fraser's acceptance of all people who arrived uninvited by boat and requested refuge. By doing so, Fraser defied the fear of not only members of the Australian public, but also of discontents within the international community. Fraser's actions in relation to the *Song Be* demonstrated that Australia was confident in its sense of national self and secure in its cultural and political independence.

Notes

1 Roy Morgan Research, 'What happened on November 10? Did the "race card" (border protection) swing the electorate?' <www.roymorgan.com/news/polls/2001/3476>.

2 Butler, D, 'Introduction' in H Penniman (ed), *The Australian National Elections of 1977*, ANU Press, Canberra (1979), p 15.

3 *The Age*, 1 December 1977, p 1.

4 Ibid.

5 *The Australian*, 29 November 1977, p 1.

6 *The Australian*, 30 November 1977, p 1.

7 *The Australian*, 2 December 1977, p 3.

8 *The Australian*, 1 December 1977, p 1.

9 *The Age*, 1 December 1977, p 1.

10 *West Australian*, 30 November 1977, p 1.

11 *The Australian*, 1 December 1977, p 1.

12 Lawrence, P, CSAAR Research Paper no 24, *Australian Opinion on the Indo-Chinese Influx, 1975-1979*, Griffith University Press, Brisbane, 1979, p 6.

13 In an infamous outburst, Prime Minister Whitlam referred to the incoming refugees as a problem of 'hundreds of fucking Vietnamese Balts coming into this country with their religious and political hatreds against us', as quoted in Viviani, N, *The Long Journey: Vietnamese Migration and Settlement in Australia*, Melbourne University Press, Melbourne, 1984, p 70.

14 Samuel, P, 'Viet Boat-People mustn't be rebuffed', *Bulletin*, 10 December 1977, p 44.

15 *The Age*, 1 December 1977, p 1.

16 Richardson, M, 'Asian boat refugees twist Australia's tail', *Australian Financial Review*, 6 December 1977, p 11

17 *The Age*, 3 December 1977, p 1.

18 *The Age*, 8 December 1977, p 1.

19 Lloyd, CJ, 'A Lean Campaign for the Media', in H Penniman (ed), *The Australian National Elections of 1977*, ANU Press, Canberra, 1979, p 246.

20 Samuel, above, n 14, p 47.

21 Ibid, p 45.

22 Federal Election Debate, 14 October 2001, transcript at <www.pm.gov.au/News/interviews/2001/interview1382.htm>.

23 Jupp, J, *From White Australia to Woomera*, Cambridge, Melbourne, 2002, p 66.

24 'Up to 2000 on way: new housing planned as illegals flood in', *Herald Sun,* 24 August 2001, p 7.

25 Marr, D and Wilkinson, M, *Dark Victory*, Allen & Unwin, Sydney, 2003, p 8.

26 Herald Sun, above, n 24.

27 *The Age*, 'The shame of Shayan', 28 August 2001, p 13.

28 ABC Television, *Four Corners*, 'Inside Story', 13 August 2001, transcript at <www.abc.net.au/4corners/archive/2001b_Monday13August2001.htm>.

29 'Suicide attempt in Woomera', *The Age*, 28 August 2001, p 2.

30 'Concern mounts for teen hunger striker', *The Australian*, 28 August 2001, p 2.

31 Scott, L, 'Hopes blown out of the water', *The Australian*, 18-19 August 2001, p 21.

32 'Ruddock holds line on mandatory detention', *The Australian*, 24 August 2001, p 4.

33 Ibid.

34 Scott, above, n 31.

35 'The human cost of our rising tide of refugees', *The Australian*, 24 August 2001, p 1.

36 'Ruddock holds line on mandatory detention', *The Australian*, 24 August 2001, p 4.

37 *Herald Sun*, above, n 24.

38 Marr and Wilkinson, above, n 25, p 15.

39 'Refugees stranded at sea', *The Age*, 28 August 2001, p 1.

40 'Unwanted: Food, Aid, but no home for 438 boat people', *Herald Sun*, 29 August 2001, p 1.

41 John Howard to Alan Jones, Sydney Radio 2UE, 30 August 2001, transcript at <www.pm.gov.au/news/interviews/2001/interview1199.htm>.

42 Pickering, S, *Refugees and State Crime*, Federation Press, Sydney, 2005, p 19.

43 'Your Say', *West Australian*, 28 August 2001, p 14.

44 'Your Say', *West Australian*, 31 August 2001, p 10.

45 Kim Beazley, as quoted by Matt Price, 'Labor lays it on the poll line', *The Australian*, 31 August 2001, p 2.

46 Kim Beazley declared in the only debate of the 2001 election campaign that the 'problem' of refugees seeking unauthorised entrance to Australia had not existed when Labor was in power and insinuated that the Liberals had let the policy of compulsory detention go to seed, 14 October 2001, <www.pm.gov.au/News/interviews/2001/interview1382.htm>.

47 *Herald Sun*, 31 August 2001, p 3.

48 John Howard in a speech to Parliament, 29 August 2001, printed in *Herald Sun*, 30 August 2001, p 7.

49 'Navy threat', *Herald Sun*, 31 August 2001, p 4.

50 'World takes Howard to task on refugees', *Herald Sun*, 31 August 2001, p 4.

51 'Navy threat', *Herald Sun*, 31 August 2001, p 4.

PART II

Coming to Australia

LYN ALLISON

Part II Introduction

In 1963 Martin Luther King Jr wrote 'Injustice anywhere is a threat to justice everywhere' and four decades later, the proof of this is evident in our treatment of asylum seekers.

Australia's once progressive asylum seeker policies have become draconian under the Howard government. The *Tampa* crisis sailed right into the wake of the 11 September terrorist attacks and the government took the opportunity to ramp up its politics of fear. The Prime Minister's infamous catchcry of 'we will decide who comes to this country and the way in which they come' set the scene of the 2001 election campaign, and underlying it was the premise that our security and freedom could only be bought by sacrificing the security and freedom of others.

Government action from then on was driven by the idea that the more harshly we treated asylum seekers, the more this would deter others and the safer Australia would become. Men, women and children were placed behind razor wire often for years while their applications for protection were slowly processed. Our policies and detention centres wrought physical, emotional and mental damage on hundreds of people seeking protection, putting Australia in serious breach of our international obligations.

The 'Pacific Solution' was and still is an astronomically expensive and inhumane solution to a non-existent problem. But it arguably served its purpose of keeping refugees well away from the public eye in camps set up in far flung and destitute Pacific nations. The most infamous are those on Nauru. Our government claimed the refugees held there were Nauru's responsibility and the Nauruans insisted (rightly) that they were ours.

The irony of making refugees stateless twice over, was apparently lost on our government.

Access to the island nation was restricted for anyone who might have criticised the plight of the refugees there, including prominent human rights figures and journalists. My Democrats colleague, Andrew Bartlett, negotiated his way on to the island three times, bringing to the refugees there an important message of hope on behalf of, I think, the majority of Australians. This paved the way for Michael Gordon, the first Australian journalist to reach the camps, and to the migration agent Marion Le who worked tirelessly on behalf of so many of the refugees there.

Back in Parliament, the government rammed through even more legislation to strike down fairness, adequacy and proper administration in the entire *Migration Act.* More power was put in the hands of the Minister and the Department, more restrictions placed on the powers of the Courts and fewer rights for those subjected to the *Migration Act* and its Regulations.

One of the more cruel regimes imposed is the Temporary Protection Visa (TPV). Back in 1999, the Democrats moved in the Senate to prevent TPVs, but government and Opposition were unmovable. Our warnings have since been vindicated. The TPV has been shown to be unjust to refugees, prolonging their state of limbo and significantly affecting their ability to settle and rebuild their lives. The lack of access to family reunion is particularly harsh and harmful to refugees. It is also against the interest of the wider Australian community, as it makes it far more difficult for refugees to settle, adapt and contribute effectively to their new country.

Family members who arrived separately were also assessed separately, even when husbands, wives and children who had arrived earlier were found to be genuine refugees. The UN Refugee Convention explicitly states that when someone is found to be a refugee, their immediate family is automatically granted refugee status.

The last decade has been a discriminatory and shameful episode in Australia's history and it is important that that history is written, that we look refugees in the eye and see their humanity and respond more humanely to their circumstances.

Yearning to Breathe Free does just that, dispelling misconceptions, analysing government spin in the media about refugees and their relationship with Islam and terrorism, challenging the economics and the fairness of this extreme reaction to 'protecting our borders' and it tells the stories of asylum seekers as they tell it.

It is a must for those interested in politics, human rights, the concept of equality before the law, our international obligations and how easily all this can be sacrificed in the quest for power.

4

PETER MARES

Reassessing the *Tampa*

Today, the *Tampa* affair is generally seen through two lenses. It is viewed as a key moment in political history – the masterstroke of Australia's wiliest Prime Minister to secure victory in the 2001 federal election – and it is regarded as a major blemish on our human rights record, a moment when Australia defied international opinion and betrayed its history as a liberal, tolerant nation. While neither view is entirely wrong, both can be misleading. When we view the *Tampa* through the first lens, as political history, it is easy to forget that the Prime Minister's stand was a high stakes gamble that nearly went awry. To see the *Tampa* affair through the second lens, as an event out of keeping with Australia's liberal traditions and good international standing, overlooks the continuities with past approaches to asylum seekers and underplays the similarities between Australia's actions and the treatment of 'boat people' by other developed nations.

A brief sketch of the *Tampa* affair

The bare facts of the *Tampa* story are quickly sketched.[1] On the morning of 26 August 2001, the Australian Maritime Safety Authority alerted the Norwegian freighter MV *Tampa* that a wooden ferry was in distress in the Indian Ocean. Captain Arne Rinnan immediately sailed to help and his crew undertook a dangerous rescue mission in heavy seas, hauling asylum seekers to safety as the overloaded and rapidly disintegrating timber boat rode up against the steel hull of the *Tampa*. Captain Rinnan was told that he should expect to find eighty or more passengers on the stricken vessel. After a rescue lasting three hours, 438 people had been hoisted aboard his ship.

Captain Rinnan opened empty containers on the deck to create shelter and makeshift toilets. His crew provided basic first aid and distributed food and drink as the *Tampa* resumed its voyage from Perth to Singapore. Captain Rinnan intended to disembark his rescued passengers at the Indonesian port of Merak. As he steamed towards Java five men came up to the bridge. According to Captain Rinnan, they were 'aggravated' at the prospect of being returned to Indonesia and warned that if he did not change course people 'would go crazy or start jumping overboard'.[2] Concerned that things might get out of control, Captain Rinnan consulted with Australia's search and rescue authorities. He was told it was up to him, the ship's master, to decide what to do. Erring on the side of caution he opted to make for the closest port, on Christmas Island, just four hours distant.

As the *Tampa* neared Australian territory, Captain Rinnan received another call from Canberra. This time it was an immigration official, warning him that he risked prosecution for people smuggling if he entered Australian waters. The captain maintained his course, but did not immediately test the resolve of the Australian government, stopping the *Tampa* outside the 12-mile exclusion zone. As the sun was rising over Christmas Island on the morning of Monday 27 August, Prime Minister John Howard convened cabinet's National Security Committee in Canberra. At a lunch time media conference, he declared that the *Tampa* would 'not be given permission to land in Australia or any Australian territories'.[3] Captain Rinnan remained outside the 12-mile limit and requested medical assistance for his rescued passengers. By Monday evening, no help had arrived. The stand-off continued throughout Tuesday, while furious diplomatic work went on behind the scenes. On Tuesday evening, Captain Rinnan renewed his appeal for help, this time signalling medical distress on board in the form of a 'pan-pan' emergency call. He repeated the call roughly 12 hours later, on the morning of Wednesday 29 August.

Still no help came. Three days after rescuing the passengers from the sinking ferry, the Master of the *Tampa* defied Canberra's warnings and entered the waters around Christmas Island. By lunch time, 45 Australian Special Air Service commandos had taken control of his ship.

The *Tampa* affair as a high stakes political gamble

When the *Tampa* steamed onto Australia's political horizon, 'boat people' were already at the top of the domestic news agenda. Three boats had arrived in the space of six days carrying almost 1000 people between them. In this climate, the government's response to the *Tampa* was canny politics. As government MP Ian Causley noted later in parliament: 'I've never had an issue in my political career – and that spans 18 years now – which has made so many people come up to me in the street, without any urging whatsoever, and say, "Don't back away"'. The government was seen to be standing up to the people smugglers and the 'illegals', the legions of 'queuejumpers' who in the words of then opposition leader Kim Beazley, 'flout' Australia's generosity. The government's tactics wrong-footed the federal Opposition: Labor's 'me too' support only boosted the Coalition's credentials for strong and decisive leadership.

Earlier in the year it had looked likely that Prime Minister John Howard would lose the 2001 federal election. By August, cuts to petrol excise, targeted spending in marginal electorates and generous handouts to the over 60s had clawed back ground for the government but a Coalition victory was still far from assured. The Prime Minister's decision to take a stand against the 'boat people' turned the tide of public opinion firmly in his favour. Border integrity and national security were pushed to the forefront of the campaign even before the 11 September terrorist attacks in New York and Washington that gave Australia a khaki election.

It was brilliant electoral politics, but in the fraught days of late August and early September 2001, the whole enterprise very nearly went off the rails.

There is some evidence to suggest that the government had been preparing to use the defence force to take firm action against asylum boats for some time. Norman Banks, commander of HMAS *Adelaide*, told a subsequent Senate hearing that a Prime Ministerial task force had discussed using the navy 'to intercept and deter' boats carrying 'large numbers of potential illegal immigrants' as early as 1999.[4] By late 2001, he said, those discussions were 'becoming a reality'.

It's unlikely however, that the government had envisaged a scenario such as that involving the *Tampa* – asylum seekers rescued at sea by a commercial freighter – and when John Howard took his stand he seemed to be acting on political instinct rather than implementing a carefully crafted strategy. The full implications of the government's actions had not been thought through. First Australia wanted to send the boat and its rescued passengers back to Indonesia, but with no groundwork done in Jakarta, the Indonesian government would have none of it. The Indonesians were angry that Australia had made its plan public without so much as a phone call to discuss matters first and accused Canberra of megaphone diplomacy.[5] In any case, there was no way that Captain Arne Rinnan could now sail to Merak. Rescuing asylum seekers at sea and continuing on his scheduled journey was one thing; setting out from a safe harbour on a new voyage was quite another, because the *Tampa* was neither equipped nor insured to sail with so many passengers on board.

The United Nations refugee agency, UNHCR, offered Australia a way out of the impasse. If Canberra allowed the asylum seekers to land and be processed on Christmas Island then it would find other countries willing to resettle those found to be refugees. (New Zealand and Norway were willing to assist and Britain and Canada were being consulted.) By facilitating the asylum seekers' disembarkation at the most convenient port, the UNHCR aimed to ensure that the ship's master would not be penalised – commercially or legally – for rendering assistance to people in distress. By refusing to accept the UNHCR's burden-sharing approach, Australia risked undermining fundamental, time-honoured conventions on the protection of life at sea: having seen the trouble that Captain Rinnan landed in, the masters of other ships might now think twice about answering a distress signal. To the Howard government, the law of the sea was of less pressing concern than domestic politics. The UNHCR's pragmatic proposal smacked too much of a back down in the eyes of the public.

In place of international cooperation, the government attempted to push emergency legislation through parliament to give it sweeping powers to force the *Tampa* – and any subsequent asylum boat – back out to sea. The Border Protection Bill 2001 (introduced on 29 August) would have enabled the Prime Minister or his immigration Minister to empower any customs officer, immigration department official, police officer or soldier, to exercise 'his or her absolute discretion' in directing the master of any ship 'outside the territorial sea' of Australia. No court would have had the power to review such action and no officer would have been subject to civil or criminal prosecution for enforcing such a directive. As opposition leader Kim Beazley pointed out, the Bill would have made it legal to order a boat that was sinking back out to sea: 'drag the boat out, sink it, people die'.[6] Up to this point the opposition had supported the government's stand on the *Tampa*, but the provisions of the Bill were so sweeping that Labor refused to pass it.[7]

By Saturday 1 September it looked like the government's impulsive decision to block the *Tampa* might come unstuck. Its draft legislation had been defeated, Indonesia's President was refusing to take a phone call from John Howard and Australia's actions had provoked a storm of international criticism. SAS commandos were on board the *Tampa* but the ship was going nowhere and remained inside Christmas Island's 12-mile exclusion zone. Meanwhile human rights lawyers were preparing to take action in the Federal Court that could force the government to bring the asylum seekers ashore. Newspapers described John Howard as 'desperate'. In *The Weekend Australian,* Paul Kelly described the *Tampa* affair as an 'inept saga of crisis management'. He said 'the astounding feature of the drama' was that John Howard 'went in without any exit strategy'.[8]

However, as Kelly noted, Australia's diplomatic resources had been 'fully mobilised' and the government had not yet exhausted all its options. Urgent cables had been sent to the heads of Australian missions around the region, instructing them to sound out their host governments about the possibility of warehousing asylum seekers on Australia's behalf. Diplomats were given to understand that they had an open chequebook. The pressure was coming from the Department of the Prime Minister and Cabinet. The gut response in Foreign Affairs and Trade was that the policy was wrong and that it would damage Australia's reputation and relations with its neighbours. Resistance to the policy ran to the highest levels of the department.

The government cast about for help from traditional ally New Zealand, from an aid-dependent former colony Papua New Guinea, even from recently traumatised East Timor, which on 30 August, was in the process of voting in its first ever free elections. Informal approaches were also made to Fiji, Kiribati, Palau and Tuvalu. In the end it was near bankrupt Nauru, another former Australian colony, that agreed to help. New Zealand also came to the party, agreeing to accept families and a number of unaccompanied teenage boys from the *Tampa* – a total of 132 people. The rest were to be taken to two camps in the lunar landscape of Nauru, the world's smallest republic, a 22-square-kilometre island rendered mostly uninhabitable by decades of phosphate mining. The 'Pacific Solution' was born.

Continuities with past policy

The federal government's stand on the *Tampa* was a decisive moment in the development of Australia's treatment of asylum seekers and refugees, but it did not so much overturn past policies of deterrence as build upon them. And the evolution of policy continued in the weeks after the *Tampa,* as another 13 asylum boats tested Australia's defences.

On Monday 3 September, after more than a week on the open deck of the freighter, the *Tampa* asylum seekers were transferred to HMAS *Manoora* for transport to Nauru. Meanwhile, Prime Minister Howard called up five additional navy ships and four extra aircraft for the 'saturation surveillance'[9] of Australia's north-western approaches under Operation Relex. The navy's mission was to 'deter and deny' SIEVs (suspected illegal entry vessels). Navy commanders were under no illusions about the politically sensitive nature of their task. Commander Norman Banks told the Senate inquiry into a certain maritime incident that he understood decisions about individual asylum boats were being made at Prime Ministerial level.[10] The navy was instructed to repair and resupply the boats when necessary, so that they could be towed back out to sea and sent back in the direction of Indonesia. If this failed, then the asylum seekers were to be held for transfer to an 'offshore' detention centre, initially in Nauru, and later in Papua New Guinea. The mission was to be achieved 'without loss of life or serious injury to any party' and the primary objective was clear: 'At no stage were unauthorised arrivals to have access to the Australian migration zone'.[11]

The first four vessels to follow in the wake of the *Tampa* were all intercepted and their passengers transferred to navy ships for transport to detention centres in the Pacific. But as a fifth boat approached, the government updated its orders, giving greater emphasis to the policy of turning boats back. Rear Admiral Geoffrey Smith told the Senate inquiry 'we received new instructions which were to, where possible, intercept, board and return the vessel to Indonesia'.[12] In subsequent weeks, half the boats intercepted by the navy were successfully returned to Indonesia – four boats in total, carrying more than 500 people between them.[13] Another four boats were too unseaworthy to send back, and the asylum seekers aboard were transferred to detention in Nauru and Papua New Guinea. One boat, the SIEV-X, ('X' for unknown) sank before reaching Australian territory, taking the lives of 353 people, most of them women and children.

More than five years later some of those asylum seekers returned to Indonesia in late 2001 remained in limbo. I am aware of the case of an Iraqi woman and her three children living in East Java. As members of Iraq's minority Christian community, they can neither return safely to the sectarian violence that wracks their homeland nor settle easily into their host community in Indonesia. The mother cannot work and the children do not go to school. They survive on a weekly stipend from an international agency that amounts to about two dollars per person per day. The family has close relatives (the mother's sister) already living in Australia but as of early 2007 their requests to Canberra for resettlement on compassionate grounds have made little progress.[14]

The return of the boat known as SIEV-12 to Indonesia marked the end of what Frank Brennan calls the 'fourth wave' of 'boat people'.[15] Many factors are recognised as contributing to stopping the boats: the 'offshore' processing regime set up under the 'Pacific Solution', the overthrow of the Taliban, Indonesia's cooperation with Australia to break smuggling rackets and the deterrence effect of the SIEV-X tragedy. What has been overlooked is the government's success in physically returning vessels to Indonesia. This was the ultimate outcome of what can be described as a shift from a policy of *deterrence by example* to a policy of *deterrence by force*.

Mandatory detention is a key element of *deterrence by example*. As Robert Manne writes, in its efforts to deter boat arrivals Australia constructed a regime 'harsh enough to wreak havoc on the lives of those it touched'.[16] Temporary Protection Visas were another attempt at *deterrence by example* – restricting the rights of refugees was intended to make Australia a less attractive destination. Even the 'Pacific Solution' was an extreme instance of *deterrence by example* – asylum seekers would have their cases heard but the route to protection would be circuitous, protracted, legally stunted and unpleasant. But when Australia used the navy to turn boats back to Indonesia it moved from *deterrence by example* to *deterrence by force* (or as Manne calls it 'naval deterrence at the border'[17]).

It is not surprising that this strategy stopped the boats. Consider the options open to asylum seekers using the established maritime smuggling route from Indonesia in late 2001. They basically had two choices: either they must travel in a vessel that is so unseaworthy that it cannot be forced back to Indonesia – and so risk the fate of those aboard the SIEV-X – or secondly, they must immediately sabotage their boat after reaching Australian waters and render it irreparable, in order to force a rescue at sea by the Australian navy. Under either scenario, the best that they could then hope for is to be dispatched to Nauru or Papua New Guinea to face a long and uncertain detention.

Australian in the international context – a step ahead but not a step apart

Implicit in much public debate about the *Tampa* is an assumption that Australia went out on a limb internationally. However, if Australian refugee policy is compared to that of other developed nations, then the similarities are as important as the differences.

For example, the United States routinely uses its Coast Guard to intercept 'boat people' from Haiti and return them to their homeland without *any* formal investigation of their status whatsoever. A Haitian (or a person of almost any other nationality) will only be interviewed as a potential refugee if they pass 'the shout test' – that is, if they spontaneously demonstrate a fear of return.[18] In the early 1990s, in what might be called the 'Caribbean solution', the US asked Caribbean and Central American nations to host the displaced Haitians on its behalf. Haitians and Cubans have been held for processing in 'offshore' places – on navy ships or at the naval base at Guantánamo Bay in Cuba[19] – and in the past the US has attempted to convince third countries to resettle those found to be refugees.[20] This approach pre-figured Australian policy in its 'offshore' detention centres in Nauru and Papua New Guinea.

In recent decades all developed nations have tended to follow a path of deterrence and containment – *deterring* asylum seekers from arriving on their shores and *containing* the refugee 'problem' to countries of first asylum, usually poorer countries in the developing world.[21]

The most important aim of that policy is to stop asylum seekers from ever crossing your frontier in the first place, in order to prevent them from invoking the protection obligations enshrined in the 1951 Convention on the Status of Refugees. Britain's Jack Straw acknowledged this in June 2000, when he was still Home Secretary and responsible for immigration. At a public forum in London, he pointed out that the 1951 convention gives people facing persecution the right to claim asylum, but does not oblige any nation to admit people through its borders so that they can make that claim. The consequence – as he admitted – is that asylum seekers are forced to break the law to seek safety.[22]

It took the *Tampa*'s arrival to reveal this truth, and those of us who were not busy applauding the government were shocked to see how crude the business of border protection can be. When the Australian government stopped the *Tampa* landing its rescued asylum seekers at Christmas Island it reached for the bluntest and heaviest instrument available: military force. But dramatic events on the high seas are rare. Generally border protection proceeds in a more mundane manner, beyond the view of ordinary citizens. All developed nations have an extensive kit of border protection tools that are essentially bureaucratic. For example, Australian immigration officials are posted at major airports in South-East Asia to help prevent travellers holding false documents from getting on a plane to Australia. Airlines are pressed to cooperate with screening procedures and large fines are imposed on any carrier that inadvertently allows an inadequately documented traveller – refugee or not – to land at an Australian airport. Airport counter checks are preceded by another level of screening. Applicants from so-called 'refugee producing countries' will be refused a visa to visit Australia if they are deemed at 'risk' of seeking asylum after arrival.

Without a visa to get you past immigration controls, the only legal route to refugee protection in Australia is the much vaunted 'offshore' humanitarian resettlement program, which during 2006-2007 has an upper limit of 14,000 places per year. This is the queue that the former Minister for Immigration Philip Ruddock so frequently accused the 'boat people' of jumping. A more appropriate metaphor (coined by David Corlett) is a 'refugee heap' out of which very few are plucked for resettlement in countries like Australia.[23]

Given the barriers erected on the legal route to Australia, it is not surprising that some asylum seekers would sell their land and whatever other possessions they have in order to scrape together the money to engage a people smuggler and risk a dangerous journey from Indonesia to an Australian territory in the Indian Ocean. When the federal government prevented the *Tampa* from disembarking its passengers at Christmas Island it was taking the next logical step in policy, closing off another route by which refugees might actually make it past our border controls, and so make a call on our obligations under the 1951 convention.

Conclusion

The government's response to the *Tampa* was the centrepiece of Howard's victory at the election on 10 November 2001. As David Marr and Marian Wilkinson write, there can be no doubt that the Coalition saw 'border protection as its most potent vote winner … [and a] fortune was spent hammering the message home'.[24] As wavering voters went to cast their ballots, they entered polling stations decorated with posters of a resolute John Howard, 'fists clenched, flanked by flags' delivering the key slogan of the campaign: '*We* decide who comes into this country and the circumstances in which they come'. In the last days of the election campaign, in the most closely contested seats, the Liberal Party 'pulled advertising on every subject but this one'.[25]

The government not only won overwhelming electoral support for its stand, it also claimed success in policy terms – by late 2001, boats carrying Middle Eastern asylum seekers had stopped arriving on Australia's shores. However victory over the 'boat people' was not complete – as we know from the subsequent arrival of boats carrying Kurds and Vietnamese and West Papuans and Tamils. And in the long term, there is no doubt that attempts to deter and contain asylum seekers (and other spontaneous migrants) have contradictory results, often at odds with the stated intention. Specifically, they lead to *burden shifting* rather than *burden sharing*[26] on the global refugee problem and encourage, rather than inhibit, growth in the illicit business of people smuggling, as asylum seekers and other spontaneous migrants circumvent border controls via new and ever more dangerous routes.

Notes

1 The best and fullest description of the *Tampa* affair in all is dramatic detail is *Dark Victory* by David Marr and Marian Wilkinson, Allen & Unwin, Sydney, 2003. A more condensed version is Chapter 5 ('In the wake of the *Tampa*') in my own book, *Borderline: Australia's treatment of refugees and asylum seekers in the wake of the Tampa*, UNSW Press, 2002.

2 Interview with Captain Arne Rinnan, *The Europeans*, ABC Radio National 1.30 pm, 5 May 2002.

3 Joint press conference with the minister for Immigration, Parliament House, Canberra, 27 August 2001, <www.pm.gov.au/media/Interview/2001/}interview1187.cfm>.

4 Australia, Senate, 'Evidence to Senate Select Committee on a certain maritime incident', 26 March 2002, Canberra, <www.aph.gov.au/hansard/senate/commttee/s5410.pdf>.

5 See, for example, Garran, R, 'Jakarta-Canberra ties to hold firm: envoy', *The Australian*, 29 August 2001, p 2.

6 Australia, House of Representatives, *Debates*, vol 13, 29 August 2001, p 30571.

7 This was the only point at which Labor opposed the government's approach to the *Tampa* and it did them no good politically. Labor's Julia Gillard recalls that for the next few days all her staff did all day was 'take abusive phone calls from constituents'.

8 Kelly, P, 'No way out for a pale imitation', *The Weekend Australian*, 1-2 September 2001, p 1.

9 John Howard, Joint press conference with minister for Immigration, Sydney, 1 September 2001, <www.pm.gov.au/media/Interview/2001/interview1206.cfm>.

10 See Commander Banks' testimony to the Australia, Senate, 'Evidence to Senate Select Committee on a certain maritime incident', 26 March 2002, Canberra, p 177, <www.aph.gov.au/hansard/senate/commttee/s5410.pdf>.

11 Ibid.

12 Parliament of Australia, *A Certain Maritime Incident,* 23 October 2002, p 26-27, Government Members Report, <www.aph.gov.au/senate/committee/maritime_incident_ctte/report/index.htm>.

13 SIEVs-5,7,11 & 12, see 'SIEV Event Matrix', *A Certain Maritime Incident*, Parliament of Australia, 23 October 2002, Government Members Report,

Appendix III, <www.aph.gov.au/senate/committee/maritime_incident_ctte/report/index.htm>. See also, Marr and Wilkinson, above, n 1, pp 216-220 (SIEV-5); pp 247-249 (SIEV-7); p 287 (SIEV-11 & 12).

14 In May 2007, on a visit to Indonesia, Immigration Minister Kevin Andrews finally agreed that Australia would resettle 120 of the 240 Iraqi and Afghan asylum seekers stranded in Indonesia since the *Tampa* affair, including the family described above. It was reported that the rest of the asylum seekers were likely to be resettled in other countries, including Canada and New Zealand. The intervention followed repeated appeals by the UNHCR and lobbying from community groups within Australia. (Mark Forbes, 'Policy backflip ends limbo for 120 asylum seekers', *Sydney Morning Herald*, 5 May 2007, p 2.

15 Brennan, F, *Tampering with Asylum,* University of Queensland Press, Brisbane, 2003.

16 Manne, R, 'For pity's sake, set them free', *The Age*, 10 June 2002.

17 Ibid.

18 The only exceptions (reflecting domestic political realities in the US) are citizens of the Peoples Republic of China and Cuba. Chinese citizens are asked to fill in a written form asking why they have left China, which provides an opportunity to express a fear of return if they have one, while Cubans are read a statement explaining that they will be given a 'credible fear' interview if they request it; Van Selm, J and Cooper, B, *The New 'Boat People': Ensuring Safety and Determining Status*, Migration Policy Institute, Washington, 2005, p 12. See also *World Refugee Survey 2001,* US Committee for Refugees, Washington, 2001, p 294.

19 Helton, A, *The Price of Indifference: Refugees and Humanitarian Action in the New Century*, Oxford University Press, Oxford, 2002, pp 86-101.

20 Noll, G, 'Visions of the exceptional', *Open Democracy People Flow Debate*, 27 June 2003, <www.opendemocracy.net/debates/debate-10-96.jsp>.

21 See Helton, above, n 19. The most obvious example of containment was the case of Kurdish refugees in northern Iraq after the 1991 Gulf War.

22 Jack Straw's comments were reported by Alan Travis, 'Straw wants to re-write Geneva refugee convention', *The Guardian Weekly*, 15-21 June 2000.

23 Corlett, D, 'Politics, Symbolism and the Asylum Seeker Issue', *University of New South Law Journal* (*The Refugee Issue*), vol 23(3), 2000, p 18.

24 Marr and Wilkinson, above, n 1, p 277.

25 Ibid.

26 Gabaudan, M, 'New Challenges in Refugee Protection and Policy', Address to the Federation of Ethnic Communities Councils of Australia National Conference, 26 October 2001.

5

ARNOLD ZABLE

Perilous journeys

Tale 1: Living in limbo

A frayed visa document, a learner's driving licence and an interim Medicare card are all that remains of Zainalabaden Aluomer's former presence in Australia. The visa, printed on cardboard, was his longed for passport to a new life. Instead, it proved to be one of the factors that contributed to his death.

Aluomer's nightmare began when his father was executed by Saddam Hussein's regime in 1982. Aluomer escaped to Iran in 1991 and languished for eight years in refugee camps in Iran and Saudi Arabia. In 1999, as the situation for Iraqi refugees in Iran continued to deteriorate, he left behind his wife and mother with the promise of reuniting with them in a country where they could feel safe.

Aluomer arrived in Australia by boat from Indonesia in September 1999, and was transferred to the Curtin Detention Centre in Western Australia. When he was finally released in September 2000, he was granted a three-year Temporary Protection Visa (TPV) and bussed to Melbourne, where he was left to fend for himself.

With help from caseworkers at the Ecumenical Migration Centre, and the Darebin City Council, Aluomer was able to find transitional accommodation in a flat in West Heidelberg. Early in 2001, Aluomer learnt that his wife and mother had arrived in Jakarta and were looking for a boat that would enable them to make the final run to Australia. He pleaded with them, by phone, not to risk the voyage.

To understand what happened next, we need to look at the provisions of Aluomer's visa. Between 1994 and 1999 asylum seekers, including those arriving by boat, who were found to be genuine refugees, were granted permanent protection visas, subject to health and character checks. This visa entitled them eventually to sponsor family members they had left behind.

In October 1999, the Howard government introduced a new visa regime. Asylum seekers arriving by boat, and judged to be genuine refugees, were to receive three-year Temporary Protection Visas. They were required to wait 30 months before being eligible to apply for permanent protection. Until then they could not be reunited with their families. If they left the country merely to visit their loved ones they could not return. In effect, this meant they could not hope to see their spouses and children for years. They could also be required to return to their countries of origin at the end of this three-year period, if it was deemed safe to do so.

Aluomer's wife and mother could not wait any longer. They decided it was preferable to risk their lives in a fishing boat than to remain separated from him indefinitely. Aluomer consulted with Haider Al Juboory who was then a caseworker for the City of Darebin and the Ecumenical Migration Centre. Aluomer was contemplating the possibility of joining his wife and mother even though it meant losing his visa. He was advised against leaving Australia, but he could not bear the thought of his loved ones taking the boat journey unprotected and alone. He flew to Indonesia on 13 July 2001.

On 18 October 2001, Aluomer, along with his wife and mother, boarded a fishing boat in Sumatra. They were among the 353 asylum seekers, 146 children, 142 women and 65 men, who drowned when the boat sank the following day, en route to Christmas Island.

Aluomer's tale was publicly recounted on Friday, 2 November 2001, at a memorial service for the victims of the SIEV-X tragedy, as the event has become known, held at the Migrant Resource Centre in High Street, Preston. Among those present were asylum seekers who had lost family on the boat. They were devastated. Their distress was compounded because, as holders of Temporary Protection Visas, they could not even visit survivors of the tragedy.

Some of those present at the memorial service had an additional reason for feeling bereft. Just weeks earlier, on 27 September 2001, the Howard government's revised visa regime had become effective. According to the new provisions, asylum seekers who, en route to Australia, had spent a continuous period of seven days or more in a country in which they could have sought and obtained protection, faced the prospect of never gaining permanent residency. Instead they had to apply, every three years, for a renewal of their temporary visas. In effect this meant they could remain in Australia, but could not be reunited with their families either in this country, or anywhere else unless they were prepared to forfeit their right to protection.

The predicament of TPV holders was highlighted by the plight of Sydney-based refugee, Ahmed Alzalimi, who lost three daughters in the boat tragedy – Eman, aged eight, Zahra, six, and Fatimah, five. Ahmed had arrived in Australia by boat and spent eight months in Curtin Detention Centre, before being granted a three-year Temporary Protection Visa. The government refused his plea to visit his grieving wife, Sondos Ismael, in Indonesia, unless he was prepared to forfeit his right to return to Australia. For the next five months, 27-year-old Sondos Ismael grieved alone as Australian immigration officials investigated the details of her visa application. She was finally reunited with her husband in Sydney on 21 March 2002.

Hazam Al Rowaimi, a 29-year-old Iraqi asylum seeker, was fruit picking in Mildura when he heard the news of his tragic loss. Al Rowaimi, who fled Saddam Hussein's Iraq in 1999, lost his wife, Akhlas, his mother, Hamda, and four children: Noor, aged eleven, Fatama, eight, Nargis, five, and Mohammed, three. Al Rowaini had also warned his family, by phone, not to embark upon the dangerous journey from Jakarta. But almost three years of separation was too much to endure. Again, the travel restriction on his Temporary Protection Visa was one of the major reasons his family chose to risk the journey on an unseaworthy boat.

Ten days after the memorial service I met a group of eight asylum seekers, now released from detention, who were trapped by the new Temporary Protection Visa regime. Their countries of origin include Syria, Iran, Iraq and Yemen. All had wives, children, or other family members who remained in the country they fled, or within refugee camps in third countries. They live in Melbourne's northern suburbs where several hundred TPV holders were then concentrated.

All eight had been found to be genuine refugees. Some had been tortured or threatened with death in their countries of origin. They had all lived, for varying periods, in third countries en route, and had arrived in Australia by boat. Several had lived in a series of refugee camps for up to a decade.

The men I spoke to did not wish to reveal their names. They fear they could be put in jeopardy by speaking out. There is an irony in this. As one of the men put it: 'We chose Australia because it was a democratic country. It was our dream to live in freedom. This is why we risked our lives'.

The pain of their situation was evident in the tears that came to their eyes as they spoke. Some have nightmares in which they have seen their families beyond reach, beyond touch. Others wake up screaming their children's names. Those who are able to speak to their children by phone sometimes break down during their conversations. One regularly walks the streets night after night. He walks because he cannot sleep. He cannot sleep because he awakes from dreams of the three children he last saw when he fled Iraq four years ago. They come to him almost every night, put their arms around him, and beg to see him. He has come to dread the night.

Several of the men I spoke to said the most difficult aspect of their ordeal was being unable to practice their hard-won skills and qualifications. The group included a journalist, a metallurgical engineer, an artist, a surgical technician and an economist. They say they have so much they wish to offer their new country. But when potential employees discover they are on temporary visas, they are overlooked for the job. Instead they work at whatever comes along. Many travel to country areas in the fruit-picking season. Others work in the abattoirs, or in other menial jobs.

Said one:

> I am floating between sky and earth. We are in Australia, but we are not a part of Australia. I want to show Australians what I can do. But in this situation I cannot focus. I feel shattered. My mind goes blank when I think about my family. Australia is a beautiful place, but we cannot enjoy it. This legislation is a rope around my neck.

According to caseworkers I have spoken to, TPV holders exhibit both physical and psychological symptoms of trauma. Some are suicidal, others severely depressed. All suffer from a sense of guilt for not being able to help their families, especially those who have relatives still being persecuted in their country of origin. The men I spoke to feel like outcasts. They believe many Australians are against them. They know the Howard government cares naught for their plight.

There is an additional catch. Asylum seekers who decide they have had enough of this agony are, in some cases, not even able to return to their families because they do not have the papers that would enable them to do so. Others cannot return because it could mean further persecution or even death. Their plight and their treatment by those who govern in our name is a blight upon the nation. As a Samurai maxim puts it. 'Even a hunter does not kill a bird that comes to him for protection'.

Tale 2: Maybe I will see you in paradise

First written for publication on 19 October 2002: the first anniversary.

On 19 October 2001, a woman gave birth on a sinking boat en route from Indonesia to Christmas Island. She was one of 421 men, women and children who had boarded the boat the previous day in the Sumatran port of Lampung with hopes of being reunited with loved ones who had preceded them, and of beginning life anew in Australia. She was last seen by survivors, drifting past with her baby attached by the umbilical cord.

At least three women gave birth as the boat sank, says Amal Hassan Basry, a survivor of the tragedy. One of the mothers was merely six months pregnant. The tragedy induced the births prematurely. Amal recalls the events of that day with great clarity. She knows the exact moment the boat capsized: ten past three in the afternoon. Many watches stopped at that time:

> Because I was waiting for my death, I saw everything. I was like a camera. I can still hear the shouting, the screaming. I see the people going under, my son swimming towards me. Everything.

More than one year later, the memory of the tragedy remains a raw wound. But before she recounts the story, Amal insists on telling me why she was so desperate to make the journey. 'I want people to know why I stayed on the boat even when I saw it was very dangerous', she says. 'I want people to know who I am. Why I escaped from Iraq. Why I risked my life. Why I wanted to come to Australia. Maybe then they will understand'.

We first meet in the living room of the Thornbury Asylum Seeker Resource Centre, a house of welcome, a place where we can talk in peace. I see the strain on Amal's face and the lingering anguish in her eyes. As if sensing my thoughts, Amal says, 'I'm a strong woman, believe me'.

Amal's troubles began in 1980, when her husband was conscripted to fight in Saddam Hussein's war against Iran. She left her job in the Bank of Iraq, in Baghdad, to look after their three young children in his absence. The eight-year war claimed an estimated one million lives.

In 1990, Saddam Hussein invaded Kuwait, and in 1991, at the height of the Gulf War, Amal's 20-year-old brother, was killed by an American bomb in the southern city of Basra, a victim of 'collateral damage'. In the wake of Iraq's defeat, a second brother, 29 years old, was executed because he had refused to take part in the fighting. 'He said he did not want to kill people, that Kuwaitis are my brothers and sisters', says Amal. 'So he got six bullets in his chest'.

In the same year, a brother-in-law was killed in Southern Iraq for taking part in a Shiite revolt against Saddam. Amal's entire family was now under surveillance. Her husband, and two of his brothers, were jailed and tortured in 1995. In 1997, the police came for them again. The family was threatened and harassed. One brother-in-law was arrested and has not been heard of since.

It was time to escape. Amal and her family found sanctuary in northern Iraq in the Kurdish zone, with Iraqi Kurds who had been persecuted by Saddam Hussein. They lived there for 18 months, in an area that was under threat of attack. In 1999, with the help of the Kurds, the family fled to Iran.

At this time, word had it that Australia was a potential haven. They would be welcomed, Amal's family was told. Her husband flew to Malaysia. He arrived by boat on Australia's northwest coast in January 2000. After eight months in Woomera Detention Centre, he was granted a Temporary Protection Visa and settled in Melbourne.

Amal was determined to join her husband as soon as possible. He phoned her in Iran and warned her that the journey was too dangerous. But Amal could not wait. Under the conditions of his Temporary protection visa, her husband could not leave Australia to visit her. Life in Iran, where refugees numbered in many thousands, had become very difficult. Deportation was a constant threat.

In July 2001, Amal left her 19-year-old son in Iran, and together with her younger son, Amjed, then aged 17, she flew to Malaysia. At each stage of the journey there were moments of great danger and payments to be made to people smugglers whose promises could turn out to be lies or half-truths.

From Malaysia, Amal and Amjed journeyed by boat to Sumatra, and subsequently arrived in Jakarta where they met people smuggler Abu Quassey:

> He told us that he had a boat that would take us to Australia. He said it was a big boat, with a lot of space, radar, satellite, plenty of food, toilets. We had to pay 500 dollars American. We went by ferry back to Sumatra, and by bus to the port of Lampung, in the middle of the night.

The women and children were the first to be taken from the beach to the boat, by launch, in the pre-dawn darkness, on 18 October. As they boarded the boat, now known as SIEV-X, Amal and her companions realised that the smugglers had lied. The vessel was just over 19 metres long, and four metres wide. A fishing boat of this length could barely carry 150 people, let alone the 421 asylum seekers who were being ferried to the ill-equipped vessel. 'We couldn't believe it', says Amal. 'We were crowded together. It was raining. There was little food. We were fed only bread and water. The sea was angry. We quickly became sick'.

Amal's teenage son sat on the roof of the cabin while she remained on the deck. Others crammed into the hold. Those on board came mainly from Iraq, Afghanistan and Iran. Later that morning 24 asylum seekers, Mandaean Christians from Iraq, disembarked near a group of islands, south of the Sunda Strait.

At dawn on 19 October, says Amal, one of the Indonesian crew informed the passengers they had moved into international waters. They were well on the way to Christmas Island. A group of children saw dolphins swimming by. For a while the refugees' spirits lifted and their fantasies were revived. 'What do you think Australia looks like?' the children asked. 'Like paradise', was a common reply. Others thought of the husbands and fathers they would soon be reunited with. 'Everyone had their special dream about Australia,' says Amal.

At one in the afternoon, the engine broke down. The backup motor proved useless. The sea was becoming rougher. 'We were very afraid. We were crying. The children were crying. We prayed to God. Everybody was praying'.

At two o'clock the boat began taking water. Passengers were instructed to throw luggage overboard. Some joined the crew in bailing water with improvised scoops. As the boat listed heavily, panic began to take hold. Soon after, the top-heavy vessel capsized. Many women and children were trapped in the hold. Amal closed her eyes, lost consciousness, and came to underwater. 'I could not breathe, so I could not swallow water, and that is why I am alive today', she says. 'I could not breathe and I could not swim'. Somehow she was able to propel herself to the surface.

When she opened her eyes, the boat was beginning to break up. Amal saw people drinking water. Drowning. Shouting:

> The doors to hell opened to us. One man was screaming – all my family are gone. My wife die. My daughter die. Then I thought about my two sons, my husband, my daughter and her children in Jordan. I had to live for them. I had to find a way.

Amal speaks with a sense of urgency. She is driven by a need to record each detail:

> I saw a dead woman in a life jacket, floating. I cannot swim, so I held onto her. I remembered that when I was a child in Baghdad I heard that bodies can float. That memory saved me. Then I saw my son. He was holding onto a piece of wood. He said, mother I want to give you one last kiss. He took the life jacket off the dead woman and helped me put it on. Then he said goodbye mother. Maybe I will see you in Paradise.

Amal clung to the woman's body. As night fell she was floating alone. She disappeared into the dark. It was cold and still raining. Says Amal: 'I spoke to the dead woman. I said, forgive me, but you save me. I was drinking in water. I was waiting for the time of my death'.

Amal saw a shark circling. She believes that it did not attack her because her clothes were saturated with fuel. She saw an island spouting water, but when she paddled closer, she realised it was a whale. During the night she saw lights. She could hear other survivors calling for help. She came upon friends clinging to debris, planks of wood. They moved together towards the lights. For two hours they fought the waves as they tried to reach the mystery boats. At one point, beams of light appeared to sweep over them, 'When we came closer, I saw three boats, two bigger and one smaller boat. I heard their horns. We cried for help, but the boats disappeared. They did not save us'.

At dawn Amal saw no-one as she drifted on. She was exhausted. She could not hold on any longer. She tried to swallow water to end it all quickly. 'I tried to swallow water', she says, 'but I could not do it. Then I looked up and I saw an Indonesian fishing boat moving towards me'. As the boat drew alongside, a crewmember jumped in to take her on board. Only when he touched her did Amal finally let go of the woman's body. She had clung to the corpse for 20 hours. She thanked her before she let go.

There were 40 asylum seekers on the boat, all of whom the fishermen had rescued. Amal was frantic in her concern for her missing boy:

> I cried: My son! My son! You must save my son. Some people told me they saw him half an hour ago. I wanted to jump in, to go after him. I asked the captain: please, turn back, you must save my son. And he did it. One hour later we found him. He was holding onto a piece of wood. He kissed me. He held onto me. He was sitting next to me like a baby.

One of the rescued was a 12-year-old girl, Zeinab, who had lost her entire family in the tragedy – her mother, father, two brothers and two sisters. Says Amal:

> She was crying. She was saying, I am all alone now. I told her I will take you. You can be my daughter. We were in the fishing boat for three nights. I dreamed of sharks. I woke up and saw it was not a shark, but my son.

After a seven-and-half-month wait in Jakarta, Amal was granted a five-year Temporary Protection Visa. She was reunited, on 7 June 2002, with her husband in Melbourne. Because of her temporary status, her future remains uncertain. She envied those survivors who had been taken in by Scandinavian countries where they had been treated far more sympathetically, and given permanent residency. At one point, in Jakarta, she had implored UN officials to allow her to go to Norway. She felt it was better to bring her husband over there where she could get on with her life with greater certainty. Australia had become the most feared destination for survivors. 'We thought Australians do not like us'.

Amal credits the softening of her feelings to 'some good people'. She speaks glowingly of the volunteers who work at the Thornbury Asylum Seeker Resource Centre, and of her teachers at Broadmeadows TAFE. 'They give me new hope. I know good Australian people who stand by me, and help me. I want to learn computer. I want to work. I want to help my son who is in Iran. He is still in danger'.

The memory of the tragedy pursues her. On the 19th day of every month, Amal relives the sinking. Every day she glances at her watch, at about 3.10 pm, and is seized by the memory of the boat capsizing. The watch was a farewell present from Zeinab, her 'adopted' daughter, who was reunited with relatives in Sydney. 'Think of me when you look at the watch', she had asked Amal, before they parted in Jakarta.

Almost every night Amal dreams she is sleeping on the ocean:

> I can't breathe. I am alone. Then I see people who are shouting: Turn back! Turn back! You are going to drown. I put out my hand to stop, and I wake up with my hand still held out. My husband hears me call out and he turns on the light.

Amal has another recurring dream. She is walking. It is dark. She sees a door. She opens it and can see paradise. Inside, she sees all those who had perished in the disaster. 'In the dream they are happy', she says. 'They are calling me. They want me to join them. But I do not want to go in. I close the door, and return to life. My true dream is to live with my family, in peace'.

Postscript

Amal Basry passed away on Saturday, 18 March 2006. Her death, from cancer, was a tragic irony, and her life's journey, a mirror to our troubled times. She understood, intuitively, that her experiences have much to tell us about who we are as a nation, and how we can become a more just and compassionate society.

Since her arrival in Australia, in mid 2002, Amal made it her mission to tell the story of the sinking. A woman of extraordinary courage, she would rise from her sick bed to address audiences in schools, colleges, memorial services, and at public meetings. She told her story with the passion of Coleridge's ancient mariner. She relived the terrifying images many times.

'I was like a camera' she said. 'I saw everything, people drowning and screaming'. Amal was finally granted a permanent visa in 2005. Her spirits soared. 'I am a free woman in a free country', she said. In November 2005, she was able to travel to Iran and Jordan to see her ailing father, elder son, daughter, and four grand children.

Before she left for the Middle East, Amal expressed a wish to be buried in Iraq should something happen. On her return in February she said she wanted to end her days in Australia. She had come to love the country, and those who had welcomed her.

Amal will not be forgotten. Her tale will live on and become an Australian legend. Those of us privileged to know her will continue to tell her story, and reveal the many tales and anecdotes she told us in the years we knew her. She was a woman of great humour and humanity who became a dear friend to people from many backgrounds. She was loved by her fellow survivors, and became their outspoken champion. She bore witness to the most tragic maritime disaster off Australian waters since World War II.

Her tale is a powerful counter to the collective amnesia that has so quickly developed about the SIEV-X tragedy. It is the story of our ancestor's writ large. It reminds us that the country has been built upon the perilous journeys of our forbears, and the wisdom of the land's Indigenous peoples. These are the two great forces that have shaped us.

6

MICHAEL GORDON

The 'Pacific Solution'

What was the Pacific Solution?
A magician used fear to create an illusion:
Smooth prestidigitation,
With one hand – watch! – he distracted the nation;
But the other hand: cruel, barbed, spiked,
That other hand did whatever it liked.
That was the Pacific Solution.
(From a poem by Emrys Nekvapil)[1]

Two events early in 2007 closed the first chapter on the Howard government's 'Pacific Solution'. The first, on 31 January, was the granting of a permanent protection visa to Mohammad Faisal, an Iraqi who had been on Nauru until August 2006, when his mental state deteriorated to the point that he was evacuated to Brisbane. The second was the departure from Nauru early in February of another Iraqi, Mohammed Sagar, to Scandinavia after he had been offered the protection that Australia had refused. Both could be described loosely as the last men standing under a policy that resulted in more than 1500 asylum seekers being processed 'offshore', 1232 of them on the remote, near-bankrupt and sweltering Pacific island of Nauru.

In essence, the 'Pacific Solution' is a policy that was crafted to deter asylum seekers from contemplating paying people smugglers to take them to Australia in often unsafe boats, mostly from Indonesia. Indeed, virtually every aspect of Australia's border protection policy after the *Tampa* episode of August 2001 was framed in terms of sending an uncompromising message to the people smugglers that Australia should be crossed off their list of prospective destinations. This meant telling asylum seekers who did come that they would be treated differently to those refugees who are chosen to come to Australia as part of this country's humanitarian program. Specifically, it meant telling them that they would always be temporary, that they would never be able to reunite with immediate family members, and that they had very little prospect of living in Australia, even on Temporary Protection Visas.

The reality was somewhat different. Of the original Nauru caseload, 274 were resettled in countries other than Australia (most of them in New Zealand): 225 as refugees, 49 without refugee status; 484 were resettled in Australia: 455 as refugees, 29 on humanitarian visas; 425 accepted the voluntary return packages, involving a payment of $2000 per individual and $10,000 per family; and 48 returned to their home country without accepting the voluntary return package. Over the period from late 2001 until 2004, there were 19 births at the two processing camps and one death from natural causes. The cost of setting up and running the Nauru camps between 2001 and 2007 was around $200 million.

Then there was Manus Island in Papua New Guinea. Of the 368 asylum seekers who were accommodated at the Manus Offshore Processing Centre, 306 of them were found to be refugees while at the centre. Twenty-six whose claims were rejected were later transferred to Nauru, where they were reassessed as refugees. Of those who were found to be refugees on Manus, 174 were resettled in third countries and 132 were resettled in Australia. Another 31 who were transferred from Manus to Nauru were later resettled in Australia (21 as refugees and 10 on humanitarian visas). Four asylum seekers on Manus accepted the voluntary return package and another five returned to their home country without accepting the package, but with the assistance of the International Organisation for Migration, the agency contracted to run the camps on Manus and Nauru.[2]

To summarise, the great bulk of those who came uninvited by boat were, eventually, found to be refugees and resettled in Australia, but at great cost to the taxpayer and the mental health of the asylum seekers.

The statistics do not, however, tell the whole story. What we do *not* know is how many of those who returned would have been found to be refugees and afforded protection if they had continued to resist the pressure to go back. What we *do* know is that many whose claims were rejected were subsequently found to be refugees on the basis of changed circumstances in Afghanistan or new information about their cases. What we also know is that mistakes were made in the processing of some of the asylum seekers that were subsequently rectified for those who remained.

Consider, for example, the case of Amin Jan Amin, one of several Afghans on Nauru who marked World Refugee Day on 10 December 2003 by beginning a hunger strike and stitching their lips together. Amin's claim that he worked for the United Nations and World Vision, and consequently was a target for persecution, was not investigated before his claim for refugee status was twice rejected. During the hunger strike, some of those who had been writing to him approached World Vision Australia about his claim and it was quickly established that he was worked on an AusAid de-mining program in Afghanistan and was remembered fondly for his character and good work by the program manager.[3]

During the hunger strike, then immigration minister, Amanda Vanstone, issued a statement urging those who were part of the protest to follow the lead of around 420 others who had accepted the voluntary return package, 19 of them on 1 December. Within one week of the minister's statement, the United Nations refugee agency, the UNHCR, announced that it was reviewing the cases of 22 Afghans on Nauru on the basis of new information. Vanstone responded by saying that, as soon as the UNHCR had completed its assessment of whether the situation in Afghanistan had changed, the government would examine the implications for those it had previously found not to be refugees. As a result, all 22 in the UNHCR caseload were found to be deserving of protection. Of the Immigration Department's remaining Afghan caseload on Nauru, 146 out of 175 were found to be refugees. Amin Jan Amin was one of them.

Looking back, no aspect of the 'Pacific Solution' better demonstrates the inhumanity of the policy than the treatment of husbands who arrived before the *Tampa* episode and their wives and children who followed and were sent to Nauru. By late 2003, there were nine cases where one spouse was living in the community in Australia on a Temporary Protection Visa while the other was in detention on Nauru with their children. As Andrew Bartlett, the Australian Democrats senator who made more trips to Nauru than the total for all other politicians, expressed it:

> It is hard to know which are the more distressed, the wives and kids on Nauru, stuck in the middle of nowhere being pressured to go back to a place they fled, or the husbands, stuck here and separated from their loved ones for almost three years.

What is very clear from the information provided to the asylum seekers is that the women *were* pressured to go back to Afghanistan and Iraq, leaving their refugee husbands in Australia. Information sheets handed to the woman told them their claims had been assessed separately from those of their husbands because they had travelled at different times:

> Under the conditions of your husband's stay in Australia, he is not able to sponsor you. Like all refused asylum seekers you cannot remain on Nauru indefinitely. You should consider voluntary repatriation now … there is no chance of you going to Australia by staying here longer.

There was also the warning that, if the wives did not opt for voluntary return, 'the government is exploring all options for return including involuntary return'.[4]

As the UNHCR pointed out on several occasions, this practice of keeping immediate family members apart was at odds with the agency's criteria for determining refugee status and in breach of Australia's obligations under various human rights instruments, including the Convention on the Rights of the Child. It also had the opposite impact than the one that was intended, encouraging entire family groups to embark on the hazardous boat trip from Indonesia to maximise their chances of staying together. In the end, New Zealand offered a solution for these families, but only after they had endured great psychological trauma.[5]

My own experience reporting on the situation of two of these families highlighted both the trauma suffered by those on Temporary Protection Visas in Australia and their families on Nauru and the folly of forcing men who had shown themselves to be valuable members of the Australian community to move to another country, albeit one with a more compassionate response to refugees. Ali Sarwari was a craftsperson who worked as a pool tiler in Melbourne and was described by his employer as the best worker, in terms of craftsmanship and character, he had ever employed. Jawed Ali received similar endorsements from the human resources manager at the Young meatworks. Both suffered from depression and Jawed was driven to a suicide attempt before the UNHCR was able to negotiate what became known as the Kiwi solution. Before the two men left for Hamilton in New Zealand to restart their lives, one of Sarwari's customers summed up what was a common reaction to their forced relocation. 'It's ridiculous that we can turn away people of this quality and it's ridiculous that he should be separated from his family. I'm just stonkered by it'.

After the cases of all Iraqi and Afghan asylum seekers were reviewed in 2004, with the vast majority being found to be refugees, the population of asylum seekers on Nauru was reduced to 54, comprising 29 Afghans, 20 Iraqis, two Bangladeshis, two Iranians and one Pakistani. It was then that I was granted a visa to visit Nauru by the foreign minister of the recently elected government, David Adeang, and became the first journalist to be afforded unfettered access to the State House processing centre.

It is very difficult to describe the sense of despair that permeated every aspect of the existence of the residents of the camp known as State House. Many were surviving on sedatives issued to help them sleep. All projected a kind of numb, all-consuming hopelessness that had nothing, or very little, to do with the conditions of their detention (which had been progressively relaxed by a new Nauru government and its young, reform-minded ministers) and everything to do with the uncertainty of the situation and their remoteness from loved ones. One of the Afghans, Ali Rezaee, who was 17 when his life in 'offshore' detention began, summed it up in an email to Halinka Rubin, a Melbourne resident who was a tireless supporter of those on Nauru:

> I am a boy who is powerless and lonely burning inside the fence,
>
> I am a boy who is solitary who has been grabbing with discrimination in the circle of human being,
>
> I am a boy whose brain is full of sorrow. I am the boy whose body is full of wound feeling of pain, does have rest for a while.
>
> I am a boy, who just sees dark and dark, and a minute is passing like one hour, a month is passing like a year. And have sleep

> without tablet, no medicine available for reducing the pain, except rolling tear on my cheek.
>
> I am a boy who in mid of night, most of the time lonely sitting in the corner side the fence, looking at the blue sky, at stars, weeping tears, during that time that none is moving around.

Rubin came to know many of the refugees personally once they settled in Australia and has no doubt that 'offshore' detention made it much harder for them to recover from the persecution they had endured before fleeing their homelands. 'While the immediate effect of detention, such as insomnia, nightmares, headaches, lack of concentration, became apparent soon after the release of the asylum seekers, the long term effects are yet to be known', she told me. 'Many of the asylum seekers felt they had lost some of the best years of their lives. They emerged from detention unsure about their self worth'.

A few weeks later, it was announced that nine of the asylum seekers I had interviewed had been granted refugee status. Then humanitarian visas were granted to the last family on Nauru and two Iraqi couples, leaving just 27. Among them were Mohammed Sagar and Mohammad Faisal, two Iraqis who had been found to be refugees, but were denied a security clearance by ASIO after they were interviewed on Nauru. Both had maintained, when I first spoke to them, that their initial ASIO interviews had been more like interrogations and that they had been wrongly accused of being uncooperative.

In the weeks that followed, the news from Nauru on the mental health of those 27 grew progressively bleaker, until there were concerns that several were at grave risk of self-harm. What had been apparent to me, a layperson, was confirmed when the psychiatrist responsible for the mental health needs of the group wrote to a superior on 12 September 2005. The letter, later obtained under Freedom of Information legislation, recommended an immediate change in the social environment of the asylum seekers. It concluded:

> I would recommend the earliest possible time for removal of the migrants from this kind of environment and atmosphere of consistent hopelessness, stressful situation, which are the main

> source and the aggravating factor for their condition ... IOM Medical cannot be held responsible for any events that may arise as a result of such above situation.[6]

Senator Vanstone responded by sending a team of mental health experts who confirmed the assessment of the IOM psychiatrist and urged the transfer of all residents to Australia as a matter of urgency. 'The extreme levels of hopelessness and worthlessness constitute major indicators of risk with regards to suicide', the team said in their report. 'These indicators when combined with other depressive symptomatology and a sense of isolation are well recognised in the literature as predictors of suicide'. The report explained that medications were ineffective in treating those who could not sleep and how in some cases nightmares cause a fear of sleeping. What was clear was that the deterioration in the mental health of those detained on the island was not sudden. As the report noted, it had been 'steady over the past two years', but had become more pronounced over the past six months. 'All cases are considered vulnerable to further deterioration. In many cases the duration of poor psychological functioning has been long-standing'.[7]

None of the above was made public when the government announced in October 2005 that 25 of the 27 had been granted visas to come to Australia as a result of a 'constant review of the failed asylum seekers caseload'. And then there were two.

Early in 2005 I reported that Mohammad Faisal had attempted suicide and been found in a semi-conscious state by Mohammed Sagar. He later told me he had been 'pushed to the edge' by the isolation and uncertainty of his situation and a sense of desperation. 'In Nauru life is black. I feel I am in hell. When I came to Nauru I was 21. My age now is 26. Everything is negative'.

Seven months later, after a plea from the Nauru government, Faisal was evacuated to a Brisbane private hospital, where he spent the next six months. Ironically, it was the inhumanity of the system that saved him. Because he was now on Australian soil he could lodge a fresh application for protection which necessitated a new ASIO assessment as to whether he constituted a security threat to Australia. This time, the spy agency ruled in his favour, clearing the way for him to be issued with a permanent visa.

The story of Faisal's experience in the hospital is typical of how hostility towards those who had been demonised as 'queuejumpers' so often was turned into a warm embrace by personal contact. One of the hospital's patients, in particular, was so upset that 'illegal immigrants' from the Middle East were taking the beds of Australians who needed treatment that he made it his mission to have Faisal and two other asylum seekers already at the hospital moved somewhere else. 'I knew nothing of him. I just put him in the same bracket I put every person who came from somewhere else – I just didn't like him', explained Alan Burrows, 59, a Vietnam veteran whose post-traumatic stress disorder was diagnosed only four years ago.

Then, late one evening, Burrows was sitting in the corridor when Faisal appeared with a plate and offered him a slice of watermelon. 'My instinct was to say no, but I finally took a slice and, later on, he came back and asked if he could sit with me'. Their conversation over the next two or three hours was, in Burrows' words, a life-changer. Faisal told his story, from his childhood in Iraq to the decision to flee Saddam Hussein's regime, to the experience with the people smugglers and, finally, what happened on Nauru. Burrows also told his story to Faisal, of how he joined the navy at 17, served in the Vietnam War and became 'a redneck racist' – and how he was prone to bouts of depression and seemingly inexplicable anger, unaware that these episodes were the result of his wartime experience as a 19- and 20-year-old. Six months later, Burrows' wife, Kaye, credited Faisal with playing a crucial role in Burrows' recovery. 'It's just been incredible', Kaye told me. 'Life in general from that day on has just blossomed'. And Burrows? He said he was honoured to have become Faisal's Australian 'father' and proud to say he is not a racist.

Sagar, meanwhile, was left to ponder whether his mental condition had to deteriorate to the point where he, too, was suicidal, before the government would end his suffering. In a letter to Australia's Immigration Department, he suggested that, if this was the case, he had two options. 'First, in order to expedite the process, I can manipulate that I am suicidal, which I'm unable to do since it isn't a feature of my character. Or, second, we will wait until the zero hour, but then I very much doubt that the Australian government would be able to react timely to save my life'. Ultimately, the UNHCR found a Scandinavian country willing to give him a fresh start.[8]

The same week that Mohammad Faisal was evacuated to Brisbane, in August 2006, two other things happened. First, the Howard government abandoned legislation that would have required all unauthorised boat arrivals, including those who made it to the Australian mainland, to be processed on Nauru. Second, eight Burmese asylum seekers were discovered on Ashmore Reef, having been dropped off by Indonesian people smugglers.

Vanstone, who was dumped from Howard's cabinet in a reshuffle in January 2007, used the detection of the eight, from the Rohingyan ethnic minority, to dramatise the consequences of the legislation being abandoned. 'If, as expected, this group was dumped by people smugglers, this is an example of why our tough border security stance is a necessity', she said. Because they were detected on an island that was excised from Australia's migration zone under the 'Pacific Solution', Vanstone explained that they would be processed on Nauru. Had they made it to the mainland, however, and been found not to be refugees, they would 'have been able to stay here for years on end contesting that decision'.[9]

Unfortunately for the eight, the converse was also true. If they were to be successful in their applications for refugee status, they faced the prospect of spending a long time on Nauru, and experiencing the same levels of despair and depression as those who had gone before them. Indeed, within six months, all said they were suffering from depression and making regular visits to the Nauru hospital. Certainly, their Australian lawyer, David Manne, who spent more than one week with the men on Nauru preparing their applications, had not the slightest doubt that all eight were deserving of protection.

On 15 December 2006, the Burmese received a letter from Australian immigration officials explaining 'two possibilities' for resolving their status. The first was to return to Malaysia, where they had lived after fleeing Burma. They would be given temporary residence and work rights and a modest amount of money to cover immediate expenses and *they* would be able to apply to the Australian High Commission in Kuala Lumpur for refugee status. If successful, they would be eligible for resettlement in Australia as part of the 'offshore' humanitarian program. The second option was for their applications for refugee status to be processed on

Nauru and, if they were successful, resettlement would be pursued in a third country.

In answers to written questions from the group, an Australian government official made it plain that the second chapter of the 'Pacific Solution' would in one sense be even less compromising than the first. The men were told that they should be under no illusions about their prospects if they rejected the offer of voluntary return to Malaysia:

> Immigration outcomes for previous groups processed on Nauru offer no indication as to the likely immigration outcome for you. Unlike previous groups, the Australian Government has decided that even if you are found to be a refugee, you will not be issued with a visa to Australia from Nauru.
>
> Depending on the outcome of the refugee status determination process, Australia will explore options for resettlement in a third country which may take some time. Some persons remained on Nauru for a long time before a durable solution was found.[10]

Despite this warning, seven of the group rejected the first option, saying it would mean returning to a place where they had experienced all manner of forms of persecution. They were also deeply distrustful of the Malaysian authorities. Manne explained:

> Their emphatic belief is that the whole proposal (for return to Malaysia) is far too uncertain, far too precarious and far too frightening. It would leave them back in the state of very dangerous limbo from which they fled.
>
> They have not a skerrick of confidence that there would be anything that would come even close to effective protection in Malaysia. It would mean going back to the lion's den, to the very place where they suffered horrific abuse for years on end. It would re-traumatise them.[11]

What the government clearly wanted to avoid was giving any hint that other asylum seekers, especially the thousands of refugees from Burma, should follow the lead of the eight and attempt to come to Australia by boat. The logical flaw of the approach would have been exposed if the eight had accepted the first option of voluntary return to Malaysia and been granted visas to bring their families to Australia. Would not this, too, have represented an incentive for other Rohingyas in Malaysia to attempt the boat trip to Australia? After all, the end result would be resettlement and protection in Australia.

As Susan Metcalfe, a researcher who became one of the strongest supporters of those on Nauru, expressed it: 'If the only justification for 'offshore' processing is on the basis of deterring other potential arrivals, then it is fatally and morally flawed by the damage it does to the individuals involved, the lack of natural justice and fairness in processing claims, and by the enormous amount of money and resources involved in its implementation'. More than five years after the policy was hastily constructed as part of the response to the *Tampa* episode – as Mohammad Faisal and Mohammed Sagar prepared for the adjustment from long-term 'offshore' detention to freedom in different countries – the Howard government was no closer to accepting this simple truth.

Notes

1 Emrys Nekvapil visited Nauru with Marion Le and assisted in the preparation of applications for refugee status. He wrote this poem in October 2005 after the Government issued 25 of the last 27 on Nauru with visas to come to Australia.

2 All figures provided by Australian Department of Immigration and Citizenship, February 2007.

3 This and other case studies mention in the chapter and dealt with in greater detail in Gordon, M, *Freeing Ali, The Human Face of the Pacific Solution*, UNSW Press, Sydney, 2005.

4 Information handed to Sediqa Sarwari on Nauru in Q&A format by the Department of Immigration, Multiculturalism and Indigenous Affairs.

5 See the UNHCR submission to the Senate Legal and Constitutional Committee on the Migration Legislation Amendment (Further Border Protection) Bill, 2002.

6 Letter from IOM (International Organisation for Migration) psychiatrist on Nauru on 5 October 2005, obtained in response to Freedom of Information request for documents relating to mental health of asylum seekers on Nauru.

7 Report of Mental Health Issues for Residents of the Offshore Processing Centre on Nauru arising from a visit of the Informal Advisory Group on 22 & 23 September 2005.

8 See Gordon, M, 'Living In Limbo', *The Age*, 30 September 2006.

9 The Hon Amanda Vanstone MP, press conference, Canberra, 14 August 2006.

10 Written response to questions from Burmese asylum seekers entitled 'Options for resolution of your immigration status', 19 January 2007.

11 See Gordon, M, 'Asylum seekers reject a return to "lion's den"', *The Age*, 17 February 2007.

PART III

Treatment of arrived asylum seekers

MALCOLM FRASER

Part III Introduction

I am honoured to write the Introduction to Part III of *Yearning to Breathe Free.* We used to be regarded as a humane, compassionate country with the idea of a fair go extended to all people, especially those fleeing tyranny.

In recent years, embracing the major political parties, policy has become harsher. We invented permanent detention centres, first in Australia and then in countries overseas. Our government is doing everything it can to deny access to the law, access to the provisions of the Refugee Convention, to potential refugees. It has called such people 'illegal', 'queuejumpers', 'evil', 'potential prostitutes' or 'drug peddlers'. It has even been suggested, contrary to advice from our security authorities, that they may involve terrorists.

In our name our government has ceased to recognise the terrors from which many people fled, whether it was from Iraq or Afghanistan. It treated people trying to reach our shores as non-people, who did not deserve the benefits of the Rule of Law and due process, the benefits of a fair go.

We have now been told that some people have come to Australia, who don't accept Australian values and that we need a stiffer test to see that it doesn't happen again. So, in our name, our government is introducing much tougher language tests which will embrace history and culture. The government indeed created a fear, as I believe falsely, and then said we can make sure that fear does not become a reality by introducing these tests.

They will penalise those at the lower end of the economic scale who do not have too much time to study, whose education might not have been so good in their own country. It will not penalise a person who wants to do us harm because, if there are such people wishing to become Australians, they will learn how to pass that test. It offers no protection at all but it will offer a means that will enable the government to keep some people out of this country whom the government thinks it does not want.

This book demonstrates that there are people prepared to work hard to expose what has happened in the detention centres, the impact on mental health of the processes that we have put in place and other aspects of a harsh, uncaring Australian regime, one that says Australian values are for the chosen ones and not for people because they are people. One that says Australian values do not extend to mateship or a helping hand for people in distress.

This book deserves to be widely read. The more people who know what has happened in our detention system over the last 20 years, the better it will be. The Labour Party began regressive methods in the late 1980s when they established mandatory detention centres for 'boat people'. That system, which they created, has been sharpened and made more inhumane in the years since by the Liberal government. It has done much to damage our reputation around the world. I commend the book.

7

LINDA BRISKMAN • CHRIS GODDARD

Not in my name: the People's Inquiry into Detention

There are few issues in Australian politics that succeed in uniting elements of the left and the right. The substantial and diverse social movements that have developed in response to Australia's policies and practices towards asylum seekers represent such a coalition. This movement has called on the Australian government to comply with international obligations and core principles of humanity. Groups have formed to condemn policies of mandatory detention, Temporary Protection Visas, the 'Pacific Solution' and the excising of islands from Australia's migration zone. One such activity is the People's Inquiry into Detention, which exposes the policies and practices of immigration detention. This chapter discusses both the processes and findings of this citizen-driven Inquiry.

The People's Inquiry was prompted by the cruelty shown to one woman and the limited response to her plight by the federal government. Early in 2005, the Australian media reported that a woman known as 'Anna', suffering from a severe mental illness, was being held in the Baxter Immigration Detention Facility in Port Augusta. It eventually became clear that 'Anna' was in fact Cornelia Rau, an Australian resident. She had been reported as missing by her family but had not been identified by authorities. Mistaken for a 'suspected non-citizen', she had been held in a Queensland jail and then Baxter for months.

As social workers Chris Goddard and Max Liddell wrote in *The Age*, the treatment of Cornelia Rau 'exposed the darkest corners of our lives'. The plight of Cornelia raised many awkward questions:

> Why was it that those who are amongst the most marginalized, the Aboriginal community in Queensland and those imprisoned in Baxter, were apparently able to recognise someone in desperate need of help when professionals were not? Why was it that it was those same marginalized people who were the ones who showed kindness and concern? Why do we treat those in need of help so brutally? Why do we imprison those who are ill? What is it that makes us place 'suspected non-citizens' behind wire in the desert, in an environment so harsh and damaging?
>
> Was it solely because Cornelia Rau was one of our own that we now recognise – all too belatedly – that such treatment is so cruel?[1]

Cornelia had much in her favour. She was young, attractive and had been a flight attendant on that Australian icon Qantas. Strangers from other countries in need of help had much less in their favour. Cornelia's sister, journalist Chris Rau, commented:

> While she was an unnamed illegal immigrant, the only treatment she got for mental illness was longer periods in lock-up as punishment for bad behaviour … As soon as she became an Australian resident, she was whisked away to a teaching hospital, seen by consultant psychiatrists and medicated. During which leg of her flight from Baxter to Adelaide did she suddenly gain the basic human right to medical treatment? Over the years we have heard of immigration detainees denied access to psychiatric care, some with horrific mental illnesses and suicidal tendencies. How many cases like Cornelia's will it take until they get the care they deserve or, more importantly, are taken out of conditions which in themselves lead to mental illnesses?[2]

Prominent QC and refugee advocate Julian Burnside points out that the treatment of Rau is commonplace in Australia's detention centres:

> The only novel feature of the Rau case is that she is uncomfortably like us. She looks like a typical Aussie girl. We are shocked at her treatment, but she received the same careless, cruel indifference that most asylum seekers receive. Why is it acceptable to treat asylum seekers this way, but shocking when it is done to one of us?[3]

The outrage at Cornelia's detention forced the government into announcing an inquiry into the circumstances of her detention, convened by former federal police commissioner Mick Palmer.[4] There were many community calls for the government to widen the terms of reference of the Palmer Inquiry but these went unheeded. The calls were in recognition that although the Rau situation depicted a scenario of incompetence and inefficiency it was in fact much more. It was driven by an obsession with non-citizens, an acceptance of ill-treatment and a philosophy of discrediting informed advocates. It was a clear demonstration of a secretive and punitive system that ensured that power remained vested with those in the public and private sector, driven by profit motives, and colluding in formulating and implementing the harsh regime.[5]

Despite the bleak political and community context, those immigration detainees inside Baxter were optimistic:

> God sent Cornelia here to send our cry to all Australian people. We are all happy that she be free from such a terrible place. We all pray that she will get well. She remains in our minds and hearts as a heroine for ever and ever.[6]

The heart of the government remained hard and unmoved. An official wider inquiry was not called and the People's Inquiry was born.

The beginnings

The Australian Council of Heads of Schools of Social Work (ACHSSW) represents social work in universities throughout Australia. Its charter includes addressing national issues in social policy, consistent with the social work quest to work towards social justice and human rights. The Council had previously taken up concerns about immigration detention through its advocacy endeavours. With the terms of reference set in place, the Inquiry's aims were twofold: to influence policy and to place the stories of detention on the public record. In bearing witness to the experiences of detention, the accounts represent 'a form of moral suasion'.[7]

The ACHSSW took the decision to convene the Inquiry believing it was beholden on those with privilege and expertise to speak out and to act, recognising the oft-quoted adage that bad things happen when good people do nothing.[8] From the beginning, the Inquiry was open, inclusive and transparent. The first announcement was made by journalist Andra Jackson in which the ACHSSW expressed concern about why people could be incarcerated for lengthy periods when they had committed no crime and conveying the need for an 'open, transparent and ethical inquiry'.[9] As Rachel Judd has stated, the extreme suffering of those detained under immigration law has long been represented by the government as an adverse side effect of a tough but benign immigration policy. For Judd, the Inquiry hence makes a contribution to placing previously concealed information on the public record.[10]

The organisers were almost overwhelmed by the response that followed the call to participate. Immediately support emerged from all around Australia and from people from all walks of life. Before long a team of advisors, organisers, researchers and others rallied to join in the quest to expose the evils of the detention regime. Volunteers included transcribers, food organisers, legal personnel and media experts. Students from a range of disciplines came forward to undertake field placements or internships, making a valuable contribution to the much-needed labour and to their own learning. Although commencing with no money, donations were received from philanthropic trusts and other supportive organisations in order to facilitate the work. The amount of money remained limited, and we were heartened by the amount of goodwill, time and energy that so many volunteers invested in the Inquiry. The comment was made by one volunteer: 'I bet Mick Palmer didn't have to sweep the floor after his meetings'.

The process

Two main methods of inquiry took place. These were public hearings and written submissions. The hearings took place in Port Augusta, Melbourne, Sydney, Launceston, Perth, Canberra, Adelaide, Shepparton, Swan Hill and Griffith. More than 200 people testified including asylum seekers and refugees, former detention and immigration staff, lawyers, nurses, psychiatrists, psychologists, migration agents, refugee advocates and activists. In addition, approximately 200 written submissions were received.

The process of running the Inquiry was somewhat organic in nature, responding to ideas and requests as hearings took place.

For example, the idea for hearings in Griffith emerged when a group of refugees in that community participated in a Canberra teleconference, which led to an invitation to visit. In every location there was a different auspice, usually a university, but sometimes other groups. Each auspice responded to the local context in the way the hearings were developed including choice of venue, type of launch, composition of hearing panels and the nature of debriefing for participants. We were guided by legal and ethics advisors and media experts.

We heard stories of great pain, stories of resilience and stories of shame about what was occurring in our nation. Those involved have cried, despaired and hung their heads in shame but have been buoyed by the resilience of those who suffered. In our endeavours, we have tried to give back to those participating by linking them to services or legal advice where required. Invariably people who have spoken out have told of the value of the experience of having their stories believed and validated. The stories told, like life narratives, put a human face to suffering and, as individual stories accumulate, 'the collective story gains cultural salience and resonance'.[11]

The findings

The first report, *We've Boundless Plains to Share*, was released in November 2006, launched in Perth at a national social work conference. The preliminary report presents an initial analysis of verbal and written testimony given to the Inquiry about boat journeys to Australia and the detention experience. Evidence from people on asylum seeker boats includes accounts of perilous journeys that were compounded by the endeavours of the Australian Navy to remove boats from Australian waters before the 2001 federal election. Evidence was received about widespread assaults in detention facilities, appalling levels of health care and a number of deaths. Representations by Australian supporters to politicians about these and other matters were largely ineffective.

The overall impression was one of needless cruelties. Former immigration detainees, visiting health workers and others reported a catalogue of callous disregard for human rights. Detention in desert locations was hard enough, but the isolation was magnified by repeated cruelties imposed on vulnerable people. The Inquiry was told about people being called by numbers alone, about being woken in the early hours of the morning for head counts, of delays in sending mail, of the lack of toilets and the refusal to allow personal photographs to be taken of their children. One witness to the Inquiry said that detention centres generated universal ill-health never seen outside a psychiatric hospital. 'You couldn't design an environment more destructive to a child's development than in immigration detention', a mental health professional told the Inquiry.

Testimony

The following examples illustrate the brutality:[12]

Testimony from asylum seekers

> [T]hey took women and children only. Single men and married men were left in this broken boat by themselves and they said we are going to take you to international waters and then from there you can go wherever you like. The wives were pleading, crying and begging them – that's how it is when you are so desperate. You are holding someone's feet and begging for their mercy and that's what our wives were doing, yet they were kicking them and telling them we have to take these people to international waters, they can go wherever they want to go but we cannot take them.

> The first day we were given a number and I was told from now on that's how I will be known. You will be ABC123. That was one of the most difficult things for us because having your normal freedom taken away from you and at the same time you lost your name.

> I had a lot of cockroaches in my room where I used to wake up in the morning and there were cockroaches on my chest and in my hair. For three months I asked either to be moved to another room or to have the cockroaches exterminated.

Testimony from visitors

> We … do our best but nothing bloody well changes. And while we do our best, we watch people get very, very, very sick – trying to kill themselves and wish they were dead.

> The overriding thing is the shame that this is Australia. There's no way of really expressing how hurt we all feel by this happening and our powerlessness to do anything about it.

Testimony from professionals

> You could have the Rolls Royce of mental health services in Baxter and I don't think it would make a scrap of difference, because the environment is so toxic that you can't treat anything meaningfully. I think that half a dozen of the most damaged people that I've ever seen are the adults I've seen in Baxter and Woomera, both parents and single men.
>
> [N]ot be able to keep children physically and emotionally safe in detention, children I know were suffering, has been the most shocking, brutal thing that's happened in my life.

Children in detention

The practice of locking up children is one that will plague this country forever. Marcus Einfeld asks 'by what cruel standards of thinking do we empower ourselves to abuse and mistreat children who have already arrived here as a weapon to deter others who have not?'.[13] Children in detention have received a great deal of public attention, particularly through the Human Rights and Equal Opportunity Commission (HREOC) report of 2004[14] and the 2005 challenge to the Howard government by federal Liberal backbencher Petro Georgiou and colleagues, which resulted in changes to policies regarding children, specifically a move to housing in the community.[15] But, as our Inquiry has demonstrated, the changes were too late for many. In 2004, we described holding children in detention centres as 'organised and ritualised abuse' by the government:

> We use the term "organised abuse" to mean that those children are being abused by many perpetrators who are acting together in ways that they know can be extremely harmful.
>
> And we use the term "ritualised abuse" to mean that the children are subject to formal and repeated acts of abuse carried out under a belief system that the government uses to justify such cruelty.[16]

The treatment of asylum seeker children has chilling similarities with the way Indigenous children were treated in institutions through the stolen generations policies and practices. Lowitja O'Donohue asks: 'How is it that this nation's First Peoples, and its last peoples, should suffer similar indignity?'.[17]

Like the stolen generations it may be many years before the full impact of locking away children is known. An analysis of Inquiry material to date reveals heartbreaking accounts. These add to the much publicised case of Shayan Badraie who, in early 2006, as a result of an out of court settlement, received government compensation. Shayan became a symbol of the evil of locking away children after developing disturbing symptoms including total withdrawal and refusal to eat and speak in detention.

Next steps

The final and more expansive report will be released in early 2008.[18] It will further develop the themes of the first report and will also explore issues of claims processing and the aftermath of detention. Although our primary concern is with asylum seekers, we will include the experiences of others who find their way into immigration detention including students, people whose visas have expired and Indonesian fishermen. Our work will not cease here and a monitoring role will continue with annual reporting on detention policies and practices. Our commitment will continue until asylum seekers are treated with humanity and decency, which includes an end to mandatory detention. The concluding comments to our first report argue the case for ongoing vigilance, for many of those released after spending years in detention still have no certainty about their future. Furthermore, there are still asylum seekers detained in Indonesia who did not find their way to Australia; Operation Relex, the activities of the Australian Defence force to prevent asylum seekers reaching Australian shores, is still in place; the building of a new custom built detention facility on Christmas Island is underway; and the policy of mandatory detention for those arriving without valid travel documents remains.[19] And:

> At a time when 'Australian values' are being publicly debated, the evidence presented to the People's Inquiry stands as

> a condemnation of those Australians who constructed and implemented policies which damaged and, in some cases destroyed, the men, women and children who fled brutal regimes and asked for our help. It condemns those who, in the face of overwhelming evidence of the destruction such policies were causing, not only failed to change them, but continued to defend them. It stands as a vindication of the thousands of ordinary Australians, activists, community and religious leaders and the few brave politicians who dedicated themselves to fighting these injustices. But above all, the evidence presented to the People's Inquiry demonstrates the extraordinary resilience and courage of those who survived their treatment at the hands of the Australian government.[20]

To our knowledge this is the first time that such an extensive citizen-driven inquiry has been conducted in Australia. The essence of the Inquiry's content and processes has struck a chord with community members from all walks of life by enabling previously silenced voices to be heard in the public domain.

Notes

1 Goddard, C and Liddell, M, 'Exposed: the darkest corners of our lives', *The Age*, 14 February 2005, p 13.

2 Rau, C, and McDonald, J, 'My sister lost her mind, and Australia lost its heart', *Sydney Morning Herald,* 7 February 2005, <www.smh.com.au/articles/2005/02/06/1107625064599.html>.

3 Burnside, J, 'The abuse of one exposes what we're doing to them', *The Age*, 7 July 2005.

4 Palmer, M, *The Inquiry into the Circumstances of the Immigration Detention of Cornelia Rau*, Commonwealth of Australia, Canberra, 2005.

5 Briskman, L, 'Can we still call Australia home?', *Forum*, No 44, Centre for Citizenship and Human Rights, Deakin University, 2005.

6 Baxter detainees' statement to refugee advocates, 2005.

7 Schaffer, K and Smith, S, *Human Rights and Narrated Lives: the Ethics of Recognition*, Palgrave Macmillan, New York, 2004, p 3.

8 Adapted from the words attributed to English statesman Edmund Burke: 'All that is necessary for the triumph of evil is that good men do nothing'.

9 Jackson, A, 'Academics to hold alternative inquiry', *The Age*, 14 February 2005.

10 Judd, R, 'The People's Inquiry into Detention', *New Matilda.com*, July 2005, p 3.

11 Schaffer and Smith, above, n 7.

12 More testimonies are available in the first report, which is available at <www.peoplesinquiry.org.au>.

13 Einfeld, M, *Address to the ACT Launch of the People's Inquiry into Immigration Detention*, Australian Catholic University, 4 May 2006.

14 Human Rights and Equal Opportunity Commission (HREOC), *A Last Resort: the Report of the National Inquiry into Children in Immigration Detention*, HREOC, Sydney, 2004.

15 ABC Television, 'Detention policy changes "meaningful"', *Insiders*, 19 June 2005, transcript at <www.abc.net.au/insiders/content/2005/s1395397.htm>.

16 Goddard, C and Briskman, L, 'By any measure, it's official child abuse', the *Herald Sun*, 18 February 2004, p 17.

17 O'Donohue, L, 'Return to Afghanistan: resettlement or refoulment', speech given at public forum, Adelaide, 27 February 2003.

18 The first report of the Inquiry is available at <www.peoplesinquiry.org.au>.

19 Australian Council of Heads of Schools of Social Work, *We've boundless plains to share: the first report of the People's Inquiry into Detention*, ACHSSW, Melbourne, 2006.

20 Ibid, p 64.

8

PATRICIA AUSTIN • DERRICK SILOVE •
ZACHARY STEEL

The impact of immigration detention on the mental health of asylum seekers

> *My world has become like upside down because I have never seen things like this. I see people who bury themselves alive one day … I see people go on the tree and just jump down just like that and I see people who cut themselves. I see officers hit woman and children with batons, or use tear gas. I just, it's too much for me, I don't know why and sometimes I wonder you know, it is very stressful to me.* (A child detained at Curtin in 2002).[1]

As part of its 'offshore' humanitarian program, Australia resettles up to 13,000 refugees annually. Refugees are processed by the Department of Immigration prior to arrival and enter Australia with permanent protection visas. Smaller numbers of 'onshore' asylum seekers apply for refugee protection after they arrive in Australia. If asylum seekers arrive with a valid visa they are allowed to live in the community under restricted conditions; however, if they arrive without an authorised visa or if their visa is cancelled they are then placed in detention while their refugee claims are processed.

The policy of mandatory detention, instigated in 1992, is applied to all persons, including asylum seekers without a valid visa or who have their visa cancelled on arrival. This shift in policy accorded with international trends to apply strategies of so-called 'humane deterrence' to asylum seekers.[2] These strategies aimed to discourage entry into developed countries of the increasing numbers of persons fleeing conflict and persecution. The parallel Australian refugee policies created two classes of refugees: those awarded permanent settlement and those who lived under restrictions in the community or were in detention. More recently, since 1999, asylum seekers eventually found to be refugees commonly are offered only temporary protection, creating a state of 'permanent impermanence'.

Asylum seekers have experienced long and perilous journeys, speak little or no English, and arrive disoriented and confused. Many have suffered persecution, arbitrary incarceration, killings, losses and torture.[3] International research suggests that prolonged detention of asylum seekers in host countries causes stress both in adults[4] and in children and adolescents.[5] In contrast, refugees who are accorded permanent residency tend to recover from trauma-related stress over time.[6]

In the 1990s, several detention centres were established in remote, semi-desert locations in Australia. These centres are located far from the coastal cities where compatriot communities and services for refugees are concentrated. Multiple layers of razor wire or electrified fences surround the centres and they are patrolled by uniformed guards. Detainees often are separated from families; face indeterminate periods in detention, experience social and cultural isolation, and uncertainties about the future. Torture and trauma survivors in particular face the risk of being repatriated to situations of danger.

Researchers have not gained authorised access to detention centres in spite of repeated requests.[7] Nevertheless, some studies have been conducted.[8] We report the findings of these studies and the conclusions of 19 successive Commissions of Inquiry (COIs) investigating concerns about detention. In addition, we draw on observations of some key health professionals who have treated detainees.

Mental health problems

Reported mental health problems amongst detainees include depression, suicidality, post-traumatic stress disorder (PTSD) and a general deterioration in emotional, behavioural and social well-being. Depression is commonly associated with acts of self-harm. The following is illustrative testimony from the 2004 HREOC

(Human Rights and Equal Opportunity Commission) National Inquiry into Children in Immigration Detention:

> In January 2002 (at the Woomera Centre), the father attempted to hang himself. He told detention staff that he was tired and upset because his three-year-old son could not go to school … Later … the mother allegedly threatened to harm herself with broken glass.[9]

A 14-year-old boy at Woomera was severely suicidal in 2002, an officer reporting that:

> He wanted to kill himself because his mother doesn't eat and she cries all the time. [He said] "I have every intention of killing myself. I'll do it again and again". Very tired of camp, getting up in the morning and seeing the fences and dirt. "We came for support and it seems we're being tortured. It doesn't matter where you keep me. I'm going to hang myself".[10]

The Department of Immigration documented a strikingly high prevalence of self-harm and suicide attempts amongst adults and children:

> Between July and December 2001 there were 688 major incidents involving 1149 detainees across all detention centres … 174 were self-harm incidents (25 of which involved children). Seventy-four percent of all the major incidents in that period occurred in the Curtin, Port Hedland and Woomera centres, where the largest number of children have been detained for the longest periods of time.[11]

A South Australian Department of Human Services, (DHS) report focusing on the Woomera Centre stated that:

> Since January 2002 a total of 50 reports of self-harm have been raised on 22 children, ranging in age from 7 to 17 years. These incidents included hanging attempts; self-harm by cutting arms or ingesting shampoo; and persistent depression and/or suicidal thoughts. The most frequent incidents occurred with children who are 10 and 12 years of age. Children aged 14 years are the next highest sub-category represented in this group … Sixty percent of these reports related to children aged 12 years or less.[12]

Structural clinical interviews undertaken as part of an independent research study of families held in detention[13] showed that the majority of adult members of families from one ethnic group held in a remote detention centre were suffering from clinical depression, severe PTSD and suicidal thoughts. Most of the children were depressed and manifested a range of other mental disorders while several had suicidal thoughts and had tried to harm themselves. The rates of mental disorder in adults and children far exceeded those in the general Australian community and those documented in studies of refugee groups living in the community.

A parallel study[14] surveyed families in a remote detention centre over a period of two years. Very young children exhibited substantial developmental delay in attachment formation and behavioural disturbances while older children commonly manifested symptoms of post-traumatic stress, major depression, suicidal thoughts and bed-wetting.

An Afghan man at the Perth centre in 2001 said:

> It's about 16 months since I arrived here. I've been under a lot of pressure. My life has been taken away from me. Within this 16 months I have become mentally and also physically ill. Every day my physical well-being is getting worse … I've become a useless person who wishes for death every day.[15]

Factors contributing to mental illness

The deterioration in mental health has been attributed to several interrelated factors: prolonged and indeterminate confinement, conditions in detention centres, and inadequate or inaccessible health, psychological and psychosocial support services.

(a) Environment of detention

The general environment of detention centres that may impact on mental wellbeing include the prison-like conditions, lack of privacy, overcrowding, and invasive procedures including frequent musters, roll calls and room searches:

> Committee members were shocked by what they saw during their visit to the six centres … shocked by the harsh picture presented by the exterior of some of the centres: double gated, large spaces between high fences topped with barbed or razor wire. The physical impact of the centres and their psychological impact on the detainees are among the lasting impressions of the visits.[16]

> [T]he effects of being restrained behind wire fences and locked gates; of knowing that one's parents are suffering depression and uncertainty, will have long term psychological and psycho-social consequences that could be avoided by allowing for release of families into the community.[17]

> [W]e were locked in and the APS (the uniformed custodial guards under contract to manage detention centres) came in each hour once every hour to check up on us during the night. A number of us did not sleep. It was particularly difficult for the women with men coming into their rooms every hour. They said that this was for our own safety but we could not imagine what these safety issues were.[18]

Unaccompanied children residing in the Curtin Centre said they felt 'like animals' and 'like you have a cow tag or something on you'.[19] The confined conditions and overcrowding increased exposure to extreme reactions of other detainees, including hunger strikes, mass acts of self-mutilation and other forms of self-harm, riots, damage to buildings, violent protest and other confrontations with authorities. Detainees have witnessed violent confrontations in which tear gas and water cannons have been used.

A father at the Curtin Immigration Centre expressed his concern:

> Unfortunately, the environment is not very healthy because every day they [the children] are witnessing people who are going on top of the tree, who are suiciding or just cutting their body by blade or jumping, shouting, doing everything violent and they are witnessing and they think this is a game they have to participate in it. It's a very dangerous situation and we cannot have any control of it.[20]

Authorities have used isolation and forced transfer to other facilities as a form of 'behavioural management' of detainees. Detainees have been transferred to State prisons for a wide range of behaviours including health-related crises such as suicide attempts and threats of self-harm.[21] In addition, chemical restraints have been used to control behaviour rather than for strictly medical purposes.[22]

(b) Prolonged detention

Prolonged indefinite detention over several years may be particularly detrimental to the mental health of detainees. A husband and wife detained in Port Hedland wrote in 1997:

> In the detention centre we pass a day as if it were a year, all our hopes dashed to pieces, despaired, puzzled … During the miserable detention, we have both been sad, despaired and helpless, and have continuous nightmares.[23]

A number of surveys conducted in the 1990s, focusing on groups of Cambodians, East Timorese and Sri Lankan Tamils revealed that psychological problems tended to mount as detention became more prolonged. Comparisons with compatriot groups allowed to live in the community suggested that detention was the key factor in the deterioration of mental health in those confined.[24]

A senior child psychiatrist who examined a family at Woomera in 2002 stated that:

> [C]hildren who are in the centre for long periods manifest a significant regression over the period of detention… many factors contribute to this regression … little opportunity for play and legitimate academic pursuits; reduced availability (physical and emotional) of attachment figures; interference with normal family rituals of feeding and caring; lack of privacy; hostile and deprived physical environment with intimidating and ever-present security measures; dehumanising use of numbers rather than names (theoretically now banned, but highly prevalent during my visit); and exposure to violence (not only witnessing intermittent full scale riots, but also equally disturbing episodes such as men burying themselves and inviting their family to sit around and watch them die). It is hard to conceive of an environment more potentially toxic to child development.[25]

Research by Steel and colleagues[26] identified a three-fold increase in psychiatric disorders amongst adults and a ten-fold increase in children after an average of two years in detention, findings supported by a parallel study of detained families in a another remote detention facility.[27]

Compromised health and mental health care

Lack of access to appropriate medical and psychological services may add to the problems generated by detention itself. Personnel from a torture and trauma services, STARTTS, commented as follows:

> The ACM (private company managing the centre) refused to provide the escort service to our office stating that it was not

> part of their contract, and we refused to provide counselling services in the counter-therapeutic environment of the detention centre for sound professional reasons.[28]

In 2004 it was noted that:

> [The detention centres] because of their location, do not have ready access to emergency services including surgical, obstetric, dental and psychiatric services nor the ready availability of consultants to offer the necessary back up to the primary care service providers.[29]

The Department of Human Services, South Australia commented on the inadequacy of services in Woomera in 2002:

> The provision of medical services does not have sufficient scope to provide for the acute and long term psychological and psychiatric needs of the detainees … The health service cannot provide sufficient monitoring of children and adolescents at risk of harm to prevent multiple episodes of slashing of arms, ingestion of tablets or shampoo and attempted hangings. This deficiency is as much a resource issue as a management issue.[30]

Mental health experts recognised that mental illnesses could not be effectively treated within the detention environment since the prevailing conditions were contributing directly to the persistence of symptoms. Numerous psychiatric reports have stated that the most therapeutic action would be to release children and their families from detention. In short, caution was needed in advocating for services when the root cause of existing psychological problems could be traced to the reality of detention itself.

The longer term psychological consequences of detention after release

Recent studies have looked at the carry-over effects on mental health once asylum seekers are released.[31] Those who had been detained showed more psychological problems than compatriots who had never been confined, even when other risk factors such as past trauma were taken into account. Furthermore, if after detention refugees were given only temporary protection, creating the risk that they would be sent back to their homeland, they suffered worse mental health compared to those on permanent residency visas.

These findings are important since they suggest that detention may have a prolonged effect on the capacity of refugees to adapt to their new environment even after release, coinciding with the crucial phase of early resettlement when they are confronted with many challenges such as learning English, finding accommodation and work, and acculturating to the new environment.

The response of authorities

During the 13-year period from 1992 to 2005, the Immigration Department resisted repeated calls by health professionals, researchers and community groups to remedy the impact of detention on the mental health and wellbeing of asylum seekers. It did so in the face of a growing body of reports from mental health professionals detailing how prolonged detention posed a risk to mental health.

The Departmental response to the HREOC inquiry stated that:

> The government rejects the major findings and recommendations contained in this report. The government also rejects the Commission's view that Australia's system of immigration detention is inconsistent with our obligations under the United Nations Convention on the Rights of the Child (CROC) … The HREOC report is very disappointing. In proposing that there should be a presumption against the immigration detention of children, and that family unity should be preserved, the report recommends a model that would in practice encourage the inclusion of children in people smuggling operations. The government will not be encouraging such activity.[32]

In 2004, Dr Simon Lockwood, a primary care physician who had worked for more than three years across a number of remote detention facilities, gave an illuminating media interview. He described how he had addressed a meeting of Immigration Department officials to inform them about how the practice of detention impacted on the wellbeing of confined families and children:

> [A]nd then towards the end of the meeting one of the bureaucrats said to me, in front of everyone there, "That sounds all well and good to us, Simon, but we don't want to make it so nice for them in detention that they won't want to leave." I knew that I'd spoken for two hours probably for nothing.[33]

In 2005, growing public concerns about Australian immigration policy were fuelled by media coverage of an incident of the wrongful detention of Cornelia Rau, an Australian citizen suffering from severe mental illness. The report detailed the poor conditions of care she was subjected to and the inadequacy of psychiatric treatment she received. Further revelations followed about the wrongful deportation of Vivian Alvarez Solon and other incidents of deportation of mentally impaired persons mistaken for asylum seekers. A major inquiry produced the Palmer Report,[34] which was very critical of the practices and departmental culture associated with detention. Intense lobbying by community leaders, health professionals and politicians was instrumental in the government softening aspects of the policy of detention. Families and children have been released from detention centres and the Federal Ombudsman now is able to make recommendations for alternative arrangements for persons held in prolonged detention, although these remain non-binding.

Commentary

The evidence provided herein, compiled as it is from a number of sources, suggests that many asylum seekers have been exposed to adverse experiences in Australian detention centres over recent years. Asylum seekers already are vulnerable because they have fled countries with repressive regimes, a significant number having experienced torture and other forms of gross human rights violations and trauma. They have undergone long hazardous journeys in their search for freedom, leaving family and possessions behind. These persons then face the baffling reality of a two-tier reception system in Australia. Authorised refugees receive state-of-the-art specialist support services such as torture and trauma counselling, assistance with housing, English-language classes, employment assistance, the potential to reunite with families, and financial support. In stark contrast, asylum seekers without valid travel documents – often those fleeing their countries in haste because they are in imminent danger – are greeted with restrictions and deprivations in Australia, the most extreme outcome being that they are held for prolonged periods in detention.

For almost two decades, the dual pathway has discriminated against persecuted persons who legitimately seek asylum but who do not have the capacity to seek prior authorisation to seek refuge here. For those held in detention, the very conditions of their confinement, and the fears and uncertainties that detention generate, appear to trigger or worsen psychological symptoms. Some of the worst consequences are now well documented and include suicidal tendencies, difficulties in providing effective parenting and loss of the capacity to adapt when released from incarceration.

In the past 30 years, much progress has been made in offering comprehensive psychosocial services to assist refugees to recover from previous trauma in their homeland and to adapt to a new life once they reach safe countries. Australia is a leader in the field. Sophisticated psychological treatments can assist recovery from experiences of torture, mass violence and forced displacement. Living in a state of security, however, is a vital condition for traumatised refugees to benefit from these treatments. Instead of creating an environment of safety and predictability, detention has the diametrically opposite effect, intensifying feelings of isolation, uncertainty, fear and despair.

From the perspective of society as a whole, policies that perpetuate and worsen mental disability in displaced persons represent an unnecessary waste of human potential. Instead of the host country capitalising on what refugees have to offer, contemporary practices are creating a generation of immigrants with long-term emotional problems who will need extensive rehabilitation in order to restore them to a state of wellbeing and effectiveness so that they can contribute to the new society. Australians of all walks of life need to consider the impact of these policies on the fabric of their society. Concerned citizens can be active in encouraging further research, insist on more information and more informed debate in the media and in the public domain as a whole, and challenge political leaders to account for their policies. Hopefully, a multi-pronged and more critical approach to this problem will give further impetus to the process of policy reform and create a deeper communal recognition that harsh treatment of traumatised refugees and asylum seekers has adverse consequences not only for those fleeing persecution, but for the moral fabric of the host society as well. An important index of the integrity of a society is the extent to which it adheres to its international responsibilities to provide genuine welcome to those persons fleeing persecution who arrive at the country's doorstep seeking desperately needed protection. We have a responsibility not to do these persons any further harm but rather to provide a healing environment that gives them the best chance to become functional members of their adopted community – which is the only outcome genuine refugees seek.

Notes

1 Human Rights and Equal Opportunity Commission (HREOC), *A Last Resort: National Inquiry into Children in Immigration Detention*, HREOC, Sydney, 2004, p 406.

2 Silove, D, Steel, Z and Watters, C, 'Policies of deterrence and the mental health of asylum seekers', *Journal of the American Medical Association*, 2 Aug 2000, vol 284(5), pp 604-611.

3 Burnett, A and Peel, M, 'Asylum seekers and refugees in Britain, What brings asylum seekers to the United Kingdom?', *British Medical Journal*, 2001, vol 322(7286), pp 485-488; Gorst-Unsworth, C, Goldenberg E, 'Psychological sequelae of torture and organised violence suffered by refugees from Iraq. Trauma-related factors compared with social factors in exile', *British Journal of Psychiatry*, vol 172, 1998, pp 90-94.

4 Keller, AS, Rosenfeld, B, Trinh-Shevrin, C, Meserve, C, Sachs, E, Leviss, JA, et al, 'Mental health of detained asylum seekers', *Lancet*, vol 362(9397), 2003, pp 1721-1723; Ichikawa, M, Nakahara, S, Wakai, S, 'Effect of post-migration detention on mental health among Afghan asylum seekers in Japan', *Australian & New Zealand Journal of Psychiatry*, vol 40(4), April 2006, pp 341-346; Pourgourides, C, Sashidharan, S, Bracken, P, *A Second Exile: the Mental Health Implications of Detention of Asylum Seekers in the United Kingdom*, North Birmingham Mental Health NHS Trust, Birmingham, 1995.

5 McCallin, M, *Living in Detention: A Review of the Psychological Wellbeing of Vietnamese Children in the Hong Kong Detention Centres*, International Catholic Child Bureau, Geneva, 1992.

6 Westermeyer, J, Neider, J, Callies, A, 'Psychosocial adjustment of Hmong refugees during their first decade in the United States: a longitudinal study', *Journal of Nervous and Mental Disease*, vol 177, 1989, pp 132-139; Steel, Z, Silove, D, Phan, T and Bauman, A, 'Long-term effect of psychological trauma on the mental health of Vietnamese refugees resettled in Australia: a population-based study', *Lancet*, vol 360(9339), 5 Oct 2002, pp 1056-1062; Steel, Z, Silove, D, Chey, T, Bauman, A, Phan T, and Phan, T, 'Mental disorders, disability and health service use amongst Vietnamese refugees and the host Australian population', *Acta Psychiatrica Scandinavica*, vol 111, 2005, pp 300-309.

7 Australian Medical Association, Media Release: 'Asylum seekers should have access to quality health services under Medicare', 8 August 2001 (cited 2005), <www.ama.com.au/web.nsf/doc/WEEN-5GB46R>.

8 Steel, Z, Momartin, S, Bateman, C, Hafshejani, A, Silove, D, Everson, N, et al, 'Psychiatric status of asylum seeker families held for a protracted period in a remote detention centre in Australia', *Australian & New Zealand Journal of*

Public Health, vol 28(6), Dec 2004, pp 527-536; Sultan, A and O'Sullivan, K, 'Psychological disturbances in asylum seekers held in long term detention: a participant-observer account', *Medical Journal of Australia*, vol 175, 2001, pp 593-596; Sobhanian, F, Boyle, GJ, Bahr, M and Fallo, T, 'Psychological status of former refugee detainees from the Woomera detention centre now living in the Australian community', *Psychiatry, Psychology and Law*, vol 13(2), 2006, pp 151-159; Momartin, S, Steel, Z, Coello, M, Aroche, J, Silove, D and Brooks, R, 'The impact of policy on the mental health of refugees: a comparison of temporary and permanent protection visa holders', *Medical Journal of Australia*, vol 185, 2006, pp 357-361; Steel, Z, Silove, D, Brooks, R, Momartin, S, Alzuhairi, B and Susljik, I, 'Impact of immigration detention and temporary protection of the mental health of refugees', *British Journal of Psychiatry*, vol 188, 2006, pp 58-64; Steel, Z and Silove, D, 'The mental health implications of detaining asylum seekers', *Medical Journal of Australia*, vol 175, 2001, pp 596-599; Mares, S and Jureidini, J, 'Psychiatric Assessment of Children and Families in Immigration Detention: Clinical, Administrative and Ethical Issues', *Australian & New Zealand Journal of Public Health*, vol 28(6), 2004.

9 HREOC, above, n 1.

10 Ibid, p 442.

11 Ibid, p 299.

12 Ibid, p 410.

13 Steel et al, 'Psychiatric status of asylum seeker families', above, n 8.

14 Mares and Jureidini, above, n 8.

15 HREOC, *The Human Rights Commissioner's Report on Visits to Immigration Detention Facilities*, HREOC, Canberra, 2001, p 207.

16 JSCFADT, *A Report on visits to Immigration Detention Centres*, Joint Standing Committee on Foreign Affairs Defence and Trade, Human Rights Subcommittee, Parliament of the Commonwealth of Australia, Canberra, 2001, p 65-66.

17 JSCM, *Asylum, Border Control and Detention*, Joint Standing Committee on Migration, Commonwealth of Australia, Canberra, 1994, p 138.

18 HREOC, *Those who've come across the Seas: the Report of the Commission's Inquiry into the Detention of Unauthorised Arrivals,* HREOC, Canberra, 1998, p 94.

19 HREOC, above, n 1, p 338.

20 Ibid, p 407.

21 HREOC, above, n 18, pp 100-101.

22 Ibid; JSCFADT, above, n 16.

23 HREOC, above, n 18, p 232.

24 Victorian Foundation for Survivors of Torture, 'The East Timorese: clinical and social assessments of applicants for asylum', in D Silove and Z Steel (eds), *The Mental Health and Well-Being of On-Shore Asylum Seekers in Australia*, Psychiatry Research and Teaching Unit, University of New South Wales, Sydney, 1998, pp 23-26; Victorian Foundation for Survivors of Torture, 'File audit of clinical assessments undertaken with Cambodian asylum seekers', 2001; Thompson, M, McGorry, P, Silove, D and Steel, Z, 'Maribyrnong Detention Centre Tamil survey', in D Silove and Z Steel (eds), The Mental Health and Well-Being of On-Shore Asylum Seekers in Australia, Psychiatry Research & Teaching Unit, Sydney, 1998, pp 27-31.

25 HREOC, above, n 1, p 397.

26 Steel et al, 'Psychiatric status of asylum seeker families', above, n 8.
27 Mares and Jureidini, above, n 8.
28 HREOC, above, n 1, p 418.
29 Ibid, p 496.
30 Ibid, p 414.
31 Sobhanian et al, above, n 8; Momartin et al, 'The impact of policy on the mental health of refugees', above, n 8; Steel et al, 'Impact of immigration detention and temporary protection', above, n 8.
32 The Hon Amanda Vanstone MP, Media Release: 'HREOC inquiry into children in immigration report tabled', Joint media release with the Attorney-General, The Hon Philip Ruddock MP, 2004 (cited 9 February 2007), <www.minister.immi.gov.au/media/media-releases/2004/v04068.htm>, p 1.
33 ABC Television, 'Woomera detention centre doctor speaks out', Lateline, 2004, (cited 9 February 2007), <www.abc.net.au/lateline/content/2004/s1229335.htm>.
34 Palmer, M, *Inquiry into the Circumstances of the Immigration Detention of Cornelia Rau: Report*, Canberra, Commonwealth of Australia, 2005.

9

CHRISTINE CANTY • CHRISTOPHER BENJAMIN

Mandatory detention and brain function and structure

Individuals in long-term mandatory detention are placed in a severe and often traumatic environment. It is likely that such experiences result in significant changes to brain function and structure. In this chapter we review evidence on the effect of environmental stress and deprivation on the adult brain. We will also discuss the additional detrimental effects of stress and deprivation on children.

The detrimental effects of mandatory detention on the mental health of asylum seekers (detainees) are well known. Detained asylum seekers have considerably higher rates of depression and post-traumatic stress disorder than the general population.[1] Rates of suicidal behaviour are 48 times the national average for male detainees, and 26 times higher for females.[2] Importantly, these effects are not the result of previous trauma alone: asylum seekers who are not detained experience significantly lower rates of mental illness.[3] These alarming figures reflect the severity of the detention centre environment. Detainees have reported witnessing such traumatic events as riots, fights, self-harm, and suicide attempts.[4] The extent of the chronic stress that they experience is evidenced by the extreme acts many of them have undertaken in a bid to change their situation, such as hunger strikes and self-mutilation (eg, sewing lips closed).[5]

The effect of this environment on detainees' brain function and structure has not, to date, been directly studied. This is likely due to difficulty in obtaining access to asylum seekers and the political nature and cost of such research. However, a wealth of relevant literature details the effects of stress and deprivation in animals. This literature is pertinent in understanding the effects of mandatory detention given that it is an environment high in chronic stress and low in social and environmental interaction.[6] In this chapter we review this literature and conclude that such environments detrimentally affect the adult brain, with the effects being disproportionately worse in the young, developing brain.

The effect of stress on the brain

The Oxford English Dictionary provides a definition of stress as 'hardship; straits; adversity; affliction' (noun); or 'to abridge the liberty of; to confine, incarcerate; to subject to hardship; to afflict, distress, harass, oppress' (verb).[7] These definitions lend themselves well to a description of long-term, indefinite detention. In addition, mandatory detention is characterised by a lack of control, high levels of uncertainty, lack of privacy, lack of resources, lack of dignity, dehumanising treatment, and exposure to a high prevalence of mental illness.[8]

The excessive level of stress experienced by asylum seekers in mandatory detention is compounded by their lack of control over the situation. Researchers have made a distinction between controllable and uncontrollable stress.[9] Periods of controllable stress lead to the formation of adaptive strategies via the strengthening of neural pathways. However, uncontrollable stress results in these adaptive strategies being abandoned as the brain attempts to change and respond to the new situation. As a result, when uncontrollable stress is prolonged and unpredictable, the person is left with an impaired ability to deal with future stress. In detainees, long exposure to uncontrollable stress is therefore likely to reduce their ability to cope with later stressful situations (eg, resettlement).

The brain has developed a short-lived stress response, which has evolved to deal with acute rather than chronic stress. The system supporting this involves several brain structures involved in the secretion of stress hormones such as *cortisol* (a neurohormone). Importantly, the main memory structure in the brain (the hippocampus) is particularly susceptible to the effects of cortisol.[10] This is important in an evolutionary sense, because it is advantageous to remember what the likely future causes of stress will be. Although the brain's stress response is an adaptive mechanism, prolonged secretion of cortisol in response to chronic stress can have a toxic effect on the body and brain alike.[11]

The effect of chronic stress on brain function

Both animal and human research indicate that clear changes in brain function occur with the experience of chronic stress, and that these changes alter the response to future stress.[12] The effects of chronic stress on the brain can be understood in terms of a continuum. Stress is a common experience in life, and the extent to which an event causes stress may differ depending on one's experience. Thus, in effect, what is stressful may be culturally defined (eg, if being verbally abused by others while driving is common in your environment, it may be less stressful than if it is your first exposure to such an event). The brain responds and adapts to ongoing fluctuations in stress levels. However, when stressful experiences become extreme, as in the experience of traumatic violence, the neural stress response increases accordingly, resulting in an extreme stress response.[13]

Ongoing periods of extreme stress can have long-term effects on the functioning of the stress response, so that the ability of the system to respond to stress appropriately is impaired. In this situation, individuals may become overly sensitive to stressors within their environment.[14] The inability to regulate the stress response has been implicated as a risk factor for the development of several mental illnesses including depression and post-traumatic stress disorder.[15] In asylum seekers, the experience of incarceration of indefinite duration constitutes a situation of chronic stress. Additional ongoing stresses often include separation from and concern about family members still at home, boredom, isolation, and loss of culture and support.[16] Detainees simultaneously face the stress of immigration applications, which frequently involve conflict with immigration officials, delays in the processing of applications, fears of being sent home and communication difficulties.[17]

Significant impairment of the brain's stress response has also been shown in depressed children with a history of abuse.[18] These differences were attributed to the experience of chronic stress. Importantly, impaired stress responses were only found in children who were living in situations of ongoing adversity. The implication from this research is that damage caused by initial trauma can be reduced if the individual is removed from the stressful situation. Conversely, placing an individual into another stressful environment, such as mandatory detention, is likely to compound the effects of previous trauma. In the case of asylum seekers in Australia, previous experience of severe traumatic stress in one's country of origin often includes abuse, exposure to unnatural death, and flight from conflict.[19] The detention of asylum seekers, then, is likely to significantly impair recovery from previous trauma.

The effect of chronic stress on brain structure

In addition to changes in brain function, animal research has demonstrated structural brain changes in response to chronic stress. Chronic stress results in structural changes to the hippocampus, the major memory structure of the brain. These changes include cell death as well as altered connections and impaired cell generation.[20] Indeed, animal studies have shown that the experience of prenatal stress has deleterious effects on the later development of the hippocampus and functioning of the stress response in the unborn infant.[21] These structural changes may also result in changes in cognition, including memory skills.[22]

In human research, evidence also suggests that stressful experiences early in life result in an impaired stress response and structural brain changes.[23] These changes can in turn cause the individual to be under or over-responsive to subsequent stressors, placing them at greater risk of psychiatric disorder.[24] Indeed, studies show that the hippocampus is smaller in individuals who suffer from depression or post-traumatic stress disorder.[25]

In summary, mandatory detention places asylum seekers in a situation of chronic stress. There is evidence that this results in changes to both the *function* and *structure* of the brain, particularly the stress response and the brain's major memory area. These changes can impair the ability of the nervous system to cope with further stressors.

The effect of social and environmental deprivation on brain function and structure

Detention not only presents asylum seekers with many threats and challenges resulting in chronic stress; it also places them in a restricted physical environment and deprives them of emotional interaction. Positive social and emotional interaction improves our health, quality of life and neurological function, while a deprived environment affects brain function negatively.[26] Studies of animals in deprived environments have consistently documented an altered biological stress response.[27] Further, altered levels of brain chemicals involved in the stress response are observed when monkeys are deprived of maternal and social interaction.[28]

The effects of social and emotional deprivation are illustrated by the brain's response to an engaging ('enriched') social and emotional environment. In animal research, an enriched environment is typically one allowing a 'complex combination of inanimate and social stimulation'.[29] Environmental enrichment results in a larger number of more complex brain connections and greater brain weight; signs of a healthy and well developed brain.[30] At a cognitive level, the benefits of such enrichment include improved learning and memory.[31]

While the growth of new neurons was thought to be limited to the early stages of development, this has recently been demonstrated in the adult brain.[32] Animal research has shown that these processes increase in response to an enriched environment.[33] By extension, it is likely that when adult humans are placed in an environment limiting physical, social, and emotional stimulation, the brain's capacity for neuronal growth will be reduced. This is likely to negatively affect cognitive abilities, consistent with detainees' reports of impaired attention, memory, and problem solving skills.[34]

In stark contrast to the Australian government's treatment of asylum seekers, the right of animals to experience an enriched environment is set out by a peak governmental health/research body – the Australian National Health and Medical Research Council (NHMRC). They state that:

> Housing of non-human primates should be designed with the aim of satisfying the behavioural, social and physical needs of the particular species. The environment should stimulate activities, improve cognitive capabilities and facilitate social interaction while encouraging the animals to display a more complete range of normal behaviours … Emphasis must also be placed on enrichment of the physical environment.[35]

In contrast, the National Inquiry into Children in Detention describes harsh, isolated and impoverished physical conditions, poor accommodation, lack of leisure resources and high exposure to mental illness and self-harming behaviour.[36] It is remarkable that in Australia a non-human primate can expect better treatment than a person who has sought asylum.

The effect of stress and deprivation on the developing brain

Historically it has been assumed that the ability of a child's brain to recover from injury is similar or even superior to an adult's. Recent studies, however, have demonstrated that the development of skills in childhood is characterised by 'critical periods' in which an early neural injury can have dramatic effects.[37] During a critical period, a particular cognitive skill develops rapidly and the health of the brain regions supporting that skill is essential. At these times the detrimental effect of negative influences, including social, emotional or other sensory deprivation, can be substantial,[38] as animal research extensively documents. Children who have been neglected have an impaired stress response system, and altered brain development.[39] These changes may result in cognitive problems and impaired emotional regulation, as well as an increased risk of mental illness.[40] Indeed, Steel et al found that the number of diagnosed psychiatric disorders in a group of children who had been detained was 10 times above expectations.[41]

The severity of a negative event's influence on brain development also depends on the stage of cognitive skill development. The effects are likely to be worst when a skill is emerging or developing, and skills the child would typically acquire later in life may also be disturbed.[42] The disproportionate effect of negative influences on the developing brain can also be understood when young age is conceptualised as a 'risk factor' that magnifies the effects of other negative influences (such as social deprivation and stress).[43] Moreover, children seeking asylum are likely subject to many other risk factors for poor outcome,[44] including exposure to widespread and violent social conflict, pre-existing psychological disorders and separation from family members. Accordingly, children in detention:

> described having witnessed detainees who had slashed their wrists, jumped from buildings … resulting in broken

> legs, and detainees attempting to strangle or hang themselves with electric cords. At times, children witnessed their parents' suicide attempts, or saw their parents hit with batons by officers.[45]

These models are also relevant when understanding the effects of detention on adolescents and young adults. For example, in humans, maturation of the brain's frontal lobe is incomplete until early adulthood,[46] with healthy frontal lobe development critical for the acquisition of attention and planning and organisational skills.[47] These skills – and attention in particular – are essential for numerous other cognitive functions. Indeed, disruption of brain development has been shown to impair the ability of children to focus their attention and quickly process information.[48] As such, stress and deprivation-related brain changes in childhood, adolescence and young adulthood are likely to have significant effects on crucial abilities including attention, memory, and planning.

Conclusion

The research reviewed in this chapter provides a compelling case for chronic stress and social/environmental deprivation having detrimental effects on brain function and structure. Animal studies have shown that these adverse experiences impair brain connections and alter important neurobiological systems. Research with psychiatric patients suggests these negative outcomes also arise in humans. It is likely that long-term mandatory detention, a situation in which chronic stress and social and environmental deprivation are endemic, will similarly impair brain function. These effects are likely to be even more detrimental in children, given the sensitivity of the developing brain to stress. While it has been shown that some of the effects of chronic stress and deprivation can be reversed, the human cost of reversing these changes in detained asylum seekers is significant.

While our motivation in writing this chapter has been to clarify in a scientific manner the likely effects of mandatory detention on the brain, it is difficult to set aside moral concerns when considering this issue. In our view, it is morally repugnant that any government should enforce policies that result in the indefinite mandatory detention of individuals seeking asylum. As clinical neuropsychologists, we deal with brain impairment and the devastating effects it has on people's lives on a daily basis. It seems perverse that a government can fund hospitals to treat Australians with brain impairment while simultaneously adding to this burden through its policies on mandatory detention. In our opinion, there are compelling scientific and moral arguments for a policy where asylum seekers are supported and integrated into the community, thereby significantly reducing the lasting neuropsychological changes experienced by this already traumatised group.

Notes

1 Thompson, M, et al, 'Maribyrnong Detention Centre Tamil survey', in D Silove and Z Steel (eds), *The Mental Health and Well Being of on-Shore Asylum Seekers in Australia*, UNSW, Psychiatry Research & Teaching Unit, Sydney, 1998, pp 27-30.

2 Dudley, M, 'Contradictory Australian national policies on self-harm and suicide: the case of asylum seekers in mandatory detention', *Australian Psychiatry*, vol 11, 2003, pp S102-S108.

3 Ichikawa, M, Nakahara, S, and Wakai, S, 'Effect of post-migration detention on mental health among Afghan asylum seekers in Japan', *Australian and New Zealand Journal of Psychiatry*, vol 40(4), 2006, pp 341-346.

4 Steel, Z, et al, 'Psychiatric status of asylum seeker families held for a protracted period in a remote detention centre in Australia', *Australia and New Zealand Journal of Public Health*, vol 28(6), 2004, pp 527-536.

5 Australian Human Rights and Equal Opportunity Commission (HREOC), *A Last Resort. A National Enquiry to Children in Immigration Detention*, HREOC, Sydney, 2004.

6 Thompson et al, above, n 1.

7 *The Oxford English Dictionary*, 2nd ed, prepared by JA Simpson and ESC Weiner, Oxford University Press, Oxford, 1989.

8 Steel et al, above, n 4.

9 Huether, G, 'Stress and the adaptive self-organization of neuronal connectivity during early childhood', *International Journal of Developmental Neuroscience*, vol 16(3-4), 1998, pp 297-306.

10 McEwen, BS and Magarinos, AM, 'Stress and hippocampal plasticity: implications for the pathophysiology of affective disorders', *Human Psychopharmacology*, vol 16(S1), 2001, pp S7-S19.

11 Cicchetti, D and Walker, E, 'Editorial: stress and development: biological and psychological consequences', *Development and Psychopathology*, vol 13(03), 2001, pp 413-418; Uno, H, et al, 'Neurotoxicity of Glucocorticoids in the Primate Brain', *Hormones and Behavior*, vol 28(4), 1994, pp 336-348.

12 De Bellis, MD, 'Developmental traumatology: the psychobiological development of maltreated children and its implications for research, treatment, and policy', *Development and Psychopathology*, vol 13(03), 2001, pp 539-56; San-

chez, M, Ladd, C, and Plotsky, P, 'Early adverse experience as a developmental risk factor for later psychopathology: evidence from rodent and primate models', *Development and Psychopathology*, vol 13(03), 2001, pp 419-449.

13 De Bellis, above, n 12.

14 Ibid.

15 Ibid; Meyer, S, Chrousos, G, and Gold, W, 'Major depression and the stress system: a life span perspective', *Development and Psychopathology*, vol 13(03), 2001, pp 565-580; Post, RM, et al, 'Developmental vulnerabilities to the onset and course of bipolar disorder', *Development and Psychopathology*, vol 13(03), 2001, pp 581-598.

16 Steel, above, n 4.

17 Thompson, above, n 1.

18 Kaufman, J, et al, 'The corticotropin-releasing hormone challenge in depressed abused, depressed non-abused, and normal control children', *Biological Psychiatry*, vol 42(8), 1997, pp 669-679.

19 Silove, D, et al, 'Asylum seekers centre study', in D Silove and Z Steel (eds), *The Mental Health and Well Being of on-Shore Asylum Seekers in Australia*, UNSW, Psychiatry Research & Teaching Unit, Sydney, 1998, pp 9-12.

20 Uno et al, above, n 11.

21 McEwen, BS, 'Effects of adverse experiences for brain structure and function'. *Biological Psychiatry*, vol 48(8), 2000, pp 721-731.

22 Ibid.

23 De Bellis, above, n 12.

24 Ibid; Meyer et al, above, n 15; Post et al, above, n 15.

25 Meyer et al, above, n 15; Bremner, J, et al, 'MRI-based measurement of hippocampal volume in patients with combat-related posttraumatic stress disorder', *American Journal of Psychiatry*, vol 152(7), 1995, pp 973-981; Gurvits, TV, et al, 'Magnetic resonance imaging study of hippocampal volume in chronic, combat-related posttraumatic stress disorder', *Biological Psychiatry*, vol 40(11), 1996, pp 1091-1099.

26 Lewis, MH, 'Environmental complexity and central nervous system development and function', *Mental Retardation and Developmental Disabilities Research Reviews*, vol 10(2), 2004, pp 91-95.

27 Maestripieri, D and Wallen, K, 'Non-human primate models of developmental psychopathology', in D Cicchetti and E Walker (eds), *Neurodevelopmental Mechanisms in Psychopathology*, Cambridge University Press, 2003, pp 345-365.

28 Kraemer, GW, et al, 'A longitudinal study of the effect of different social rearing conditions on cerebrospinal fluid norepinephrine and biogenic amine metabolites in rhesus monkeys', *Neuropsychopharmacology*, vol 2(3), 1989, pp 175-189.

29 Kempermann, G, Gast, D, and Gage, F, 'Neuroplasticity in old age: sustained fivefold induction of hippocampal neurogenesis by long-term environmental enrichment', *Annals of Neurolology*, vol 52(2), 2002, pp 135-143.

30 Lewis, above, n 26; Nithianantharajah, J and Hannan, A, 'Enriched environments, experience-dependent plasticity and disorders of the nervous system', *Nature Reviews Neuroscience*, vol 7(9), 2006, pp 697-709.

31 Nithianantharajah and Hannan, above, n 30.

32 Eriksson, PS, et al, 'Neurogenesis in the adult human hippocampus', *Nature Medicine*, vol 4(11), 1998, pp 1313-1317.

33 Kempermann, G, Kuhn, H, and Gage, F, 'Experience-induced neurogenesis in the senescent dentate gyrus', *Journal of Neuroscience*, vol 18(9), 1998, pp 3206-3212.

34 Steel et al, above, n 4.

35 Animal Welfare Committee of the National Health and Medical Research Council, 'Policy on the Care and Use of Non-Human Primates for Scientific Purposes', 2003.

36 Australian HREOC, above, n 5.

37 Wiesel, T and Hubel, D, 'Single-cell responses in striate cortex of kittens deprived of vision in one eye', *Journal of Neurophysiolology*, vol 26, 1963, pp 1003-1017.

38 Mogford, K and Bishop, D, 'Language development in exceptional circumstances', in D Bishop and K Mogford (eds), *Development in Exceptional Circumstances*, Lawrence Erlbaum Associates Ltd, Hove, 1993, pp 10-28.

39 De Bellis, above, n 12.

40 Ibid.

41 Steel, above, n 4.

42 Dennis, M, 'Language and the young damaged brain', in T Boll and BK Bryant (eds), *Research, Measurement and Practice*, American Psychological Association, Washington, 1989, pp 85-124.

43 Anderson, V, et al, 'Functional plasticity or vulnerability after early brain injury?', *Pediatrics*, vol 116(6), 2005, pp 1374-1382.

44 Thompson et al, above, n 1.

45 Steel et al, above, n 4.

46 Klingberg, T, et al, 'Myelination and organization of the frontal white matter in children: a diffusion tensor MRI study'. *Neuroreport*, vol 10(13), 1999, pp 2817-2821.

47 Anderson, V, et al, *Developmental Neuropsychology: a Clinical Approach.*, Psychology Press, London, 2001.

48 Catroppa, C and Anderson, V, 'Children's attentional skills 2 years post-traumatic brain injury', *Developmental Neuropsychology*, vol 23(3), 2003, pp 359-373; Catroppa, C and Anderson, V, 'A prospective study of the recovery of attention from acute to 2 years following pediatric traumatic brain injury', *Journal of the International Neuropsychological Society*, vol 11(1), 2005, pp 84-98.

10

MARGARET THEOLOGOU • WINSOME ROBERTS

The invisibles: asylum seekers holding bridging visas[1]

People seeking asylum are those who, having arrived in Australia, hope to be recognised as refugees and so granted rights to permanent protection and settlement. The legal process governing determination of refugee status 'onshore' is complex and, taking account of appeals processes, can take years to achieve a final outcome. The plight of those arriving by boat, without documentation, and placed in mandatory detention has rightly been publicised. However there is a larger, less visible group of approximately 8000 to 10,000[2] asylum seekers who entered Australia with a valid visa who may also be subjected to inhumane treatment through the bridging visa regime.[3] A bridging visa grants legal permission for asylum seekers to remain temporarily in the community while their application for protection is subject to the refugee status determination and appeals process.[4] But the bridging visa regime, especially the Bridging Visa type E (BVE), prevents asylum seekers from joining the community.

This chapter seeks to bring to light the largely hidden experience of what it means to live as an asylum seeker in Australia under the BVE regime. It does so by drawing on the findings of research that asked support workers to describe what these asylum seekers went through as they waited lengthy periods in destitution.[5] What emerges is a picture of continuous and debilitating struggle. Asking asylum seekers to 'live on thin air', as the BVE does, is inhumane and punitive and that this is demanded of them over a long period, in indeterminate circumstances, challenges the will to survive and undermines the courage to hope. It is particularly damaging for families because it makes the nurturance intrinsic to family life so problematic. We highlight here some of what support workers reported they had witnessed to give an idea of what these asylum seekers on bridging visas must contend with day to day.

An invisible population

All asylum seekers holding bridging visas are denied access to Centrelink, public housing, interpreting services, and English language training. Further, children and young people have no automatic right to enrol in primary or secondary school and are ineligible for the Higher Education Contribution Scheme (HECS).[6] Some asylum seekers may be eligible for the Asylum Seeker Assistance Scheme (ASAS)[7] which provides very limited financial assistance and health care. Some may be granted the right to work but others not. The BVE is used to deny asylum seekers the right to work and Medicare, and it is granted to asylum seekers who take longer than 45 days after their arrival in Australia to apply for refugee status or those who seek to have their case reviewed by judicial appeal or the Minister for Immigration. As at April 2006, there were 3900 asylum seekers holding a BVE.[8] At least, 3600 of these asylum seekers did not have access to ASAS[9] and were living in the community in a state of enforced destitution. It is their plight and their suffering that needs to be highlighted. Without the right to work and income support they face not only an indeterminate future but a hand-to-mouth existence. Relegated to the ranks of less than human, they must scrounge like stray animals for their survival and bear the continual humiliation of seeking out kindness from strangers.

Little is known of the composition of this floating population of individuals and families on bridging visas seeking asylum: the Australian government has placed virtually nothing on public record. It has never released information as to how many asylum seekers hold bridging visas at any given point in time nor the length of time they have been waiting in limbo for a final determination of their application. There is no information on their age or family status. We call on the government to provide more transparent information. It is only indirectly, by looking at the records of community-based organisations that are working with asylum seekers, that we are able to gain some information about those on bridging visas.

Melbourne's Asylum Seeker Project (ASP), run by the Hotham Mission, is one such organisation. It provides limited specialist housing, a basic allowance and some casework support. As at February 2006, it assisted 269[10] of an estimated 750 to 900 of those seeking asylum under the BVE regime in Victoria.[11] Over one-quarter who received assistance from ASP were under the age of 15 years and so especially vulnerable. As to country of origin, almost half came from Sri Lanka, and nearly one-quarter came from either Turkey (Kurdish), Albania, Russia or India.[12] In a survey of its cases, between 2001 and 2003, ASP found 55% had been waiting four years or more for a final decision on their refugee status and 28% had been waiting more than six years.[13] So it seems reasonable to assume that a significant proportion of those on a BVE are families and families who have been left both stateless and destitute for long periods.

Living on thin air

Asylum seekers holding a BVE are asked to live on thin air, denying the reality that they are human and cannot survive without shelter, food and health care. Shelter is the most pressing of all bodily needs; it provides privacy and protection against the elements; it provides a place to rest and prepare a meal, and a place where families and friends can come together and care for one another. Shelter is hardest for asylum seekers to obtain because of the increasing lack of affordable housing in metropolitan areas. By withdrawing work rights and restricting access to ASAS, BVE asylum seekers are relegated to a permanent state of homelessness. Shelter, when found, is impermanent because their hosts are usually ill-equipped to provide it on an indefinite basis, given their guests' inability to make a financial contribution. This makes it very difficult to achieve stability and necessitates frequent movement from one place to another. Large families can make this particularly problematic. In one case, a sole mother and her five children aged two to 18 years moved six times in six months. The accommodation itself, when found, is often cramped and not conducive to family life: it may simply be a room, even a garage, at someone's house, a hospital floor or a welfare agency office. Sometimes there is the luxury of a vacant church property or a rental property paid for by donations made to asylum seeker welfare agencies. On very rare occasions emergency and transitional public housing is used. The transience of this way of life means that such families are rarely able to settle down and become part of community with the usual network of neighbourly supports.

Shattering peace of mind

Without the right to earn income or entitlement to social security, day-to-day existence is fraught with anxiety and uncertainty. Moving from one place to another, with no certain knowledge of where the next meal is coming from, is deeply unsettling and disturbing, especially for parents trying to look after children. Each individual or family is required to act on their own behalf and search out other people or agencies that may be able to provide humanitarian relief. Some are better placed than others. A sole parent, for example, may be in an excruciatingly difficult position of trying to find food, even carry a food parcel, with young children in tow. Inevitably what results is a 'lottery of care' whereby securing goods or services necessary for survival becomes simply a matter of chance or good luck: of making the right connection with the right person at the right time. In one case, a family periodically came to receive donated food from a basket placed at a neighbourhood house only because someone working with asylum seekers had happened to talk at that neighbourhood house and chose to speak about the plight of that particular family. Usually, there is no guarantee that goods or services obtained on one occasion will be available on another.

Even if the supply of goods or services needed is available on a charitable basis, it is humiliating to ask for help. Most asylum seekers are used to providing for themselves and they find their state of dependency deeply troubling. A volunteer managing an asylum seeker welfare agency commented, 'One man said to me, "I know you people are doing a great job but I hate asking for help"'.

The human spirit gives people the courage to hope for a better future and the strength to carry on struggling through adversity. However many asylum seekers holding a BVE are particularly fearful for their future because they have already had their application for protection rejected. Not knowing when a final decision on their application will be determined or what that will be increases anxiety. And being subjected to a punitive regime of enforced destitution further devours confidence and courage. These cumulative psychological burdens understandably paralyse the ability of many to actively plan for their future.

The plight of children

Adolescents are especially vulnerable to an overwhelming sense of fatalism. They are unable to prepare for independent life as an adult because they do not know in which country they will end up. This inability to plan for adult life is made more unbearable by their exclusion from rights to vocational and tertiary training, which is an extension of the denial of a right to work. For school children it is hard to see the point of striving to do well academically if there is nowhere to go at the end. Some State governments, for example in Victoria, have given adolescents some limited access to TAFE, but this may also lead to a continuing emotional rollercoaster of hope and despair. In one case, a 17 year old doing a TAFE course in hope of earning money if granted residency, constantly worried about whether he would be able to finish his course and perhaps marry his girlfriend, or whether he would be deported. He has had the courage to work for a future, fall in love and dream of a life for himself in Australia but he is also tormented by the very fact of having done so. He lives in constant inner turmoil and asks, 'Why are we in this mess? Why is it taking so long? When is it going to be over? Are we ever going to be normal?'

Some children seeking asylum were actually born in Australia and/or have spent their formative years in Australia and consider themselves Australian. The prospect of returning to their parents' country of origin is frightening because it is utterly foreign to them: they cannot speak the language and have no knowledge of its culture and society. Receiving news of pending deportation or a rejection of a claim for refugee status throws such families into further crisis. For some children this is the first time they have learned of their status. In one case, a 10 year old arrived in Australia when he was four months old and had no recollection of his country of birth. When he learnt of the rejection of his family's refugee claim he could not sleep, continually stayed up watching television until 3 am, and was fearful of being separated from his father.

Tormented by memories

Being kept in legal limbo and not knowing if, or when, you will be offered protection is especially traumatic for those asylum seekers who have experienced torture or trauma in their country of origin. The memories of their persecution continue to torment them because they do not yet feel safe. They do not know if, or when, they will be told to return to the country in which the torture took place. In one case, a 17 year old had been waiting for more than three years for an outcome of his claim for refugee status. He was detained and tortured when he was 14 years old and he lived in constant fear of having to return and being tortured again upon his return. While some asylum seekers consider torture/trauma counselling premature because they see themselves at risk of further persecution, others who might be helped by counselling do not seek it out because they are so busy struggling to survive and it seems a secondary consideration.

Undermining family life

Parents bring themselves and their children to Australia in hope of a better life but as they are kept waiting in destitute circumstances, family life can be seriously eroded. Parents can lose faith in themselves and their children can come to have a diminished sense of security and trust in their parents.

Parents have their capacity to make basic day-to-day decisions about child-rearing usurped because they are dependent on charitable individuals or agencies to supply them with the means to care for their children. For example, a parent has little choice over what food to give their child when they have to accept whatever food is available at food banks or in food parcels. Parents, forced to scrounge for shelter, food and health care, and whose children must accompany them – either because they do not have access to child care or require their children to interpret and beg on their behalf – are belittled in front of their children.

Children, especially vulnerable to the mood of their caregivers, who receive so little support, often experience the family environment as tense. A volunteer managing an asylum seeker welfare agency commented:

> Parents are so traumatised … living on a knife-edge all the time and not knowing when they are going to be sent back, sets up in a household a kind of tension that is over and beyond tension in other families. It is constant ... that has to affect kids.

Children cannot feel secure because their parents are insecure. They sense their parents' insecurity not only by directly witnessing their parents beg but they can sense this from their parents' mood: by the way their parents act, the way they reach decisions, and their diminished capacity to respond to their emotional needs. Those reaching out to such families expressed their admiration for the strength parents showed, continuing parenting their children the best way they could under conditions of extreme hardship.

Growing up before their time

Many children seeking asylum present as prematurely earnest because they are required to take on responsibilities beyond their emotional maturity. Eldest children and children without siblings were particularly likely to have such burdens placed on them.

The BVE regime places children at risk of failing to undergo normal childhood development because the child is deprived of the experience of familial sheltering.

Some parents are so incapacitated by their circumstances that their child becomes their carer and/or the carer of a sibling. In one case, a mother was so distressed that her seven-year-old daughter stopped attending school so she could comfort her mother and care for her little sister, still a toddler.

Many of these children are better equipped to deal with Australian society than their parents, especially if their parents have managed to get them the opportunity of going to school. This allows the children to acquire English and learn about Australia from classmates and teachers. It is common for professionals to ask children to interpret for their parents. But this role can also be burdensome, even traumatic. In one case, not informed of interpreting services, a 15 year old was required to interpret legal papers for her parents from the age of seven. Eight years later, this child continues to worry that she did not understand everything she was told and is still feeling confused by what she heard. In another case, a 13-year-old daughter interpreted on behalf of her father at legal and welfare appointments where he needed to talk about his friends and relatives who had been killed in the country of origin. Needless to say, the 13 year old was very frightened by what she heard.

Alongside being deprived of protection and having to take on burdensome responsibilities, children in these circumstances are also denied many of the joys that would normally be part of childhood. Their parents simply do not have the income to pay for things that secure the experience of childhood, such as kindergarten, toys and leisure. Yet they need to have fun just like other children and sadly experience the deprivation of witnessing other children having fun. A four year old, for example, sharing a one bedroom with his mother (who was dying of cancer) and his older sibling in a relative's high rise commission flat, could not get out of the flat and play or attend kindergarten.

The challenge to Australians

This chapter bears witness to the plight of those largely invisible to most Australians: those who, under the BVE regime, are trying to survive enforced destitution, to live on thin air, and in the face of extreme mental and emotional anguish, to keep human courage and spirit alive. Theirs is a predicament of appalling and sustained suffering and anguish. Yet they are rendered further invisible because they are effectively voiceless. They fear that if they voice their protest to the government or to the media their chances of ultimate sanctuary will be reduced. Not being able to voice protest, their suffering creates an overwhelming sense of impotence.

Providing community support for asylum seekers is difficult and demands a similar kind of tenacity to that required of asylum seekers because it requires constantly having to ask for donations and assistance, rather than being able to rely on a given and dependable source. Although State governments, like the Victorian government, provide special funding for work with those granted Temporary Protection Visas, financial support available for those helping BVE holders remains problematic.

The enormous effort of community agencies and volunteers is inspired by having witnessed the dehumanising impacts of the BVE regime, a regime that gives those seeking asylum the legal right to temporarily live here but deprives them of the natural justice of leading decent lives. These workers seek to minimise the harm of this regime, while advocating an end to it. We join them in arguing that the BVE regime should be abolished and all asylum seekers should be given the right to work, to access Medicare, to be eligible for income support if they cannot work, to be given the opportunity to learn English, to access interpreting services and, their children, offered age-appropriate education. By allowing the BVE regime to continue we become complicit in its brutality and our own humanity and sense of a civilised community is diminished.

Notes

1 We would like to thank the staff and volunteers of the community agencies, and Dr Lynda Campbell of the School of Social Work, The University of Melbourne, who contributed to this study.

2 Amnesty International cited in McNevin, A and Correa-Valez, I, 'Asylum seekers living in the community on Bridging Visa E: community sector's response to detrimental policies', *Australian Journal of Social Issues*, vol 41(1), 2006, p 126.

3 A very few asylum seekers in mandatory detention may be released with a Bridging Visa E before refugee status being determined.

4 Department of Immigration and Multicultural Affairs, *Bridging visas Form 1024i*, <www.immi.gov.au/allforms/pdf/1024i.pdf>.

5 Research carried out by Margaret Theologou at the School of Social Work, The University of Melbourne.

6 McNevin and Correa-Valez, above, n 2, p 129.

7 The window of opportunity in which asylum seekers holding a BVE can access ASAS is very small. They can only access ASAS if they have waited more than six months for the Department of Immigration and Citizenship (DIAC) to assess their claim for protection and they cease to be eligible for ASAS when DIAC completes its assessment. Certain categories of asylum seekers in severe hardship (such as, unaccompanied minors, parents with children under 18 years of age, women with high risk pregnancies) may be eligible for exemption from the six month waiting period and/or eligible to receive ASAS while they are seeking a review of their application before the Refugee Review Tribunal (RRT). No asylum seeker is eligible for ASAS if they are seeking an appeal before the judiciary or the Minister for Immigration (Department of Immigration and Multicultural Affairs, *Fact Sheet 62 Assistance for Asylum Seekers in Australia*, <www.immi.gov.au/media/fact-sheets/62assistance.htm>.

8 Department of Immigration and Multicultural Affairs, *People and Place*, vol 14, 2006, p 40.

9 We have estimated this figure on the basis that as at April 2006, 3600 of the 3900 people seeking asylum holding a BVE were seeking judicial and ministerial review of their application (Department of Immigration and Multicultural Affairs, ibid). All of these 3600 asylum seekers were ineligible for ASAS. Moreover, it is likely that some of the 300 people seeking asylum holding a BVE with protection visa applications subject to review by DIMA or the RRT as at April 2006 were also excluded from ASAS.

10 Asylum Seeker Project, *Annual Report April 2006*, <http://asp.hothammission.org.au/>.

11 Cited in McNevin, A, *Seeking Safety, not Charity: a Report in Support of Work-Rights for Asylum Seekers Living in the Community on Bridging Visa E*, Network of Asylum Seeker Agencies, Victoria, 2006, p 17.

12 Asylum Seeker Project, above, n 10.

13 Asylum Seeker Project, *Welfare Issues and Immigration Outcomes for Asylum Seekers on Bridging Visa E: Research and Evaluation 2003*, <http://asp.hothammission.org.au/>.

PART IV

Resettlement in Australia

SIR GUSTAV NOSSAL

Part IV Introduction

Forced to seek refuge in Australia to escape the madness of Adolf Hitler's '1000-year Reich', I welcome *Yearning to Breathe Free* with particular interest. Let me first nail my colours to the mast on some central issues. I fully understand the need for border protection and I support measures to deter people smugglers who exploit desperate refugees. The question then is what to do about those relatively few individuals who do make it to Australia unauthorised. These could be treated anywhere along the spectrum from great compassion to extreme harshness. It seems to me the compass needle has swung too far in the latter direction. I find the 'Pacific Solution' both contrived and expensive. I believe detention should be as brief as possible and particularly women and children should be allowed to avail themselves of offers made by the Australian Red Cross and others to house them within the community. We appear not to have learnt the lesson that most asylum seekers eventually make first class Australian citizens.

The following three chapters make riveting reading. The two stories of 'real life' asylum seekers serve as a reminder of how harsh and difficult life can be in certain countries and what indomitable courage is then required to succeed in the resettlement process. Yusuf survived his two years of detention in Maribyrnong by writing 55 articles seeking to disseminate his message of 'humanity, peace, justice and equality'. On release, he underwent a kind of rebirth and is now a successful Australian citizen committed to a vibrant multiculturalism. 'Jennifer' (not her real name) fought for three years to prove she was a genuine refugee, and graphically describes the half-life of an asylum seeker without the right to work or to receive medical care or welfare support. Her dependence on a series of voluntary welfare agencies was near absolute.

As a result, when she finally won her protection claim, her sense of belonging in Australia has been a difficult and ongoing process.

Pamela Curr gives us a moving account of the various community volunteer groups who have sought to help asylum seekers and also of some of the more dramatic protests from the detainees themselves. She takes us back to *Tampa* and the 'children overboard' affair and finally to the Cornelia Rau case which at last caused some improvement in detention centres, particularly in access to mental health care. This chapter is a passionate indictment of government policies. Some readers may find it harsh; if so, they should consider the frustrations which volunteer supporters of asylum seekers have had to face.

Tipping, Bretherton and Kaplan take us in a different direction. They dissect the challenges faced by refugees from Sudan in resettling in Australia. Some 22,000 mainly young people have arrived over the last decade or more, many of them deeply scarred by the years of conflict and trauma in their old country. Their search for meaning in life, social connectedness and useful education or employment is soberly described. Once again, the courage and tenacity of these migrants shines through. As well as simply providing services, we must learn the importance of continuous and intense dialogue with these, and indeed all, new settlers.

Part IV leaves me with a sense of awe and gratitude about the many Australians who have worked so hard on the resettlement process; and also with the sincere conviction that the great majority of the new settlers will contribute strongly to Australian life. Great humanitarian struggles such as seeking a 'fair go' for asylum seekers have a symbolic as well as a practical dimension. How well we respond helps to define us as a nation. I have no doubt that this book will materially aid understanding of a complex issue and will bring new players into the fray.

11

ERIN TAYLOR

Two asylum seekers' stories

Jennifer's story

Jennifer has been accepted as a refugee and is now a resident of Australia. While she has been afforded protection, she fears for her family members still living in her home country. To protect them from any reprisals that may have resulted from the publication of her story, Jennifer's reasons for fleeing her country have been omitted. Identifying features such as cultural background, age, method of entry into Australia and year of arrival, have also been omitted and her name has been changed. The following story is therefore restricted to Jennifer's experience of applying for asylum in Australia.

Jennifer had been living in the Australian community on a valid visa when, due to circumstances outside of her control, it was unexpectedly cancelled. Fearing for her life if she was deported, she sought the advice of the Refugee and Immigration Legal Centre (RILC). When they decided to take on her case her assigned legal representative explained to her that applying for asylum was a long and complicated process, with no guarantee that her application would be successful.

For Jennifer, it was a process that lasted for three long years before she was finally approved as a genuine refugee. During those years she was able to remain lawfully in the Australia community on a Bridging Visa E – a visa class for asylum seekers who lodge their application for protection more than 45 days after their lawful arrival. It provides no right to work, medical care or welfare support. Jennifer explains that:

> I didn't think that anything like that would exist, in the sense that it has no work rights, no study rights, no volunteering – nothing … It was like basically I was allowed to breathe.

With no income to buy food, let alone a public transport fare, Jennifer's life shrank down to the four walls of her home. She describes how the isolation affected her:

> I got to a point where I couldn't read, I couldn't sleep, I couldn't eat … It was just so bad that I would be indoors and would literally spend four or five days without actually talking to anyone … I felt like I was actually going insane.

The forced idleness resulting from her lack of work rights also adversely affected Jennifer:

> I used to go for walks in the morning but when I saw people dressed up, or in uniform, they have a purpose to their day … I would have loved to be up and have had a purpose to my day. So I didn't like seeing that … I preferred sleeping flat through the day and being up at night because no one is doing anything at night. I didn't feel like I was the only one not doing anything.

The RILC referred Jennifer for counselling at the Asylum Seeker Resource Centre (ASRC), which, along with St Vincent De Paul, had already been providing her with food parcels. The decision to access their counselling service was difficult for her. She explains that seeking assistance for mental health problems is alien to her culture:

> When you have a problem you solve it on your own … So when you get out there you put a smile on your face, you dress up, you clean up and just look great. No one is supposed to know what you are going through … It was so hard for me to sit down and actually talk, because I felt like, gosh, then the whole world knows what I am going through and it wasn't ok for people to know that that was how it was.

Jennifer also experienced physical health problems as a result of the stress she was under and her inability to obtain adequate food. She describes constantly feeling tired, and dealing with continual body and head aches. Without a Medicare card, accessing medical care was impossible. Eventually, with the assistance of the ASRC she was able to see a doctor. Jennifer was diagnosed with a 'list' of illnesses, including Type II diabetes and iron deficiency. She was told she needed to improve her diet to bring her iron and blood sugar levels under control. Specifically, she recalls being advised to eat more red meat, advice she found impossible to follow given her income restrictions. She lived in the Australian community for over a year under these conditions, unable to access proper medical care, while she waited for the outcome of her protection claim to be decided.

While Jennifer was dealing with these issues, her case for protection was slowly moving forward. After the initial interview she was again placed in limbo: 'They don't tell you anything, they don't call you, they don't send you a letter. From the day you leave the interview they just tell you that they will get back to you. That's it'. She waited for almost a year before the decision was given to her. It was negative: 'They said no. And yep, it's like you sort of have a bit of hope and then it is just crushed back to dirt – the hard rock bottom'. With the assistance of the RILC, Jennifer lodged an appeal against this decision with the Refugee Review Tribunal.

Jennifer's loss at this initial stage had real consequences for her ability to survive in the community. Six months after her original protection application was lodged, Jennifer had qualified for monetary support through the Asylum Seeker Assistance Scheme (ASAS), administered by the Red Cross. This income assistance had been just enough to pay her rent with a small amount left over for food. When her case moved to the appeal stage, she no longer qualified for the ASAS, and with the cessation of this income support Jennifer was in real danger of becoming homeless. She needed to find somewhere to live with no income beyond the $100 a month that the Hotham Mission could provide. Eventually a concerned member of the community offered a solution, inviting Jennifer to live rent-free in her home.

The appeals process was a long and difficult one. Jennifer's initial interview with the Refugee Review Tribunal (RRT) was a horrible experience for her. She describes the RRT Member who interviewed her as 'terrible' and 'nasty':

> He was not sensitive at all. I don't expect them to sympathise and cry with me, but he was just crazy. It was question after question … and you're not answering this and this. It felt like, oh well, what was the point of asking me if you are going to treat me like this. I know that you are going to say no.

Jennifer's prediction was correct. Months later, she was again given a negative decision. The RILC lodged an appeal in the Federal

Court, based on irregularities in the evidence the RRT Member had used to support his decision. The appeal was successful and gave Jennifer 'another chance' to have her case reviewed by the RRT, with a different Member assigned to conduct the assessment.

While this Member was 'really nice' and 'very casual', the interview was still fraught with stress for Jennifer, causing her to vomit frequently throughout the process. Despite the trauma, the process gave her renewed confidence that her claim for protection would be successful. Jennifer describes her conflicting emotions at the completion of that interview:

> I wanted to be happy but I suppressed my happiness with the fact that when you come down from that level you hit the bottom really harder than when you sort of keep yourself, you know, in the dirt. You sort of sit back, not fall back. So, it felt good. I was relieved, but it still had that, what if, what if, thing.

Months passed, and the hope created by the second RRT interview was beginning to fade for Jennifer. She was sick of the continual waiting: 'Finally, I just told myself, I am going to gather my guts and go to Immigration'. She met with opposition at the Department and was told she wasn't allowed to speak to anyone about her case. Jennifer refused to take no for an answer and was eventually given assistance. It was discovered that her case had stalled because a letter had been sent three months prior, but not received, asking her to undergo her medical exam. After completing this process Jennifer was called into the Department to be told the decision. It was positive: 'That was the happiest day of my life … It was like the long battle had come to an end and it meant that I could just be a normal person again'.

Jennifer finally had the peace of mind of permanent protection, and access to government benefits, health care, and work rights. Despite these gains, the adjustment to 'normal' life has been difficult. Her happiness over getting protection is offset by her worry about her family members at home. Some of her siblings are interested in coming to join her in Australia, however her parents, despite being 'quite miserable', are not: 'When I explained the experience of what I went through it was so painful for them. Such that, for me to turn around and say, "Australia's great!", it sort of looked stupid'. Jennifer describes the thought process behind their decision: 'I would rather be in a place and die in a place that I have a sense of belonging and know … how bad my devil is'.

For Jennifer, finding that 'sense of belonging' in Australia has been a complicated and ongoing process. She has faced issues such as racism, which have made her life here difficult:

> [When] it happens it's like a hard punch … It is like I'm nobody again … and you feel like, gosh, what am I doing here? I would rather be elsewhere, but I don't know where elsewhere is.

Despite these challenges, Jennifer is happy she can stay and has made tentative plans for the future. She feels a debt to society as a result of the kindness and assistance she has received from groups such as the ASRC and would like to pay this back through her future work. Her goal is to study to be a social worker so that she can 'earn a living but still help people as well'.

Yusuf's story

Yusuf Sheik Omar journeyed to Australia in 1999, seeking asylum as a refugee. His home country of Somalia had been wracked by civil war for much of that decade. He grew up in the Somali countryside, in a nomadic pastoral environment. He describes his culture with pride, emphasising that Somalia is an oral society which values language highly and thus is a country of poets. Yusuf's own mother is a poet and her teaching of the country's rich oral traditions was a great influence on him: 'It was my mother, Ardo, who introduced me to poetry. I learned lots of wisdom from her'. Yusuf believes that people are a product of their environment and so it is little wonder that he too is a poet and educator. The greatest wonder, given that the Somali people's experience with the written Somali word is recent (1972), is that Yusuf also became a writer and a researcher.

When Somalia descended into civil war in 1991, Yusuf was in Sudan, working towards a degree in education. The poetry and articles Yusuf wrote while abroad were often critical of those aspects of Somalia's social structure which he felt were the main source of the war in his country. These included the war lords and the social system, including some clan values and tribal traditions. Having won another scholarship for postgraduate study, Yusuf travelled from Sudan to Malaysia in 1995, where he continued to write critical fiction and novels about the situation in Somalia, highlighting the plight of his people. In 1999, with only 21 days left on his student visa, and fearing retribution for his criticisms if he returned to his country, Yusuf faced a tough decision: to remain illegally in Malaysia or attempt to journey to a country which would accept him as a refugee. He chose the latter and decided on Australia as his destination. It was a pragmatic decision, for Yusuf had very little money. He explains:

> Australia was the closest country realistically to Malaysia … I was confident of my case. I was a genuine refugee … So I chose the closest [country] that accepted refugees and the cheapest one to come to.

Yusuf arrived in Australia by plane and was placed in immigration detention at the Maribyrnong Immigration Detention Centre in Melbourne while his case was being determined. He disputes the argument that his method of arrival was illegal: 'I don't believe I was illegal. I believe I was legal. Because when you are just wanting to be safe, or salvage a life from death, any option you use is legal'. When he arrived at Maribyrnong, Yusuf was warned to prepare himself for a long stay by a fellow Somali detainee, who had himself been in detention for over two years. It was a situation Yusuf had no choice but to accept, as deportation back to Somalia was not an option: 'Deportation meant anytime you could be murdered or killed for your personal views, or civil war, or the poetry I did, or the criticism that I made in the past'.

Yusuf was finally accepted as a refugee and released from immigration detention in 2001. When he speaks of his two years in detention he does so with quiet dignity. He emphasises the way in which this experience affected him and his fellow detainees emotionally and psychologically, rather than materially. For Yusuf:

> The morale level, it is very low. People are experiencing difficulties and come here to get protection and a safe place and get themselves in a difficult situation that's not better really … They don't understand what the future will hold for them or when their cases will be determined – they don't have any idea. It is good when you have some idea how long you will remain here or be here. But it is open, and that makes it difficult.

He explains that the conditions of detention erode trust:

> People lose trust. They don't have anything. Even if you have your visa, your case has been accepted, but you don't trust it. When you get out of the detention centre it takes you time to restore the trust and accept what is true and what is not true.

Yusuf describes his experience in detention as 'painful' but also as life-changing. He believes that humans learn and gain great experience through pain, and through this insight he was able to learn how to use his nightmare in detention in a positive way, 'not to give up and become a victim'. Yusuf explains the need for balance between reality and not giving up to that reality, wisdom he drew from his Somali upbringing:

> Every aspect, every step in this life depends on how you think, how you act … So it depends on you, whether you give up or whether you gain … Understand where you start – be realistic – but at the same time you have to have aspiration and ambition, and know how to change that reality.

For Yusuf, continuing to write was an integral part of this process:

> Just when I realise I would be there for a long time, I said it is my time. It depends on me whether I damage or destroy myself or develop myself … And at that time I felt that to manage and to do some good stuff that would help me later on, and I started to think about writing articles.

Over the course of the two years Yusuf spent at Maribyrnong he wrote 55 articles, in Somali and Arabic, for publication in the United Kingdom and Australia. Those who visited him at the detention centre, from both the mainstream and the Somali community, aided him in disseminating his work and his message of 'humanity, peace, justice and equality'.

Yusuf was also lifted from dwelling on his own situation by those he saw as more vulnerable detainees – women, pregnant women, women who had babies or children, and young people. Their plight drew him to 'think about the human being, how to help, particularly the vulnerable groups, weak people who are victims'. His commitment to aid such groups, particularly young people, has been the focus of Yusuf's life, as well as his employment, since his release.

Adjusting to life in the community after his release was challenging for Yusuf. Some of these challenges were the result of the lingering physical and psychological effects of detention. The prolonged period spent confined with inadequate space for exercise meant that for the first six months of his life in the Australian community even relatively small activities, such as walking to the shops, left him tired and dizzy. Yusuf also had to rebuild his self-reliance after two years of enforced dependence on the authorities of the detention centre for necessities such as food and clothing.

Other challenges stemmed from the inevitable adjustments to living in a different culture and establishing a new life. Yusuf admits to having some trepidation while detained about what living in the Australia community might be like:

> When you are in the detention centre in a difficult situation, just seeing everyday some, I can't say brutal, but some difficult officers, you develop some image – the whole society could be the same as the ones that are in front of you.

Despite these fears, Yusuf has had many positive experiences since he was given permanent protection six years ago, and has found Australians on the whole to be 'peaceful and helpful and actually very encouraging towards your culture'. He has made many friends from all faiths and cultural backgrounds. Such friendships have allowed him 'to forget some of my past experiences, such as my experiences in detention'.

Yusuf has confronted the challenge of learning English; completed his Masters of Educational Leadership and Management at La Trobe University; worked as a multicultural aide at schools in Heidelberg; helped to establish the Australian Somali Youth Association; given numerous lectures at universities and to community groups about his experiences, his culture and his views of life; and is now undertaking his PhD through the Refugee Health Research Centre, also at La Trobe University. And of course, he has continued to write[1] and to compose and perform his poetry.

Yusuf's successes have been tempered by the emotional difficulty of his situation as a refugee, cut off from his homeland, his culture and particularly his family, who he has not seen for 17 years. However, he describes his release from detention as a kind of rebirth, and he has committed himself to his new life and his new country, becoming an Australian citizen in 2003. Yusuf is 'happy and proud' to be an Australian citizen and reflects deeply on the responsibilities and privileges of this role. He has embraced multiculturalism and says, 'Diversity is power. It is so beautiful. If we utilise it in a positive way we can create a life that never existed before'. He hopes for a new generation of leaders who can strengthen Australia's commitment to multiculturalism through greater understanding, management and promotion of the concept. Yusuf also hopes to prepare and encourage Somali young people to take on such leadership roles through his research.

Notes

1 For some examples of Yusuf's work please see: 'Beware of the dogma', *The Age*, 10 January 2007; 'The education and employment aspirations of Somali high-school students in Melbourne: insights from a small study', *The Australasian Review of African Studies,* vol XXVII(2), December 2005, pp 63-87; 'Young Somalis in Australia: an educational approach to challenges and recommended solutions', *Migration Action* vol XXVII(1), pp 6-18, 2005; and, 'I am a new Australian citizen', *Migration Action* vol XXVI(2), pp 14-15.

12

PAMELA CURR

Supporters of asylum seekers

Every Tuesday three young women with children in tow climb the stairs at the Asylum Seeker Resource Centre (ASRC) in Melbourne. Here they settle the children and then begin their volunteer shift answering phones, making appointments and welcoming the refugees and asylum seekers who arrive seeking help. This is the Tuesday morning administration team:

> After my son was born I felt the world was going in the wrong direction and I wanted to change it – that's why I am here (Bec, mother of two who volunteers at the ASRC every week).

Meanwhile downstairs 84-year-old Alec and 74-year-old Val are packing grocery shelves before opening the food bank for the day. Soon asylum seekers with no right to work and no right to income support will arrive to do their weekly shop:

> *Tampa* brought me here – I was so angry I had to do something and now I come every week (Val).

The spin

Six years after the metaphorical war on refugees began, the refugee movement is as strong as ever although the focus has shifted. In the beginning it was the activists who sounded the alarm and demanded that Australians take a good look at what was being done in their name. It was not an easy task because the politicians and their spin merchants had deftly placed refugees in the same basket with border control, terrorists, disease and criminals. While both minor parties supported refugee rights, they could not over rule both major parties who saw an electoral advantage in beating the border control drum:

> We will decide who comes to this country, and the circumstances in which they come (John Howard, Prime Minister).

As the boats arrived during 2000, Australian political leaders engaged in a campaign of fear mongering which filtered out into the community with predictable results. Talkback radio and tabloid newspapers had a field day carrying predictions of invasion, disease and criminal activity:

> As many as 10,000 people could be packing up now, in the Middle East, with a view to trying to access Australia (Philip Ruddock, Immigration Minister).

The dissidents

As in any community, not all Australians were receptive to the messages of hate, fear and racism and it was these people who formed the core of dissenters. The refugee supporters of 2007 grew out of these divisive times. At the ASRC there are 700 volunteers providing settlement services to people who have just come out of detention and supporting people seeking asylum while living in the community. These Australians, like many others around the country in similar agencies, give their time on a regular weekly basis to make available services which the government refuses to provide. They come from groups as diverse as churches, unions and students across all ages, stages of life, education and background.

Refugee supporters have been the bane of this government. While never an electoral majority, they still constitute the most committed, bloody minded, stubborn, unyielding group of dissidents this country has seen in a long while. The discomfort they have inflicted on both the government and opposition benches has resulted in them being variously disparaged as 'bleeding hearts' or 'latte-sipping elites' in an attempt to despatch them to oblivion.

What is common to the many community initiatives like the ASRC is that they operate without federal government funding and with a bare minimum of paid staff and hundreds of volunteers. They demonstrate the capacity of people of good will to step into the void left by government, existing by sheer imagination, generosity and goodwill. They provide services across the board from English classes, casework, employment, medical, legal, food bank to friendship and support, relying on volunteers, fundraising, philanthropy and donations to provide the infrastructure. Australia, which was prided itself on 'a fair go for all', has now become a country with a multi-tiered system with settlement services available only to humanitarian refugees who have been invited to Australia. People who seek a refugee visa from 'onshore' are denied these services.

Before these community networks were established there were individual people all over Australia wanting an outlet for their rising concern and dismay with the government's treatment of refugees. They came from left wing groups, church communities, many ages, life stages, faiths and political affiliations. They did not always agree on how to change refugee policies but they all agreed that the government was wrong.

The internet was an essential tool for this movement. Computers in lounge rooms and kitchens ensured that supporters were linked. When a detainee walked out the Baxter gate, the joy passed from Perth to Sydney, Melbourne, Brisbane and all points in between in minutes. The movement was blessed with a number of committed and gifted communicators who established email lists and spent their days on computers.

The response from people opposed to government policy was diverse. Vigils began outside suburban detention centres throughout 2001. Every Sunday people gathered from suburban churches, Jews for Justice, unions, Socialists, secondary and tertiary students and individuals to protest and call out messages of support. Within weeks they learnt their first word in Farsi – 'Azadi' (Freedom), which became a catchcry across the camps.

Protest from within

In August 2000 the first protest began. It came from within, when detainees walked out of the camp and up the road to Woomera township. They sat peacefully on the road all night in the freezing cold and next day with no food or water. These protesters later told me that some townsfolk rolled apples to the people and tried to give them blankets but guards stopped them. The protest was about the lack of communication from the Department of Immigration[1] (DIMA). The detainees had been in the camp for months with no word about their future. No one knew when or if they would be released.

Many people were tired of 'separation detention' where they were held in isolation with no access to radio or newspapers or even a phone to call home to tell their families that they had survived. In Curtin, people were held in this manner for 11 months. After the protest DIMA began processing their claims and issuing visas.

Release

> "Mr and Mrs Visa" walked around the camp knocking on doors telling people – you have 10 minutes to pack and go to the gate. All the children followed them calling out. We got on the bus with a bottle of water and a cheese sandwich for the 19 hour journey to Melbourne. We were so happy (Sarah, 16 years old, on arrival in Melbourne, September 2000).

The release of detainees marked a new stage amongst refugee advocates. For the first time refugees and Australians came face to face. As they listened to stories of flight and survival so far removed from their own comfortable, easy lives, hearts opened and many became friends:

> We were so scared – a boat was circling us. It was too dark to see. It could be pirates. Some people were praying, some crying. Then the sun was coming. We looked out and people were laughing. We saw men with short pants and long socks on the other boat. We knew then that we had reached Australia because we had heard about these strange clothes (Sarah, 15 years old, when she arrived on Christmas Island in 2000).

The sudden releases from detention created a new problem. Help was needed desperately to find places for people to stay. The government provided nothing for those released, except the lowest payment from Centrelink. It was difficult to rent a house when Minister Ruddock was your previous landlord. People needed assistance to find their way in this new country. Jobs, English classes, schools, real estate agents – there was nothing organised to assist these people and the established migrant resettlement services were forbidden to assist at risk of losing their funding.

This drew a new group of supporters. The community too, found that refugees did not have horns but rather were remarkably like 'us'. As trust grew, ordinary Australians heard at first hand the stories of why people took the risky trip to Australia and also what happened to them in the camps. It was inevitable that as the reality of the harsh government policy was revealed, many of those people who were previously unconcerned would change their attitude.

And then came *Tampa*

Into this confusing mix came *Tampa*. Many of those who still give their time, energy and money cite the *Tampa* as a turning point. Many in Melbourne remember the Saturday morning in August 2001 when the Federal Court was convened at short notice. People arrived from everywhere and packed the Court to witness this historic challenge. When the *Tampa* was stormed by Australian SAS forces, many people wept. Operation Relex had many victims.

In 2001 the 'children overboard' story was the last straw for many advocates. Many supporters by now had changed lifestyles, some lost friends, neglected gardens and houses but could not turn away from the need to support the refugees and asylum seekers through the system. When advocates heard from these released refugees, the stories of their experiences at the hands of our government, something changed inside many, forever:

> The water began to rise up. Some people lifted their kids up in the air so the Navy could come and take the kids before they drowned. But the sailors told us by loud speaker, that they couldn't help us until we were in the water. The captain said – we will only rescue when you are in the water. One sailor took a little baby from the mother. We had to jump. I couldn't find my family. People were crying and vomiting. I don't know how long we were in the water before we were rescued (A girl, 12 years old, on the 'children overboard' boat in 2001).

> After two weeks on Christmas Island, they told us that we were going to Australia – to Sydney. At night we boarded an army plane without windows. When we got out it was dark. We saw jungle and people with black faces. There were no buildings. We knew that this couldn't be Australia. They lied to us (Zahra on arriving in Manus Island).

When HMAS *Manoora* reached Nauru, it was known that the Afghans who had been held below deck next to the engine room for three weeks would disembark gladly. However it was suspected that the Iraqis would be another matter:

> A few days before we came to Nauru, they put hot chilli in all the food even the rice. No one could eat it. Mothers cried to the sailors – please not in the children's rice. The children cried, their lips cracked – no one could eat and then the water got smaller. We could do nothing (An Iraqi woman describing the strategy to get them to leave the boat at Nauru).

Australians organise

As the movement grew, groups and individuals across the country began to organise around different aspects of the policy. Some advocates reached out to the people 'offshore' in Nauru and Manus Island setting up websites and email lists. They wrote letters and sent gifts. Others visited the desert camps, driving and flying to parts of Australia they did not know. There they made friends and when they returned home, they wrote letters and kept in phone contact with detainees. People set up visiting rosters at the city detention centres. Others set up accommodation lists.

Strong friendship and support networks grew. Rural Australians for Refugees (RAR) began in the Southern Highlands of NSW, Australia, in October 2001. Chilout[2] was born after the airing of a 'Four Corners' television program about Shayan Badraie, a little boy who became catatonic in detention with shock from the terrible things he had seen.

Alongside these support networks there were activist groups who organised protests outside immigration offices, the Federal Parliament and the city and desert detention centres. No place was too far. They booked buses, mobile communication units, camps, water and food, and the people climbed aboard to Woomera, Port Augusta and Canberra. The Freedom Bus toured all the detention centres in 2002. Many refugees tell us now how much it meant to them to 'see these people come from so far away for us'. After being continually told that they were not wanted and to go home by immigration officers and the ACM guards, they were surprised by these 'wonderful people' who came with tears and songs and support.

The Woomera Easter protest in 2002 was organised to draw Australian's attention to a hidden hellhole. By going to Woomera, activists drew the media and made both the electorate and politicians look at the misery their brutal policies were inflicting on people seeking refuge in our land. The Woomera escapes were a spontaneous explosion of hope and despair as protester and detainee met through the bars. Unplanned and on the spur-of-the-moment the imprisoned jumped into the crowds and ran gleefully across the desert protected by the protesters. Some gave themselves up and returned to the detention centre after a night in the tents and others kept running in spite of the police road blocks. Every car was searched as it left Woomera.

The trip to Baxter Detention Centre the following year was a maximum security event with hundreds of police, horses and helicopters. At night activists were buzzed by helicopters and blinded by high powered lights. The event culminated in an excess of zeal when policemen drove into camp with machine guns strapped across their chests. It was hard to remember that this was Australia as police in full riot gear, helmets and batons marched around with no riot in sight.

As the communication between people in detention and supporters grew, so did our understanding of the harshness of their conditions. Details such as the identification of everyone including children by number shocked many of us. The way in which women had to line up for sanitary napkins shamed us. The fact that mothers had to take their babies to the dining hall at 7 am in order to get milk broke our hearts. Sometimes it was the small things that really hurt. Knowing that these young mothers had to wake their children and take them out of the huts and dongas into the cold morning or get no breakfast. In Port Hedland parents were searched to stop them taking extra food for children who did not eat. In the Maribyrnong detention centre as late as 2003, children were still denied schooling even though there are schools within a few kilometres. It was only after constant lobbying for eight months that two little girls were allowed to go to school.

Long-term detention and fear

After the initial releases of people the department hunkered down and the long-term indefinite detention began in earnest. Many advocates' hearts were broken as the time in detention grew year after year, taking its toll on the physical and mental health of those whose hope of freedom faded. It was the conditions of imprisonment and the lack of sleep through constant night-time monitoring and musters which broke people's spirits. There was also the uncertainty of removals, deportations and transfers. Advocates fought hard for the refugees. Usually advocates were rung by other detainees to alert us that someone had not returned to the compound after being called for an appointment. These sudden disappearances caused great fear and mimicked the disappearance of family members in their own countries. It played havoc with mental health.

When all the camps were operating it was hard to know if the detainee had been summarily transferred to another camp or 'removed'. Some detainees went through almost every camp. I remember meeting three Iranian men in Maribyrnong who had been woken at 4 am and taken out of Port Hedland without prior notice. They were flown to Perth and then to Melbourne. It was a cold May morning when they arrived in pyjama shorts and t-shirts with bare feet. Such transfers meant a loss of friends and property, as when their possessions eventually arrived the valuables would be missing. At one time in Port Hedland no one would go to the doctor because they believed that they would be grabbed and removed.

Learning new skills

By 2005 advocates knew airlines schedules and routes. They set up a National Anti-deportation Alliance with a phone number which is still alive. This activated a team which tracked likely routes and times while legal advice was sought. Legal routes were eventually closed off as the government sought and received rights to deport people no matter what their mental or physical condition. Injunctions were only useful to bide time if there was an unresolved legal matter. Refugee lawyers generously tested the legal avenues but in the end to no avail. The government has the legislation on its side; human rights are not enshrined in law so these cases failed.

Advocates made appeals to the UN Human Rights Committee sparingly for extreme cases, and in so doing saved a number of people who were most in danger. We also tracked people being removed and in two cases managed to get them back from Africa and the Middle East when they were refused entry to the country to which DIMA had sent them. DIMA's track record on 'removals' is littered with mistakes, diminishing any trust in the process. The department can always find a doctor to state that a person is fit to travel as we saw with Vivian Alvarez Solon. There have been other cases where DIMA took the risk with a person's life such as the transfer of 'Ali' back to Nauru following a respiratory arrest and clot in his lung. Supporters stood first outside the motel and then the hospital for eight hours but in the end the hospital collaborated and 'Ali' was taken out through a laundry exit. Fighting these battles only strengthened the resolve of supporters.

Refugee supporters' lobbying and advocacy skills were honed through sheer necessity as the government's tactics hardened. They learnt about the media and tried to get the stories of the refugees as real people into the consciousness of Australians. There were always constraints. People were punished if they spoke publicly. Editors were not always generous. Government policy was to keep refugees hidden. The military was given guidelines to ensure no personalising or 'humanising photographs' were to be taken.[3]

And then came Cornelia

However in the end it has been the Immigration Department's own failures which caused Australians to question government policy towards refugees and asylum seekers. As one detainee said after the uproar when Cornelia Rau, an Australian resident was found in a detention centre, 'Cornelia was an angel for us and she does not know it'. He understood only too well the value of this blond, blue-eyed, ex-Qantas air hostess and her effect on the conditions in detention centres. It was the first time that the government and Immigration Department had been called to account by the electorate and the media.

Ultimately it was neither the children distressed and weeping behind bars, nor their parents depressed and hopeless, nor even the single men and women who became suicidal, that forced a reappraisal of the treatment of refugees. It was the fact that DIMA locked up an Australian resident. Many are grateful to Cornelia's family, who saw what had happened as not only a tragedy for their sister but as a tragedy for all those imprisoned in the detention centres.

Advocates who lobbied hard for mental health care for detainees have not forgotten that until the case of Cornelia, the regime for suicidal detainees was solitary confinement in the Management Unit, in a suicide belt with hands shackled to the belt plus feet cuffed and helmet. Very few detainees were taken to hospital and treated for depression and mental illness despite calls from advocates begging immigration staff and politicians for a suicidal detainee to be given treatment in hospital. It took the combination of Cornelia and then a feisty South Australian barrister taking the cases to Court to change this situation. It seems incredible to think that in Australia a person had to go to Court to access the medical services which the rest of us take for granted.

Cornelia's treatment demonstrated that human rights stop at the detention centre gates. When Cornelia was thought to be an 'unlawful immigrant' she was locked up in solitary confinement 23 hours out of 24, and no one cared that she was sick. When she was found to be an Australian resident with an Australian family, she was flown to a hospital in Adelaide postehaste. There was no clearer example of the difference in human rights. It is another reason why refugee advocates fight with such fury:

> Anger, anger, anger – it's a great incentive (Bec, on why she is in the refugee movement).

Reflection

What happens to a nation's heart when its citizens can lock a child behind bars and feel nothing? Where was that outrage so keenly felt for blonde, blue-eyed Cornelia when a 10-month-old baby was pulled out of his cot at 5 am and flung into a van in his wet nappy and driven with his brothers and sisters back to detention? Where was the anger when the tear-stained face of Monte was caught in the glare of the cameras in the back of the police car on his way back to detention? Where was the outrage when Ali flew to Melbourne to see his boys who had been lost, only to find that the minister had ordered them removed in a private plane at 5 am to Woomera? Terrible things were done to men, women and children in these years and Australians looked away. Many of these cruelties were witnessed by advocates and supporters who do not forget. How was it that a small boy went in and out of hospital many times for rehydration before hospital staff got the courage to say no more? When this child's catatonic state became public, his desperate parents were vilified by the Minister and the child was taken away from them and fostered by strangers for nearly a year before slowly first his mother and then his father were restored to him.

The laws underpinning this brutal regime are still in place. The government has won the right to continue indefinite mandatory detention from the High Court.[4] This decision has diminished faith and respect in the legal process and strengthened resolve to see a Bill of Human Rights enacted which protects and makes inalienable precious human rights.

While these have been dark days in Australia and hard times for refugees and their supporters, ordinary people have found a capacity to operate outside government. They have discovered the strength that people of good will have. They have reached out to people seeking refuge and welcomed them and been rewarded with warm friendships and deeply moving human relationships. Many advocates hold hopes for a Royal Commission to expose the truth of this time and to set in place laws to ensure that it can never happen again. They reject the government claims that detention is administrative not punitive. These Australians stand beside the refugees as witnesses, waiting for the day when Australia is ready to face the truth of this time.

Notes

1 The Department of Immigration and Multicultural Affairs with acronym DIMA has recently become the Department of Immigration and Citizenship with the acronym DIAC. During the period of writing the department was known as DIMIA then DIMA and now DIAC.

2 Chilout (Children out of Detention) is a group of parents and citizens formed in 2001 to oppose the mandatory detention of children in Australian immigration detention centres. See <www.chillout.org>.

3 'We were being told it was all to protect the asylum seekers but we were also hearing from Defence PR that they were not to take humanising photographs … ', Statement from Craig Skehan, Defence Correspondent, Sydney

Morning Herald, <www.abc.net.au/mediawatch/stories/220402_s2.htm> and <www.theage.com.au/articles/2004/07/01/108848.8090060.html?from=storylhs>.

4 <http://wopared.parl.net/Library/pubs/rb/2004-05/05rb01.htm#exec>. In August 2004 Australia's High Court declared by a bare majority (4:3) that failed asylum seekers who have nowhere to go and who pose no danger to the community can be kept in immigration detention indefinitely.

13

SUSANNAH TIPPING • DI BRETHERTON •
IDA KAPLAN

Meaning in life and social connectedness: the experience of Sudanese young people (re)settling in Australia

> *I have been all along running and trying to struggle with life, hoping that tomorrow, that when the sun rises tomorrow it is going to be better … So we all go along with this life until we are now here … Now most of us can see a little bit of horizon whereby you can go to school, you can have Medicare, you can have security, but the only thing that is missing is that you can never have peace of mind because of what you thought back and the people who remain there. So that little part is just still empty in everyone, including me* (Sudanese young man).[1]

Introduction

The opportunity for resettlement[2] is a profound time in a refugee's life. Arguably, it marks a point where life transitions from chaos and trauma to the promise and hope of a new and peaceful existence. However, gaining this opportunity is only the first step in rebuilding a life shattered by war, conflict, and persecution. After arrival in Australia, refugees face the task of belonging in a new society very different from their country of origin. People from refugee backgrounds bring with them the ongoing influences of their pre-arrival experiences, including the nature of the conflict in their country of origin and its psychological impact, previous levels of education, and cultural beliefs and practices.

This chapter is based on research which explored the importance of meaning in life and social connectedness for young people from Sudan who have recently arrived in Australia. They have not been asylum seekers in Australia and the story of their flight from conflict in Sudan to a neighbouring country where they sought refuge is not often told in the asylum seeking context. Nevertheless, these Sudanese young people have typically spent years outside of their country of origin under dangerous circumstances facing a completely uncertain future. Their plight has come to be recognised and they have arrived in Australia under the Humanitarian Program with permanent resident visas.

Over the past decade, approximately 22,000 Sudanese refugees have been (re)settled in Australia,[3] mostly in the capital cities, with some (re)settled in rural areas such as Toowomba in Queensland. Young people aged less than 25 years have formed a significant proportion of Sudanese humanitarian entrants to Australia, including a large number of unaccompanied minors. The Sudanese young people's descriptions of their experiences in Australia provide invaluable insight into the challenges faced at (re)settlement. Such knowledge can be used to guide services and members of the Australian community who want to promote the wellbeing of all those who have undergone a similar journey.

In this chapter, we provide a brief overview of refugee mental health research, including the current research. Next, a brief background to the conflict in Sudan is provided, and its disruptive impact on the lives of young people through trauma, dislocation and the breaking down of social ties is discussed. This is followed by descriptions of the (re)settlement experience of Sudanese young people. Based on our research, we suggest implications for research, policy and practice for work with (re)settling refugees. Finally, significant lessons learned from the research are summarised in the conclusion.

Refugee mental health research

Research on the impact of the refugee experience on mental health has been dominated by a Western psychiatric approach.[4] Questionnaires measuring post-traumatic stress, depression and anxiety are commonly used to explore the effects of pre-migration and post-migration stressors on mental health at (re)settlement, with both found to contribute to psychological distress. Not surprisingly, refugees are at high risk for developing mental health problems, with children and young people particularly vulnerable.[5]

Our research took a different approach, concerned that the subjective voices and stories of the refugees themselves have been lost in psychiatric research. Thirty Sudanese young people aged 18 to 30 were interviewed and asked about what gave their life meaning in the past, present, and future, and about their social connectedness in Australia. The research was informed by holistic frameworks developed to understand the psychological effects of human rights violations and extreme trauma encountered as part of the refugee experience.[6] A key element of holistic frameworks is the belief that refugee trauma poses a threat to meaning in life and to a sense of connection to others. Our research has also been influenced by existential psychology, which stresses that the ability to find meaning and sense in our everyday lives and our overall existence is an integral component to health and wellbeing.

Conflict in Sudan

There is a long history of conflict in Sudan between the North and the South. The North has traditionally been home to mostly Arabic-speaking Muslims while the South is made up of diverse African ethnic groups of Indigenous and Christian beliefs with distinct languages, religions and customs. Since independence in 1956, Sudan has experienced an almost continuous civil war between the North and the South, with the latest starting in 1983 and ending in January 2005 when a comprehensive Peace Agreement was signed. Generally speaking, Northern government forces fought Southern rebel forces. However, within the North and South, major divisions also aggravated the violence. The majority of refugees have come from the South, as this is where most of the violence has occurred. Famine and disease have exacerbated the conditions. Since 1983, an estimated four million people have been displaced and an estimated two million have been killed.[7] In the late 1980s there was an upsurge in the civil war and attacks by the Northern government's militia destroyed villages in the South. An estimated 17,000 children, some as young as three or four years of age, were forced to flee. The majority of the children were boys from the Dinka and Nuer tribes, who have become known as 'The Lost Boys of Sudan'.[8] Since early 2003 a separate conflict has occurred in the Western region of Darfur.

The experience of war and life in exile

Given the nature of the conflict in Sudan, Sudanese young people (re)settling in Australia have an extensive trauma history with little experience of life ever having been 'settled'. Sudanese young people have spent the majority of their formative years fleeing conflict, spending little time settled in one place. War, displacement and separation from their family and community have severely disrupted educational opportunities. Experiences of the war and life in exile vary, particularly according to whether Sudanese young people come to Australia via Egypt, Kenya, or Uganda. Sudanese young people who have come via Egypt have spent most of their life in Khartoum and have had time in cities. In contrast, those coming via Kenya and Uganda tend to come from rural areas and have spent many years in refugee camps. A young man commented that each group has 'their own way of thinking about themselves, thinking about life'.

The impact of traumatic events

The experience of traumatic life events endured by Sudanese young people is a breakdown of meaning in life and a sense of life being on hold. In the words of a young man:

> I didn't have the opportunities to go to school all the time, war, people moving up and down … there is a cycle of moving around from camp to camp, from town to town, news of war, people dying … you could say that there was nothing in life.

During the immediate experience of war, another common experience is that 'you are valued as meaningless'. Little thought is given to the future as life becomes about 'survival': 'My life at that time it was just day to day because you don't know maybe what will happen tomorrow'. When some young people reach relative safety, meaning in life may begin to be restored. After reaching Kenya, a young man who had been in the army stated:

> I regained meaning when I came to know that I could go to school, tomorrow there would be no more trekking, tomorrow I would not worry that when it is going to rain … because shelter … [and] I am going meet new friends.

However, even once the 'safety' of a refugee camp or country of exile is reached, previous social networks have been ruptured, with ongoing separation from family and friends a common experience. Given the importance of family to meaning in life, a breakdown in social ties poses an ongoing challenge to the experience of a meaningful life in Sudanese young people.

Some of the young people contemplated the deleterious impact of pre-arrival traumatic experiences on mental health, acknowledging that it can be long-lasting. One young man stated that 'a lot of people like me have gone crazy you know, they have lost their minds'. Another reflected:

> I don't think anything can be done … maybe I will gradually forget it, but I don't really think so, it is like a scar that is there, you can't do anything about it … Sleep is a trouble, I can't sleep, I can't concentrate … I can't sometimes think straight … I forget … you find yourself thinking about something else – flashbacks.

Another commonly reported effect of trauma is the difficulty trusting others, particularly the government and its representatives. Contact with officials in Sudan or the country of exile is likely to have involved corruption or, in some cases, the disappearance of family members. A young woman reflecting on why she finds it difficult to fully trust the government in Australia stated that:

> [T]he government itself is the one who abuses people in Sudan. They arrest people, they do a lot of things. That's why I don't trust the system, but I think the longer I am here [in Australia], you know, the more time I am here, I will learn to trust the government if they do the right thing.

Life in Australia

The Sudanese young people that we interviewed found meaning in life and social connectedness were inextricably linked. The majority experience life as meaningful and have a sense of connectedness and belonging in Australia.

Australia's social, political, and legal institutions play a prominent role in the lives of the young people, enabling a sense of freedom, peace, security, justice, equality and opportunity that has previously been lacking. Having the same rights as non-Sudanese Australians, including the protection of the law and educational opportunities, is important to a sense of connectedness and meaning – 'there is no different from me and Australian citizen, we are all the same'. For a young woman, being accountable for her attendance at school and receiving letters from Centrelink is significant: 'Before I came to Australia nobody knows me in society … but when I came here … I feel the government knows me, that's why they are sending me letter'. The outstanding experience of the young people interviewed is both the previous and current role of education in creating a meaningful life. Access to education is commonly experienced as significant in keeping young people's hopes about the future alive; for example, a young woman commented:

> Since I was very young, I have been thinking that one day … I will finish my education and get a good job and get to be in a better life, so … in every situation I will always say, oh, something better is coming, you had better not give up now.

Education is also seen as a way to potentially assist those that remain behind: 'you know that you are doing something that will in the future put you in an area that you can help … that is why you see that the education will really make a meaning in your life'. Employment opportunities were also viewed as key to a meaningful life, and as a way to ensure a secure future.

Positive interactions with representatives of institutions, teachers and support workers in particular, can enhance a sense of connectedness and meaning, whereas conflict or tensions between Sudanese young people and representatives of Australia's institutions detracts from it, largely due to a subjective experience of discrimination or racism. For example, a young man reflecting on his contact with the police stated that:

> you can't feel happy because if they pull you over quite often for no reason … sometimes you can't feel like being here … maybe they pull you over because of your colour.

Struggles with education, even when pre-arrival education is relatively intact, lead to feelings of disadvantage and difference compared to young Australians. For example, one young woman who completed high school before arrival in Australia and is now pursuing a university education reflected:

> [H]ere you have to compete with people who have never even experienced what hardship is like. They had the best education, they went to the best schools … they came from very affluent families and now you have to compete with them, it is a distressing experience.

Young people's commitment to education and the amount of extra study time needed to make up for disrupted schooling can impact on the time available to them to connect socially with others, as illustrated by a young woman who stated: 'I feel isolated … I have been very busy with school'.

The presence of immediate family in Australia adds to feeling good about life and connected with others. As one respondent said, 'family is everything'. Further, connections with other members of the Sudanese community, both here and abroad, are viewed as important. In reference to her membership of a Sudanese youth group,[9] a young woman stated that:

> [T]he group is important to me because we talk, we make discussion about the life, about what happened, about how we are going to make something good of Sudanese in Australia and how we are going to help … our youth … left in Africa or in the camp.

Separation from family members and extended social networks can lead to a sense of isolation, especially given that family is a major source of meaning in life for Sudanese young people. Many young people are here without their parents, which is viewed as being 'really rough … to live without no-one guiding you, you actually tend to be very vulnerable to any situation'. For those attempting to be reunited with family, the process is a frustrating one: 'you wait and wait … and we just keep holding on and thinking of something that is not going to happen … and you just can't move on with your life'.

The multicultural nature of Australian society was identified by many young people interviewed as an important element of their (re)settlement. Further, positive contact with non-Sudanese Australians plays a significant role in a sense of connectedness: 'people treat you like one of them, they are friendly'. Learning about Australian cultural mores is vital to Sudanese young people's sense of belonging. One young man commented on the difficulty of this: 'I have to learn how to be an Australian, but if I have no Australian people close to me, how can I handle this?' Experiences of racism and discrimination, including in the workplace, were raised by Sudanese young people as detracting from a sense of connectedness. One young woman found when working as a cashier that:

> [S]ome customers would never come to my register … I could be completely without a customer … this guy, he never, ever comes to my register, regardless of how full or empty the store is … that sort of affects you.

Feelings of isolation can lead to problems: 'If my social life improved I'll feel I belong to Australia, but if it doesn't improve then that is why everything goes contrary and the people behave bad in the street'.

The impact of war on cultural identity and differences between Australian and Sudanese cultures can pose challenges for Sudanese young people. A consequence of war for some Sudanese young people may be a disconnection from their Sudanese culture and identity. One young woman suggested that 'we are losing our identity because of all the horror and everything that we have been through'. Further, the ongoing effect of this is that because 'people have missed out on culture and values … there is a problem with identity … and once they come here they try to share themselves with people who are black American, that they see from TV'. Cultural differences between Sudanese and Australian cultures can challenge a sense of belonging. Our interviewees reflected on the individualist nature of Australian society, including difficulties associated with moving from a more communal society. For example:

> Australia is different to Sudan … I don't even know who is my neighbour, there I know my neighbours, I know the whole neighbourhood and here is about individuals, it is not about community … where everybody cares for one another.

Culturally, Sudanese young people hang out in groups. One young man reflected on Sudanese youth hanging out together:

> If you see them hanging out in the street it is because they need a place away together … to play basketball … to play soccer … that's the main reason like you can see most of the Sudanese youths are hanging out on the street, they need a place to meet, but they can't find where they can meet. … it has been mistaken like they are going to the [train] station … to look for trouble, or they are just gangsters.

There are many other themes emerging that highlight what contributes to or detracts from a sense of meaning and connectedness in the lives of Sudanese young people. Religion was viewed as a major source of meaning. Difficulties with language, especially in understanding and being understood by others, can be frustrating for young people and highlight a sense of feeling different from non-Sudanese Australians. Further, language difficulties pose barriers to education and the ability to connect with non-Sudanese Australians. Our research also revealed diversity in (re)settlement experiences and views regarding the nature of assistance which is required.

A lasting impression of the Sudanese young people interviewed was a strong sense of courage and tenacity, despite having endured horrendous traumatic events beyond the experience of most Australians. Sudanese young people bring with them enduring personal beliefs developed out of their experiences, which help them cope with the difficulties in their lives. For example, 'my past experience has actually strengthened me a lot, so I don't actually fear anything or I don't really worry, even if I have a current problem'.

Implications for research, policy and practice

The current research points towards several implications for policy, research and practice in the context of working with Sudanese young people who face the challenges of (re)settlement after years of displacement and uncertainty. While it is important to keep in mind that refugees from different cultural backgrounds will have different (re)settlement needs, war, trauma, lost opportunity, dislocation, disruption and the breakdown of social networks are very much part of the refugee experience. As such, general principles and findings drawn from the current example of research with Sudanese young people can be applied more broadly.

Identification of needs is clearly the basis for planning (re)settlement responses. How this process occurs is important to ensure that diversity can be expressed. The process itself can be a basis for developing mutual understanding and trust, enhancing the experience of (re)settlement. The current research paints a portrait of Sudanese young people that contrasts starkly with the one portrayed in some of the recent media coverage. The negative media coverage depicted this newly arrived community from Africa as a burden and a danger, sending a message to Sudanese young people antithetical to the purpose of (re)settlement, and it risks undermining their motivation to identify with other Australians. In contrast, when Sudanese young people are engaged in a two-way interaction, a different understanding emerges. The opportunity to hear Sudanese young people reflect on their experiences in their own words provided the researchers with insight into the diversity of challenges faced at (re)settlement and an 'insider's' view of the refugee experience. For some participants, the chance to have 'a voice', discussing their difficulties and needs as well as their strengths, enhanced (re)settlement through contributing to a sense of empowerment and the amelioration of frustration and isolation. The process of forming a relationship based on trust with genuine regard for the needs expressed by young people cannot be overemphasised as it is the very basis for bringing hopes to fruition and is at the core of restoring safety and dignity.

It is equally important to address specific needs of (re)settling refugees for information, cultural and systems orientation, and educational and training opportunities. Sudanese young people identified a number of key (re)settlement needs. Foremost amongst them were better engagement with key institutions representing the justice system, policing and welfare, and a better understanding of how those systems work. These findings reinforce observations made in the course of providing services to newly arriving communities whereby much trust is placed in institutions which provide for both necessities and opportunities for rebuilding lives. However, those institutions can easily become a source of threat and insecurity for (re)settling refugees when there is little opportunity for dialogue or accommodation of their fears. Educational opportunities consistently emerged as the most critical pathway for rebuilding a meaningful life, as were current and future employment. Providing young people with opportunities to learn about educational and career pathways in a sensitive way is important in order for Sudanese young not to feel discouraged, especially given the prominent role of education in creating a meaningful life.

In those interviewed, foundations for connectedness were seen to lie in understanding and trust between Sudanese young people and non-Sudanese Australians, including representatives of institutions. Many believed learning about the nuances of Australian culture would enhance a sense of connectedness, and could be achieved through further cultural orientation, or building connections between Sudanese young people and non-Sudanese Australians or more established Sudanese young people. Opportunities for organised recreational activities and the provision of physical space where people can meet are ways to enhance connectedness. Participants expressed a desire for non-Sudanese Australians to learn about their journey to Australia, including the traumatic experiences they have endured and the ongoing impact of those experiences. Many Sudanese young people are seeking opportunities to tell their stories. They would also like greater appreciation from non-Sudanese Australians of the struggles faced by Sudanese young people in juggling two very different cultures. Other needs identified by Sudanese young people were learning 'life skills', including 'managing money' and 'time management'.

More generally, our work indicates that it is essential to engage in consultation with a diverse range of (re)settling refugees, and to involve them in decision-making and the generation of possible solutions to (re)settlement issues. Using the current example, opportunities for Sudanese young people to come together formally to share their past experiences and current struggles, and to discuss their concerns and hopes about (re)settlement, are needed on a regular basis and are likely to prove helpful.

Conclusion

Our research provided a space for young people from Sudan to tell their stories and to put forward some ideas as to what would assist them in the process of (re)settlement. Responding to the needs of Sudanese young people, and more broadly the needs of all refugees (re)settling in Australia, will entail more than just providing services. (Re)settling refugees need to be listened to, understood, and genuinely invited to create solutions for emerging (re)settlement challenges. As well as appreciating their vulnerabilities, it is important to acknowledge their strengths and attend to the factors they identify as contributing to meaning in their lives. This approach calls for a sense of equality in relationships between (re)settling refugees and those they encounter in Australian society.

Notes

1 The authors have attempted to be as literal as possible with quotations. Occasionally an authorial interpolation will appear within [square brackets]. Any omission from the quotation will be indicated by (…). Further, [*sic*] will not be used to represent idiosyncratic expression.

2 Despite its inherent limitations, the term 'resettlement' will continue to be used in this chapter. However, it will be written as (re)settlement in an effort to convey the limitations associated with using the term in the current context given the highly disrupted nature of Sudanese young people's lives before arrival in Australia.

3 Department of Immigration and Citizenship, <www.settlement.immi.gov.au/settlement/enterSelectReport.do>.

4 See Schweitzer, R, Greenslade, J and Kagee, A, 'Coping and resilience in refugees from the Sudan: a narrative account', *Australian and New Zealand Journal of Psychiatry*, vol 41, 2007, pp 282-288, for a more detailed discussion of the limitations of refugee mental health research.

5 Goodman, J, 'Coping with trauma and hardship among unaccompanied refugee youths from Sudan', *Qualitative Health Research*, vol 14, 2004, pp 1177-1196.

6 Victorian Foundation for Survivors of Torture Inc, *Rebuilding Shattered Lives*, Victorian Foundation for Survivors of Torture Inc, Melbourne, 1998, <www.foundationhouse.org.au/publications.php>; Silove, D, 'The psychosocial effects of torture, mass human rights violations, and refugee trauma: toward an integrated conceptual framework', *Journal of Nervous & Mental Disease*, vol 187, 1999, pp 200-207.

7 United States Committee for Refugees and Immigrants, *World Refugee Survey 2001*, <www.refugees.org/article.aspx?id=1565&subm=19&ssm=29&area=Investigate&>; United States Committee for Refugees and Immigrants, *World Refugee Survey 2004*, <www.refugees.org/article.aspx?id=1565&subm=19&ssm=29&area=Investigate&>.

8 Goodman, above, n 5.

9 There are many Sudanese youth associations in Australia. For example, the New Sudan Youth Association, the Kongor Students Association, the Bor Youth Association, Sudanese Youth for Reconciliation and Hope, Nuer Youth Association, and Equatorial Youth Association, amongst others.

PART V

Public opinion about asylum seekers

PHILLIP ADAMS

Part V Introduction

In the 1940s, when I was living on one of the few tiny farms that had survived in the Melbourne suburbs, I'd a choice of two playgrounds. One was official – the small asphalt area between the East Kew State School classrooms, the dunnies and the shelter sheds. The other was far more expansive – the unsupervised wilds of the nearby Yarra River.

The first 'reffo' children from Europe suddenly appeared in the official playground, the offspring of the 'DPs', or displaced people. The cosmetic term 'New Australian' was yet to be successfully marketed and these poor haunted youngsters became the new targets of playground cruelty. Instead of chanting 'Catholic dogs stink like frogs' to the kids in the playground across the street – echoing the bigotries of our Protestant parents – we'd bully refugees with 'why don't you go back to your own country!'.

Our unofficial playground stretched between the Kew Lunatic Asylum, a magnificent and gloomy complex of high Victorian buildings, and the muddy river's banks. From time to time we'd glimpse some of the 'trusty' inmates who were allowed to work in the institution's vegetable gardens. Terrified of these 'loonies' we'd scream abuse at them. And then run like hell.

During the carefully choreographed panic, pre- and post-*Tampa*, those shameful memories came rushing back. The new 'reffos' weren't from Europe, which made them even easier to fear and hate. And they were destined to be incarcerated in conditions even worse than those in the Kew Asylum. And somehow the word 'asylum' as applied to those seeking it, became blurred with those under lock and key on a Kew hillside. It was another time of madness.

But this time round the madness afflicted the Australian public whose collective insanity became a national shame and an international scandal. To close the circle, we'd soon be driving asylum seekers to mental destruction – to self-mutilation, clinical depression and suicide.

The White Australia policy, all but unquestioned during my childhood, would be re-introduced and repackaged for political advantage – in a cynical appropriation of the One Nation phenomenon and collaboration between Howard, tabloid pundits and the shock jocks. Australians were swept up in a vortex of vilification and vindictiveness that swept away our proud claim of 'tolerance' as the principal social glue. I remember it as the shameful period in my lifetime.

But in the eternal 'now' of the 21st Century, when today's events, trumpeted in an unprecedented media barrage, eclipse yesterday's (let alone yesteryear's); when collective memory lacks the shelf-life of yoghurt; when an effort to repress memory perhaps adds to its abbreviation, we need to be reminded of how we surrendered, as a people, to antique fears and bigotries. And it is important to be reminded of the moral collapse of the Australian Labor Party (ALP) under Kim Beazley – something so deeply shaming to the 'progressive' side of politics that the ALP is still struggling to live it down.

Attacking the attacks on refugees that began before *Tampa*, I asked my readers to sign up for a civil disobedience campaign. Immigration Minister Philip Ruddock had announced that anyone harbouring an escapee from Villawood or Woomera would be jailed for 10 years – a somewhat longer term than many get for murder. I proposed a public list. We would identify ourselves. Ruddock boasted that 'only a couple of hundred' people would be so silly. But within a few days I had 10,000 volunteers. It was the biggest response to a newspaper column I'd had in a 40-year career – and another great wave followed after *Tampa* – along with a million dollars in donations used to set up an organisation for refugee advocacy, A Just Australia. And this from readers of an ostensibly conservative broadsheet.

Almost every letter (and it was all 'snail mail', not email) echoed the same sentiment. Of shame in being Australian. Of shame in the ALP. But the 10,000 dissidents were drowned out by the overwhelming majority who chose to believe the 'queuejumpers' 'illegals' 'probable terrorists' line. We'd seen plenty of moral panics organised by the mainstream media – but this pandemic of panic and prejudice was unprecedented.

And this time of political and social lunacy must be remembered – and understood.

14

CARMEN LAWRENCE

Those people

Who we are and where we've been are questions that intermittently grab the Australian imagination with a peculiar intensity. The questions are often posed in ways which make it clear that what is being asked is what defines 'us' as opposed to 'them', how we differ from 'those people'. At various points in our history, the 'other', named or implied, has included Indigenous Australians, the Chinese, Communists, Catholics, 'New Australians', the Vietnamese and Cambodian 'boat people', 'people of Middle Eastern appearance', and Muslims in general. In much of this public debate, 'those people' lack the virtues which 'mainstream', 'middle' or 'ordinary' Australians possess: we are generous – they are mean ('cheating "queuejumpers"'); we are trustworthy – they are devious; we love our children – they would sacrifice and exploit theirs; we are moderate – they are extremists; we are law abiding – they are law breakers; we are peace loving – they are violent; we belong here – they are interlopers and refuse to integrate: 'we grew here, you flew here', as the rioters at Cronulla insisted.

This is one of those times; a time when debates – indeed demonstrations – about our identity, our values and our past have been given particular force by our fear of further terrorist attacks on western targets, attacks we've been invited to understand as motivated by hatred of 'who we are' and 'what we stand for' (whoever 'we' is). There is nothing new in this. Australia's history, like that of many nations, could be written through the prism of the ebb and flow of fear, punctuated by occasional outbursts of moral panic, more than occasionally fanned by our elected representatives. Fear is a potent political force and, even in a democracy like ours, the exploitation of fear is a seductive weapon in the politician's armamentarium. Few resist its appeal, not least because it appears to be very effective as a method of social control in assisting those who hold power to retain it. As RG Menzies suggested in his *Forgotten People* broadcasts in 1942:

> [F]rightened people are much more pliant instruments and much readier receptacles for notions of hatred and revenge than people who move and have their beings in the brave daylight of a free mind.[1]

Fear not only triggers hatred, but sustained fear-based propaganda can railroad even otherwise rational minds, causing them to regress to more primitive modes of thinking. Fearful people typically reason less clearly, are less able to learn new material and seek to avoid new situations.[2]

There is mounting evidence that when people anywhere are frightened by constantly being reminded of their own mortality, they react with increased prejudice and aggression toward those who differ in some way from themselves – in language or appearance or apparent worldview. In these circumstances, people become more intolerant of those who question their beliefs, more nationalistic, more likely to endorse stereotypes based on race and culture and more closely identified with those who share their religious and political beliefs.[3] These patterns of behaviour were all on view in the lead up to the 2001 election when the Howard government steadily increased the emotional temperature around the so-called 'illegals', asylum seekers who were arriving on our shores having fled war and persecution in the Middle East. After the atrocities committed in the US on 11 September 2001, government ministers suggested, none too subtly, that there might be terrorists among the asylum seekers; the Defence Minister suggested that the leaky boats might provide a possible 'pipeline' for terrorists. The fact that those seeking asylum were Muslims played no small part in the government's success in demonising them, there was no doubt of this, since they were already seen as the most socially distant by Australians (surveyed by Forest and Dunn in 2001).[4]

However, the current obsessive bout of anxious, government-sponsored navel gazing about our destiny, our values and our past, had its genesis well before the planes slammed into the twin towers and the bomb blasts in the bars in Bali, cutting short so many lives, and before the attacks on Afghanistan and Iraq produced their own gruesome and mounting body counts. Rather, it began, as it so often does, with uninvited strangers seeking to join us. It began when men, women and children from Iran, Iraq and Afghanistan cast up on our northern shores in increasing numbers, pleading for protection from sadistic tyrants and civil strife. It began, as it so often does with a story about invasion, about strangers trying to take what was not offered, about people who were not like us; strange tinted people whose language and culture were alien and who had not observed the niceties of queuing up (where?) in an orderly fashion and waiting their turn. It began because a government seemed a spent force and needed a compelling story to deflect attention from its deficiencies. It owed more than a little to a leader intent on refashioning a monocultural Australia: the White Anglo Australia of his childhood; one set of values to define us; one identity – 'Australian' everyman with his cricket bat and Gallipoli nostalgia; one image of the nation, all virtue and no vice; one account of our history and settlement.

Fear of invaders

Our periodic panics about alien invasion have a uniquely Australian character; while it is true that 'fear of strangers' is a nearly universal human emotion, we have evolved our own peculiar variant of xenophobia, directed with particular virulence against those who arrive, unbidden, in unseaworthy boats. It's a fear that seems to have its roots in the nature of the conquest of this land and the recurring – if repressed – nightmare of being displaced by the unannounced; of having done to us as we have done. Given their relatively small numbers, these 'boat people', as we have come to be call them, elicit a disproportionate level of community anger and fear and excessively punitive responses from governments intent on 'sending a message' to deter other would-be interlopers.

One of the recurring notes in these alarums is the idea that we are losing control of our borders; that our capacity to decide who will migrate is being eroded by lawless 'queuejumpers'. As Anthony Burke pointed out in *In Fear of Security*,[5] Australian political figures have often portrayed Australia as vulnerable to loss of sovereignty and have incited levels of fear and anxiety that are disproportionate to the actual threats. It is no accident that the responsible minister, Philip Ruddock, chose to represent the arrival of an increased number of asylum seekers during 2001 as an 'urgent threat to Australia's very integrity' and invoked the phrase 'national emergency' to describe the increase in numbers. This was no spontaneous opportunism, but rather a carefully calculated application of 'wedge politics' founded on a sophisticated understanding of Australians' attitudes to race and migration.[6] The Howard government knew which buttons to push and had no compunction about pushing them, despite the potentially damaging consequences to our social fabric.

Robert Manne has noted the 'ugly symmetry' in the fact that the first Commonwealth Parliament started with a debate on the *Immigration Restriction Act* and marked its centenary in 2001 with the passage of the *Border Protection Act*. Both had the exclusion of 'others' at their core.[7] The *Immigration Restriction Act* gave national legislative effect to the 'White Australia' policy, foreshadowed by statutes already enacted in the colonies. It provided that only those who passed a dictation test in a European language of the customs officer's choosing could enter Australia. The new Federal members eschewed a more direct, overtly race-based measure out of deference to the 'Mother Country' who presided over an empire of many races and colours. But their speeches reveal a near unanimous intention to exclude the Chinese and 'other coloured peoples' and the recognition that failure to do so would earn them the voters' ire. The Member for Parramatta, Joseph Cook, was adamant that the voters were implacable on this question:

> It is not a matter of what we consider in this House, but a matter of what the Australian people consider. We had to pledge ourselves very definitely to the people of Australia during the recent elections that we would lose no time in dealing with the race question; otherwise, many of us would not have been here and others would have been in our places ... It is believed deep down in the hearts of the people of Australia that we cannot deal with this matter too promptly or, indeed, too drastically.

Much the same could have been said – indeed was said – by MPs seeking election in 2001 following the manufactured panic about 'illegals'. Although the Prime Minister and senior government ministers were quick to reject any suggestion that their victory resulted from an exploitation of voters' primitive and exaggerated fears of asylum seekers, there were those who were more honest. In 2006, the members for Canning and Makin, both marginal seats in 2001, agreed that they owed their re-election to the post-*Tampa* border protection policy.[8]

There is historical continuity too in the justifications proffered for the 'White Australia' policy and the arguments that asylum seekers should be made unwelcome and preferably repelled altogether. The members of parliament in the 1901 debate spoke not only of the racial inferiority and immorality of the Chinese and the coloured races, but of their inability to integrate, of the likelihood that they would form separate enclaves; that they would be a corrupting influence in the society; that they were not Christians and that they were very numerous – 'swarms' and 'floods' who would overrun us. In speaking to the Bill, Sir John Forrest quoted his earlier speech to the WA Assembly on a similar piece of legislation:

> We desire that this country shall not be overrun with races whose sympathies, manners and customs and religion are not ours. There is another reason … There are millions of them, and if we do not place some restrictions on them, they will overrun the country.

As Ien Ang has argued, 'while the legal and formal-political structures of the White Australia policy itself are no longer in place, the mentality it nurtured is still part of the deep structure of Australian culture'.[9] Turning back refugee boats, as David Marr observed,[10] was always going to be popular in Australia. In ordering the Norwegian freighter *Tampa* to turn around and take the four hundred or so asylum seekers away – anywhere but Australia – John Howard knew that he was tapping a rich vein of prejudice, that he was speaking to a significant minority of Australians who had often demanded that such 'boat people' be turned away. From the time the first boats arrived from Vietnam in the 1970s, opinion polls consistently showed around 30% believed they should be turned back. During the *Tampa* incident, a truly astounding 77% of Australians said they approved of the government's action in refusing to allow the asylum seekers ashore.[11]

Previous governments had largely resisted the temptation to gain political traction by assuaging these demands and exploiting the most vulnerable of all people, although the Labor government did enforce mandatory detention of asylum seekers in 1992. The Howard regime, however, after careful research and analysis of the public's mood, embarked on a deliberate campaign of intensifying our fear of being overwhelmed by strangers envious of our good fortune; they spoke directly to our old dark fear of invasion. And the Opposition stumbled along behind them, anxious to avoid appearing 'soft' on national security. In the end, both major political parties broadly supported the crude politics of the *Tampa* and the misuse of the Navy in Operation Relex, although they disagreed about where to locate the dumping sites for those who were turned away.

While successfully playing on these fears, our Prime Minister would have us believe that, above all the world and despite our history, Australians are incapable of racism and that their hostile responses to asylum seekers have not been driven by any racist sentiments, but rather by an innate sense of 'fair play'. During the *Tampa* incident and the high drama of the confected 'national emergency', Howard insisted that:

> I don't find any racism in the Australian public … I don't find, as I move around the community, people expressing racist sentiments about the illegal immigrants at all.

He must have had his ears stuffed with cloth or have been so protected by his minders at stage-managed 'community functions' that he wasn't exposed to the unpleasant diatribes that most of the rest of us had to endure. More likely, however, he did hear the throb of racism in conversations and talkback radio and the letters pages, but refused to call it by its name for fear of offending the voters expressing these views and because he'd more than once been accused of racist views himself. Intent on protecting us from any discomfort – or adult self-insight – he argued that to say that Australians are racially prejudiced is 'self-flagellation' of the Australian spirit – and we couldn't have that. Those who had the temerity to suggest that perhaps we have made mistakes in the past and may indeed be less than perfect were – and are – condemned in this climate of rising Australian fundamentalism, as Ghassan

Hage puts it, as 'the Bad Other, hell-bent on undermining the essential Goodness of Australia and the pride of its people'.[12]

Were he more honest, the Prime Minister would acknowledge that it is a very rare person indeed who has never entertained prejudicial ideas about other people, whether the basis for that prejudice was race or religion or culture or sexual preference or sex or disability. Recognition of this near universal tendency is the reason we have developed a legislative framework to outlaw discrimination on these grounds. It's why we have signed international instruments to protect everyone's human rights. It's why, at least in the recent past, political leaders have been assiduous in eschewing language and behaviour which gives the impression that some people are, because of certain characteristics or beliefs, less than fully human and undeserving of our concern. It's why a great many people have devoted their lives to breaking down the barrier of mutual incomprehension which often underlies prejudice. It's why a bipartisan policy evolved of respecting the variety of cultures and races which make up our nation; indeed of embracing our multicultural complexion. It might entertain certain commentators to sneeringly describe this as 'politically correct', or as Howard has done to express relief that being able to say such unpleasant things about our fellow citizens things lifts 'a pall of censorship', but such restraints are needed precisely because prejudice does exist and because it can lead to discriminatory and even violent behaviour toward those who are labelled.

Populate or perish

I grew up in country Western Australia at a time when the White Australia policy was firmly entrenched and supported by both major political parties; a time when local Aboriginal people were unseen on the town fringes; a time when the shadow of the feared Japanese invasion in the Second World War and the increasing tempo of the Cold War gave force to the slogan, 'Populate or Perish'. There was constant speculation, especially by Mr Menzies, about the risk from the 'yellow peril', the millions of Chinese communists poised to overrun the country – at least, unless he was elected. Race and invasion were inextricably linked in people's minds, as they so often are in our country.

I was only dimly aware that there was a massive immigration program underway bringing tens of thousands of 'white' families, some with their passport photographs carrying the inscription, 'Labourers for Australia'. In my country backwater a few families – refugees from war ravaged Europe, people we called displaced persons – came to make a life in farming and labouring: the Rossis, the Troppianos, the Tasseffs and Mr Zinn. They stood out in the largely Anglo-Celtic community, although I don't remember them being included very often in the local social events. They were seen as outsiders; 'they kept to themselves'. It was a long time before I appreciated just how difficult the transition to the new world was for so many postwar migrants, with no mastery of English and no language classes, with little understanding of the culture and few opportunities to experience the lives other Australians led, with little wealth and no safety net if things went wrong and with no easy, comforting support from family and friends. All this, while having to deal with often barely suppressed impatience and aggression from those whose forebears had also migrated here sometime in the previous 150 years. We needed 'those people', the reffos, the wogs, the ones with strange things in their lunchboxes and funny accents, for our safety and progress, to help build Australia, but we didn't welcome them as friends or neighbours.

By the time I entered University in the 1960s, the tenor of public and political discussion was changing. The White Australia policy was under more critical scrutiny. Demands for rights for Aboriginal Australians were firmly on the political agenda as the reverberations from the Black civil rights movement were felt around the globe. Racial discrimination and xenophobia were named and judged unfair and undesirable and by the beginning of the next decade the White Australia policy was abandoned altogether (although there were many who remained – still remain – unconvinced that it should be). The children of the postwar European migrants gradually took their places in universities and the professions, in workplaces other than factories and shops. And the idea of multiculturalism officially replaced the racial exclusiveness that has featured so prominently in our history. Despite widespread apprehension in the community, the Fraser government and the Labor Opposition had cautiously defused the more alarmist reactions to the arrival of Vietnamese 'boat people' in the

1970s and seen them settled successfully into our midst. Finally, enough of us seemed willing to accept that Australia was big enough to survive, indeed thrive, on accepting migrants from all corners of the globe.

What was shocking about the *Tampa* incident and Australia's embrace of the 'Pacific Solution' and the cruel detention regime which followed, was the apparent regression to a mode of thinking and acting which many of us thought was defunct. As Paul Keating said, we had moved from being on the brink of creating a tolerant, creative society in which xenophobia was on the wane to one in which 'tolerance looks fragile and xenophobia more robust'.[13] It would appear that the public discussion on ethnic issues has regressed to the primitive form abandoned by (most) of our political leaders more than 30 years ago and the deterioration show no signs of abating. It will take time and dedication to reverse.

Notes

1 Menzies, R, *The Forgotten People*, 1942, transcripts of radio broadcasts, <www.menziesvirtualmuseum.org.au/transcripts/ForgottenPeople/ForgottenCont.html>.

2 These effects have been extensively investigated over many decades. Summaries can be found in most introductory psychology texts. For more advanced analysis, see Eysenck, M, *Anxiety and Cognition: a Unified Theory*, Psychology Press, Hove, 1997.

3 For summaries of this research see TA Pyszczynski, S Solomon and J Greenberg (eds), *In the Wake of 9/11: the Psychology of Terror*, American Psychological Association, Washington DC, 2002; and Pyszczynski, T, 'What are we so afraid of? A terror management perspective on the politics of fear', *Social Research,* vol 71(4), 2004.

4 Several surveys have been conducted by collaborative research teams at Macquarie University and the University of New South Wales, eg Dunn, KM, Forrest, J, Burnley, I and McDonald, A, 'Constructing racism in Australia', *Australian Journal of Social Issues*, vol 39(4), 2004, pp 409-430.

5 Burke, A, *In Fear of Security: Australia's Invasion Anxiety*, Pluto Press, Sydney, 2001.

6 Marr, D and Wilkinson, M, *Dark Victory*, Allen & Unwin, Sydney, 2003.

7 Manne, Robert.

8 Dodson, L and Coorey P, '*Tampa* won us votes Libs told', *Sydney Morning Herald*, 21 June 2006.

9 Ang, I, 'From White Australia to Fortress Australia: the anxious nation in the new century', in L Jayasuriya, D Walker and J Gothard (eds), *Legacies of White Australia: Race, Culture and Nation*, University of Western Australia Press, Crawley, 2003, p 52.

10 Marr, D, 'The shape of the argument: Overland Public Lecture', *Overland*, Spring Issue, 2004.

11 *Sydney Morning Herald*, 4 September 2001; see also Betts, K, 'Boat people and public opinion in Australia', *People and Place*, vol 9(4), 2001, pp 34-48.

12 Hage, G, *Against Paranoid Nationalism: Searching for Hope in a Shrinking Society*, Pluto Press, Sydney, 2004, p 77.

13 Hon Paul Keating, 'A time for reflection: political values in the age of distraction', Third Annual Manning Clark Lecture, Canberra, 2002.

15

ANGELA ROMANO

The news media's representation of asylum seekers

There has been a surge since 1999 in the number of stories in the Australian news media about asylum seekers, even though the overall number of people accepted into Australia under our refugee and humanitarian scheme has not radically changed. This chapter describes three significant issues that led these asylum seekers to become far more visible in the public and media eye than those who had arrived in preceding years. The chapter then presents an analysis of the quality of the media coverage, and the reasons why stories about asylum seekers have often been unbalanced or limited in the way that they have approached the issues involved. The chapter finishes with an exploration of what sources of information shape journalists' coverage of asylum seeker and refugee issues today, and what information the public needs to be able to make decisions about those issues.

The first wave

Between 1999 and 2001, issues relating to asylum seekers and refugees ignited in media and public debates. The sudden explosion of concern resulted from at least three factors. First, changes in global politics meant that increasing numbers of 'boat people' were heading to Australia to lodge applications for refugee status after reaching our shores (see Table 15.1, over the page). This contrasted with preceding years, when the majority of asylum seekers applied for refugee status in their home or other outside countries. These asylum seekers attracted little controversy or attention because the Australian government itself organised for them to fly to Australia only after their applications had been processed and granted.

Table 15.1: Numbers of people arriving in Australia on unauthorised boats[1]

Year	Number
1997-1998	157
1998-1999	921
1999-2000	4175
2000-2001	4137
2001-2002	1277
2002-2003	0
2003-2004	82
2004-2005	0
2005-2006	43

Source: DIMIA 2005/2006

Secondly, the majority of the arriving 'boat people' were Islamic and originated from Afghanistan, Iraq and Iran. Mass media coverage, particularly in the tabloid media and on talkback radio, reflected the unease of many Australians who had limited experience of people from Islamic faiths or from Afghanistan and the Middle East.[2]

Thirdly, most 'boat people' had paid so-called 'people smugglers' to help them reach Australia. The media in Australia has historically dedicated far more attention to people smuggling via boat, even though until 1999, most cases of people smuggling occurred by air.[3] The then editor of the *Sydney Morning Herald*, Paul McGeogh, presented a picture of the smugglers 'shipping people out of the Middle East, putting them on very good boats for big fat cheques, [and] giving them GPS satellite navigation systems'. McGeogh argued that it was this 'criminally organised passage' that distinguished the 1999 'boat people' from those who had come previously. For him, that factor logically became 'the central focus of the media's reporting, rather than the conditions the new arrivals had left and why they were presenting themselves as refugees'.[4]

Missing the boat

The increased media coverage might have served a valuable community service by focusing attention on the social, economic and political causes and implications of the increasing boat arrivals. However, analyses of the news stories of the time found that journalists largely 'missed the boat' in terms of how that they framed and represented the issues.

Journalists employed a 'language of fear', which 'undermined the possibility of any public sympathy' for 'boat people'[5] or for calm, considered deliberation about how to respond to their arrivals. Many stories described the 'boat people' arrivals with words like 'national emergency', 'invasion', 'attack', 'assaults on our shores', 'contagious disease', 'floods' or 'tidal waves'[6]. The news media uncritically circulated both direct and implied suggestions from politicians that 'boat people' might endanger our national security and stability, and might even be terrorists.[7] *Sydney Morning Herald* reporter Margot Kingston also says the image of the 'boat people' was shaped by the 'overt criminal activity of the people smugglers', in contrast to the 'romantic images' of 'boat people' from previous decades, who braved the seas on 'little tin boats' and who were 'dying and starving'.[8]

Some journalists misunderstood or failed to check even very fundamental facts about the issues that they covered. Newspaper headlines and stories mixed up terms such as 'asylum seekers', 'refugees', 'boat people', 'illegals' and 'illegal immigrants' and used them interchangeably.[9] When journalists use words like 'illegal immigrants', 'asylum seekers' or 'refugees', they set up different premises about how the reader should understand who the 'boat people' are and what their arrival means. When journalists misuse these terms or jumble them together, they create a situation where readers are highly likely to misinterpret the news.

Such problems persist today. For example, one front-page headline in Queensland's *Courier-Mail* newspaper recently proclaimed: 'Boatload of Illegal Refugees Seized'.[10] The story described the 'boat people' as 'illegal immigrants', a term that refers to criminals who have broken immigration law (and readers might assume that, by implication, these 'illegals' might be prone to other criminal behaviours). The story also described the 'boat people' as 'asylum seekers', a term with very different connotations. If they were 'asylum seekers', then they came to Australia to take up a legally recognised right to apply for asylum, even if their mode of entry was unauthorised. To add to the confusion, the story also called the people 'illegal refugees'. If people are defined as 'refugees', that would normally indicate that the government had checked those people's backgrounds and had determined that they did indeed have a well-founded fear of persecution in their home countries. There is no such thing as an 'illegal refugee', but readers might think that the journalist was intimating that the 'boat people' were making fake claims about being refugees or facing persecution. *The Courier-Mail*'s mixture and misuse of these various terms in this story created a situation where readers had to rely on guesswork and assumptions to make sense of the story.

Many studies repeatedly indicate that politicians and government officials, particularly those from the federal Immigration Department, were highly and disproportionately influential in framing public discussion on asylum seekers and refugees from 1999 to 2001.[11] Further analysis of the coverage indicates that few journalists immediately recognised the degree to which the public and media debate was being skewed by vested political interests in the lead-up to the 2001 federal election.[12] Asylum seekers and refugees were themselves rarely quoted, despite the obvious gaps in public understanding that might arise if they remained silent or unheard.

Although most academic and industry analysts found that mainstream journalists generally created negative typecasts of asylum seekers, a small numbers of critics insist that the opposite problem existed. Conservative columnist Piers Akerman is a typical example. He argues that the media were replete with journalists who were lax and over-indulgent towards 'would-be illegal immigrants'. Akerman says the news coverage of the time was characterised by 'hysteria', 'screaming front pages' and leftist columnists who vilified all who disagreed with them and provided readers with only 'a thin, pathetic grasp on historical reality'.[13]

The challenges for journalists

Some of the faults discussed above arise because of challenges that journalists face due to the reticence of asylum seeker and refugees to speak with media people.[14] Asylum seekers and refugees may hold well-founded fears that speaking publicly or having their photographs published may jeopardise their residency within Australia. Such publicity may also threaten the safety of relatives and friends who may still be at risk in their countries of origin. Asylum seekers and refugees may believe that journalists are affiliated with the government, because this is often the case in their home countries. They may face distress in talking about past traumas and knowing that the indignities they have suffered will be exposed to others. Newly arrived asylum seekers and refugees often lack the fluency or confidence to speak in English in a public forum.

These factors mean that there is a very small pool of well-spoken, presentable and accessible asylum seekers and refugees who might be available for media interviews when an event or topic becomes a major news issue. Refugee support groups complain that when issues or crises do arise, journalists from different media organisations tend to barrage this small pool of 'media savvy' asylum seekers or refugees with requests for interviews and photographs – which the journalists often need almost immediately due to tight deadlines. This pressure on the limited numbers of asylum seeker and refugees who have the will and competence to talk with journalists may result in those people becoming increasingly selective about when and how they deal with the media.

A second set of challenges arose in 2002, when the federal government began routinely rejecting almost all journalists' requests to enter immigration detention centres to see conditions or speak with asylum seekers. The government's restrictions were considered so severe that Reporters Sans Frontières (Reporters Without Borders) downgraded Australia's rating on its international Press Freedom Index in 2003, from 12th to 50th most free country for reporters to work in. The government claims that the restrictions protect the asylum seekers' privacy and shield them from the risks discussed above. *The Australian*'s editor, Michael Stutchbury, dismisses this explanation as 'a sick joke' and calls the restrictions 'a disgrace to our political system'[15].

A third challenge is that many non-government organisations (NGOs) have been uncharacteristically reluctant to speak with the media. Some journalists and NGO representatives claim that

Amnesty International, church bodies and NGOs with relevant expertise to discuss asylum seeker and refugee issues failed to do so for two reasons.[16] Some NGO representatives feared losing federal government funding or public support if they spoke out against the prevailing public perspective; other NGO representatives found it too difficult to battle journalists' pre-set agendas and limited mindsets in relation to 'boat people'.[17] By contrast, some sources argue that NGOs have not been under-represented or reticent to speak. Akerman, for example, claims that journalists have freely given NGO spokespeople 'the opportunity to make various unchallenged and nonsensical statements'.[18]

An inclusive public debate?

Opinion polls, talkback radio programs and other measures of public opinion show that the Australian community felt high levels of tension about and hostility towards 'boat people', particularly between 1999 and 2001.[19] Relatively few Australians had direct contact with incoming 'boat people' and few were immediately affected by their arrivals, so it can be assumed that much of the information that fuelled this public antagonism was delivered via the mainstream mass media. This raises a question: who provides the information to the journalists, who in turn appear to have such a significant influence on public opinion?

In an attempt to determine who is providing journalists with their information, I studied all the news and feature stories, editorials and opinion pieces in the national newspaper, *The Australian*, and the Queensland newspaper, *The Courier-Mail*, from 1 September to 30 November 2006.[20] This content analysis involved checking the sources of news: that is, who the journalists quoted or named as providing information in stories that mentioned asylum seekers or refugees. In the period studied, *The Australian* published 35 stories about asylum seekers and refugees, and these stories quoted or mentioned 103 different sources. *The Courier-Mail* printed 16 stories with 36 sources in the three months concerned.

Several decades of research shows that sources with habitual, privileged access to the news media tend to heavily influence what issues and information the story will focus on – what is known as story 'framing'.[21] The three-month-long study of *The Australian* and *The Courier-Mail* suggests that journalists rely heavily on sources from government and the law – politicians, government officials, judges, magistrates and lawyers – to provide information and set the agenda for discussion. Their influence far outweighs that of asylum seekers and refugees, the community organisations which work with them, and the Australian community which forms the audience for the newspapers. (See Table 15.2, over the page).

Given the federal government's attempts to dominate discussions about asylum seekers and refugees, it is not surprising to find that politicians and government officials were the leading sources of quotes and other information in *The Australian* (49.5% of all sources) and *The Courier-Mail* (22%). Legal professionals and legal or court documents were the second-most commonly used sources of information. It is desirable that journalists scrutinise the words and behaviours of politicians, government officials, judges, magistrates and lawyers given that they create, enact, enforce or contest the rules and regulations relating to asylum seekers and refugees.

While it is critical for journalists to continue their monitoring of these political and legal sources of information, the debate is not complete unless all stakeholders in the issue are given an adequate voice. Although *The Australian* has dedicated considerable space to asylum seeker and refugee issues, indicating the importance that the newspaper's staff attach to those issues, the dominance of government sources and perspectives seems to have come at the expense of other important stakeholders.

Inclusive discussion means that ideally journalists should speak *with* asylum seekers and not simply *about* them. Despite this, asylum seekers and refugees comprised just 3% of all sources that *The Australian* used for quotes and information in its many stories. Although *The Courier-Mail* ran far fewer stories than *The Australian*, each of its stories used more asylum seekers and refugees as sources (14% of all sources). *The Courier-Mail*'s effort seems impressive given that journalists need to work hard to develop contacts with asylum seekers and refugees and win their trust.

When marginalised groups cannot represent themselves directly in the media, then they are often represented by NGOs, such as support groups, church bodies, charities, voluntary organisations and others that work closely with the marginalised individuals or sub-communities. These NGOs can also represent or explain the

Table 15.2: Types of sources quoted in *The Courier-Mail* and *The Australian*

Type of source	*The Courier-Mail* % (Number of sources)		*The Australian* % (Number of sources)	
Politicians and government officials	22	(8)	49.5	(51)
Legal professionals or legal/court documents	16.5	(6)	11.5	(12)
Asylum seekers and refugees	14	(5)	3	(3)
Community members	11	(4)	0	(0)
Refugee support organisations	8.5	(3)	7	(7)
Migrant/multicultural organisations	0	(0)	3	(3)
International government	8.5	(3)	6	(6)
Church/religious groups	5.5	(2)	0	(0)
Other migrants (non-refugee/asylum seekers)	0	(0)	1	(1)
United Nations/World Bank	5.5	(2)	1	(1)
University lecturers and other academics	5.5	(2)	9.5	(10)
Police/military	3	(1)	4	(4)
Business	0	(0)	5	(5)
Charities, voluntary sector and other NGOs	0	(0)	0	(0)
Total	**100**	**(36)**	**100**	**(103)**

Source: Author

basis of concerns or sentiments that the broader community has about the marginalised groups. *The Courier-Mail* again showed a slightly greater proportional representation of NGOs (14% of all sources) than *The Australian* (10%).

University lecturers and other academics can also be important sources when dealing with complex social issues because of the insights that they gain through their research and theorisation. *The Australian* used a greater percentage of academics (9.5% of all sources) than *The Courier-Mail* (5.5%), reflecting the intellectual approach that *The Australian* adopts for its comparatively well-educated audience.

In inclusive deliberation, input from ordinary community members is important. Otherwise, community members are relegated to the position of mere spectators of political processes, rather than active participants. The greatest disparity between the two newspapers studied was their use of regular citizens as sources. *The Courier-Mail* had a reasonably high percentage of ordinary citizens as sources (11%), while *The Australian* used none at all.

Public concerns

In an attempt to explore the kinds of information that ordinary community members felt that they needed from the news media, I conducted five focus groups with residents in Brisbane and nearby Ipswich in 2004.[22] Across the focus groups, the participants' comments consistently indicated that they lacked knowledge about very basic issues relating to asylum seekers and refugees. This lack of knowledge hindered their ability to understand what was happening, the different responses that Australia might take to 'boat people' and other asylum seekers, and the implications of those different responses. Surprisingly, the kinds of information that the focus group participants most needed could have easily been provided to them by journalists.

The first issue that arose from the focus groups was confusion about what a refugee is. Focus group participants were generally unaware that under Australian law, refugee status is only granted to people who are deemed unable to return to their homeland due to a fear of being persecuted because of their race, religion, nationality, political opinion or membership of a social group. The participants felt that *any* person escaping problems in his/her homeland might be legally eligible for refugee status. Although the definition of a refugee can be explained in a few judiciously chosen words, journalists almost never include such explanations in their stories. Comments from the focus group participants suggested that their fear of Australia being 'overrun' by 'boat people' may have arisen in part from misunderstandings about what a refugee is and thus who might be accepted into Australia under our refugee program.

Such problems may persist because journalists themselves still regularly fail to understand that there is a difference between legally recognised *refugees* and other kinds of people who *seek refuge* from problems. For example, in the weeks following the 2004 Boxing Day earthquake and tsunami and Hurricane Katrina in the United States in 2005, Australian newspapers published hundreds of stories that incorrectly used the word *refugees* to describe people who had left their homes to *seek refuge* from these natural disasters.[23] Such people are more accurately called *evacuees.*

Focus groups participants also clearly differentiated between *boat people* and *refugees* – a trend which is also borne out in opinion polls.[24] One focus group participant rationalised the paradox of his acceptance of East Timorese refugees in 1999, but his rejection of 'boat people' in 2000 and 2001, by asking: 'How can you take *genuine refugees* and compare them to *boat people*?' Fr Frank Brennan explains why Australians differentiate between 'boat people' and refugees:

> Many Australians see no need for desperate people to force their way through the back door without an invitation when there is a front door through which the per-capita quota of refugees and humanitarian cases entering each year is greater than in most other countries.[25]

Focus group participants often expressed pride about times when Australia had aided refugees in need. At the same time, they also expressed a view that Australians should 'look after their own first' and were sceptical about the authenticity of 'boat people's' claims to being refugees. Because of this, they were concerned about spending taxpayers' money looking after 'boat people' when they first arrive in Australia, given that they might not have their claims to being a refugee recognised as 'genuine'. The federal government was thus shrewd in 1999 to 2001 when it used the media to promote the concept that 'boat people' were 'queuejumpers'. The 'queuejumper' terminology portrayed 'boat people' as 'illegals' who forced themselves into the country. The expression also implied that they took the places of those more deserving asylum seekers who were patiently following the rules by waiting overseas while their applications for refugee status were considered. By contending that the 'boat people' might not be those who were most worthy of Australia's support, the federal government was able to reduce community attention to the value of 'helping those in need' in favour of 'looking after Australia first'.

Journalists could easily help the community to understand the issues and reconcile the competing values of 'helping those in need' while also 'protecting one's own' by regularly providing explanations about why asylum seekers would choose passage by boat over other means. Furthermore, journalists writing stories about asylum seekers and refugees should regularly include a brief explanation about why many do not stay in the countries that they may transit on their way to Australia. As Fr Brennan notes, 'most refugees who arrive in Australia are presumed to have had the option of seeking protection at a place closer to their home country' because of Australia's geographic isolation.[26]

Focus group participants expressed a range of other concerns and queries about asylum seekers and refugees, which deserve ongoing media attention if citizens are to reach informed decisions about how to understand and respond to asylum seeker and refugee arrivals. These include:

1. Whether increasing numbers of Islamic and Middle Eastern/Afghanistani refugees would impact on Australia's culture and way of life;
2. Why detention centres are often portrayed as problematic environments rather than a 'step up' compared to the dangerous environments that a 'genuine' refugee might come from;
3. Whether the arrival of 'boat people' and refugees in general poses a security risk to Australia;

4. Whether refugees should be obliged to go to the 'country', to support rural industries and regional industries, rather than create further pressures in major urban centres;
5. Whether refugees threatened Australian jobs and were a net economic loss or gain to Australia; and
6. What costs are involved in processing 'boat people's' claims to asylum.

Although journalists have addressed these issues in occasional stories, ordinary citizens do not usually follow all of the news about a given issue in a strict and systematic way. Even if they read, watch or hear the news every day, they might miss or forget pertinent facts that are essential for a complete and balanced understanding of the snippets of news that they do encounter. Journalists could have addressed these information gaps very easily by regularly providing the background details discussed above.

Conclusions

Australian journalists have struggled with a variety of challenges in covering asylum seeker and refugee issues since 1999. The news media's discussion agenda has been dominated by politicians. Asylum seekers and refugees have had far less input than is desirable, given their central role in the issues. The study of *The Australian* and *The Courier-Mail* in 2006 suggests that a heavy imbalance still exists.

The study also indicates that there is much variation between Australian newspapers as to the priority that they placed on using asylum seeker-refugee sources and that an individual newspaper's performance can vary with time. *The Courier-Mail* printed fewer stories about asylum seeker-refugee issues than *The Australian*, which meant that the journalists arguably had fewer opportunities to develop contacts with asylum seekers and refugees. However, the Queensland newspaper provided a greater percentage of asylum seeker and refugee sources in the stories that it did print. *The Courier-Mail*'s relative success in 2006 in building and using a network of contacts among asylum seekers and refugees contrasts to the situation that existed at the turn of the century. In 2000, Sharon Pickering found that the newspaper had 'not been interested in listening to the voices of asylum seekers, nor of home country conditions or of conditions of flight'.[27]

The total absence of ordinary community sources in the stories published by *The Australian* suggests that the newspaper needs to strengthen its community connections in relation to its reporting on asylum seeker and refugee issues. Given *The Australian* is known for being a quality newspaper with a commitment to research, in-depth reporting and developing community contacts, the research findings suggest that such problems with community connections would exist across the broader media industry. The combined silence in *The Australian* of both civil society groups and citizens has significant implications for both the framing and content of stories. An absence of input from asylum seekers, refugees and the mainstream community reduces the potential for journalists to create stories that resonate with community concerns and help citizens to fully understand and respond to changing conditions.

Given the reliance of the mainstream public on the news media for information about asylum seekers and refugees, journalists play an important mediation role in public debates and deliberations. Journalists must negotiate between the interests of the sources who provide the information for news stories and the audiences who use that information to understand the problems and issues and how they might be addressed. To fulfil this mediation role, journalists must continue to play their traditional 'watchdog' role of checking the behaviour of governments, public servants and the legal institutions. However, journalists also need to step beyond this role. They must work to access all stakeholders, even marginalised ones. Journalists also need to develop a nuanced understanding about what the public needs to know about the issues, which issues Australians remain unclear about, and what values community members use when they judge how to respond to those issues.

Notes

1 Table 15.1 has been created using figures from 'Unauthorised Arrivals by Air and Sea', Department of Immigration and Multicultural and Indigenous Affairs, Canberra, 2006, and *Managing the Border: Immigration Compliance*, 2004-2005 edition, Department of Immigration and Multicultural and Indigenous Affairs, Canberra, 2005.

2 Poynting, S and Noble, G, '"Dog-whistle" journalism and Muslim Australians since 2001', *Media International Australia*, (109), 2003, pp 41-49.

3 DIAC, 'Managing Australia's borders: unauthorised arrivals', Department of Immigration and Citizenship, Canberra, 2007, <www.immi.gov.au/managing-australias-borders/border-security/unauthorised.htm>.

4 Stani, N, 'How the media treats ethnic diversity', *The Media Report*, ABC Radio National, 27 January 2000, <www.abc.net.au/rn/talks/8.30/mediarpt/stories/s97348.htm>.

5 Ibid.

6 See, for example, Lygo, I, *News Overboard: the Tabloid Media, Race Politics and Islam*, Southerly Change Publications, Anglesea, 2004; Mares, P, *Borderline: Australia's Response to Refugees and Asylum Seekers in the Wake of the Tampa*, UNSW Press, Sydney, 2002; Pickering, S, 'News discourses and asylum seekers in Australia', *Journal of Refugee Studies*, vol 14(2), 2001, pp 169-186; Stani, above, n 4.

7 Betts, K, 'Immigration and public opinion: understanding the shift', *People and Place*, vol 10(4), 2002, pp 24-37; Mares, above, n 6; Price, M, 'Talkback callers turn off sympathy: stand-off on the high seas', *The Australian*, 29 August 2001, p 2.

8 Stani, above, n 4.

9 Mares, above, n 6.

10 Porteus, C, 'Boatload of Illegal Refugees Seized', *The Courier-Mail*, 23 February 2007, p 1.

11 Klocher, N and Dunn, KM, 'Who's driving the asylum debate? Newspaper and government representations of asylum seekers', *Media International Australia*, no 109, 2003, pp 71-92; Mares, above, n 6; Romano, A, 'Journalism's role in mediating public conversation on asylum seekers and refugees in Australia', *Australian Journalism Review*, vol 26(2), 2004, pp 43-62; Saxton, A, '"I Certainly Don't Want People Like that Here". The Discursive Construction of "Asylum Seekers"', *Media International Australia*, (109), 2003, pp 109-120; Slattery, K, 'Drowning not waving: the "children overboard" event and Australia's fear of the "other"', *Media International Australia*, (109), 2003, pp 93-108; Stani, above, n 4; Taylor, S, 'The importance of human rights talk in asylum seeker advocacy', *UNSW Law Journal*, vol 24(1), 2001, pp 191-199; Ward, I, 'The *Tampa* affair, wedge politics and a lesson for political journalism', *Australian Journalism Review*, vol 24(1), 2004, pp 21-40.

12 Klocher and Dunn, above, n 11; Mares, above, n 6; Saxton, above, n 11; Slattery, above, n 11.

13 Akerman, P, 'Immigration policy, sovereignty and the media', Paper presented to the *14th Conference of the Samuel Griffith Society*, Menzies Hotel, Sydney, 14-16 June 2002, <www.samuelgriffith.org.au/papers/html/volume14/v14chap7.html>.

14 The information in this paragraph arises from my own experiences as a journalist, as well as from interviews conducted with 24 stakeholders with an interest in asylum seeker and refugee issues. These stakeholders included refugee support workers, lawyers active in refugee issues, academics, members of NGOs representing multicultural interests, staff from museums that regularly curate exhibits about immigration, a journalist with an alternative media organisation, and a senior public servant.

15 Herman, JR, 'Access to refugees', *Press Council News*, vol 14(1), 2002, pp 1-2.

16 Romano, above, n 11; Stani, N, above, n 4.

17 Ibid.

18 Akerman, above, n 13.

19 Betts, above, n 7, p 30; Price, above, n 7; Rehame Australia, 'Callers go overboard', *The Australian,* 9 December 1999, p M5.

20 I wish to thank Candeeda Hill-James for her hard work and diligence as a research assistant for this content analysis. Other findings will be published at a later stage.

21 Ericson, RV, Baranek, PM and Chan, JBL, *Negotiating Control: a Study of News Sources*, Open University Press, Milton Keynes, 1989; Hall, S, Crichter, C, Jefferson, T, Clark, J and Roberts, B, *Policing the Crisis: Mugging, the State and Law and Order*, Macmillan, Houndmills, 1978; McNair, B, *The Sociology of Journalism*, Arnold, London, 1998.

22 Three focus groups were conducted in Brisbane, one in the city of Ipswich and one in the nearby outer-Brisbane suburb of Forest Lake. The focus groups included both male and female participants, aged from 15 to 80. The participants' education levels ranged from junior high school to completion of multiple undergraduate degrees, and their occupations included manual trades, service industries, white-collar occupations and the unemployed. The focus groups facilitated a discussion about what the participants knew about asylum seekers and refugees, the key issues that they felt were the most important, and how well the media served their information needs.

23 This figure was obtained with the aid of the Nexis database, which archives stories from the 35 Australian newspapers.

24 Betts, above, n 7, page 30.

25 Brennan, F, *Tampering with Asylum, a Universal Humanitarian Problem*, rev edition, University of Queensland Press, St Lucia, 2007.

26 Ibid, p 11.

27 Pickering, S, 'The hard press of asylum', *Forced Migration Review*, (8), 2000, pp 32-33.

16

MICHAEL CLYNE

Words excusing exclusion of asylum seekers[1]

The language of exclusion has made a comeback in mainstream Australia in recent years. The 'war against terror' has renewed the historical tension in Australia between the forces of inclusion, openness and tolerance of diversity and those of exclusion and xenophobia. Being such an ill-defined notion, the 'war against terror' allows the hearer/reader to imagine an enemy among the unknown and the 'other'. This includes not only prejudice against all Muslims, especially easily identifiable Muslim women, but also against Asians and Africans. An example was the unashamedly racist discourse of academic Andrew Fraser claiming the racial inferiority of Sudanese and the racial undesirability of people of Chinese background in his letter[2] to the *Parramatta Sun*. Another is the overtly racist outburst against Sudanese refugees by Councillor Peter Brown of the City of Greater Dandenong, following a brawl, arguing that by allowing Sudanese to settle in Australia, the government is merely importing the ethnic problems of Africa.[3] Two important sources of exclusionary language have been Pauline Hanson's overt racist discourse and the public debate on asylum seekers. This paper focuses on the latter, drawing on statements of Australian politicians and, where appropriate, making cursory comparisons with the contemporary European discourse on refugees. I concentrate on the choice of vocabulary in the representation of asylum seekers in some public discourse in 2001 and put the exclusionary discourse in historical context.

Two incidents mark the occasion for the discourse – the *Tampa* affair (August 2001) and the 'Children overboard' affair (October 2001). Both incidents provided the Howard government with an opportunity to demonstrate its strong 'leadership' in the face of what it projected as a national threat.

Synonyms for 'refugee'

In the initial media reports, the asylum seekers in the leaky boats were excluded through dehumanisation – being described as 'boatloads' and 'cargo'. When more attention was given to them, they began to be demonised. In this discussion on the public discourse concerning asylum seekers, I will focus on the field of words around 'refugee' and the items 'queuejumper' and 'border protection'.

A *refugee* is a person who flees (religious or political) persecution. In Australia this word tends to have positive connotations, especially once the people are settled in Australia. Refugees are basically nice people who are worthy of compassion and will usually make a positive contribution to the Australian nation. Most Australians can give examples of such people from their own circle of friends or among well-known personalities. So if the government wanted people to approve of their treatment of asylum seekers, they would have to find another label, one that does not have positive connotations. The contrast is very blatantly expressed in the Prime Minister's statement on 7 October 2001 during the 'children overboard' affair:

> Genuine refugees don't do that.[4]

He was in effect passing judgment on the asylum seekers before their case had been heard by any refugee tribunal on grounds other than whether they were fleeing from persecution. But more importantly, he was 'leading' public opinion with the follow-up words:

> I don't want people like that in Australia.

This exclusionary statement echoes ones from Pauline Hanson and David Etheridge of One Nation on 'unassimilated' Asian migrants made repeatedly several years earlier: 'We don't want people like that in Australia'. They professed to be speaking on behalf of 'ordinary Australians' whereas the Prime Minister gave 'leadership' in the opinions of ordinary Australians.

The projection of these harmless people constituting a threat to the nation's moral standards was continued by Foreign Minister Alexander Downer the same day:

> Any civilized person wouldn't dream of treating their own children that way.[5]

There are parallels here with discourse on refugees in Europe – the differentiation between real and bogus refugees has been reported in parliamentary debates in Austria, Britain and the Netherlands.[6] There is also a European precedent, in Austria, Britain and France, of conservative governments taking over the discourse on refugees and migrants of right-wing fringe groups.[7]

The *Herald Sun* of 8 October 2001, conducted a poll on the pre-emptive question:

> Should boat-people who threw their children overboard be accepted into Australia *as refugees*?[8]

Unsurprisingly 95.67% of those responding voted no.

If these people were not refugees, what were they? Parliamentarians from both major parties taking part in the debate on 29 August had no difficulty finding the right vocabulary: 'illegals', 'illegal refugees', 'illegal immigrants', and 'illegal arrivals'.[9] What these terms do is to declare the unauthorised arrivals as 'non-people' which enables them and their children to be treated accordingly – detained without trial, under sub-human conditions.

The Minister for Citizenship and Multicultural Affairs, Gary Hardgrave, preferred to designate them as 'occasional tourists':

> The people on board MV *Tampa* are not refugees, they are occasional tourists, who have contracted criminal elements or crime gangs who are often involved in the transportation of drugs to our shores … It is offensive to those who are genuine refugees who have come to this country and experienced the generosity that this nation has without a doubt offered them.[10]

It was not until 18 June 2004 that the Australian Press Council finally published a guideline[11] cautioning the media against 'such unqualified terms' as illegals.

Bullies and criminals

Not only was the behaviour of the asylum seekers deemed by Alexander Downer to be contrary to the national family values.

They were sometimes depicted as bullies and criminals, for instance, by Immigration Minister Philip Ruddock:

> We will not let people force their way into this country by undesirable behaviour.[12]

Because they were brought to Australia by people-smugglers, asylum seekers were linked to criminality. This came out in Opposition Leader Kim Beazley's ambiguous statement, defending his party's failure to adopt a different policy from that of the government:

> It is *not unhumanitarian* to try to deter criminals.[13]

The Prime Minister linked 'boat people' with 'drug trafficking' and other activities, for instance in the election campaign:

> Our nation must be protected from the activities of people smugglers, drug traffickers and the introduction of diseases and dangerous goods.[14]

Asylum seekers were the result of the activities of people smugglers in the same way as dangerous goods resulted from the activities of drug traffickers.

'Queuejumpers'

Another negative label for the asylum seekers was 'queuejumpers', or as government member Kay Elson put it in Parliament on 29 August 2001:

> [Q]ueue jumpers over the many *genuine refugees*.[15]

This widely employed term was intended to demonstrate how distant the 'boat people' are from the traditional Australian values propagated by John Howard. It directed public antagonism towards the asylum seekers in three ways:

(i) It appealed to the mythical Australian national value of fairness (including 'first come, first served').

(ii) It appealed to migrants and earlier refugees from non-English-speaking countries who have been trying to get their relatives to Australia under the family reunion scheme or their friends in from refugee camps under the humanitarian scheme.

(iii) It was based on the British dominance of the straight line as a basis of orderliness in society as well as in academic discourse, sport, and the conduct of meetings.[16]

There were, however, two fallacies. First, there were no Australian embassies in Afghanistan, Iran, Iraq or the Palestinian Territories in front of which the asylum seekers could queue up. Secondly, the humanitarian category is quite distinct from the family reunion category and in fact, the former was not filled in 2001. The government was able to juggle a position against the asylum seekers which was not blatantly opposed to cultural diversity and therefore not opposed by migrants.

Border protection

It will be remembered that the terrorist attacks on the United States occurred between the arrival of the *Tampa* and the 2001 federal election. The term 'border protection', which dominated the 2001 election campaign, cannot be freed from its association with terrorism even though most of the asylum seekers were claiming to be fleeing from regimes harbouring terrorists. The 2001 election saw strong competition between the major parties as to who could protect Australia's borders best. The first of the following examples actually implies a link between terrorism and asylum seekers:

> The tragic events of 11 September *and* the challenges to the integrity of our borders will require more resources – and stronger decisions.[17]
>
> We will protect our borders and our nation's sovereignty.[18]
>
> Only Labor is committed to … provid[ing] the best protection of our national borders.[19]

Pauline Hanson's pronouncement '*We* decide who comes to Australia' now became a favourite saying of the Prime Minister, with the extension 'and the circumstances under which they come'. It featured in the Liberal Party's newspaper advertisements for the 2001 election.

The above analysis indicates that politicians, especially of the government, have skillfully employed language to present asylum seekers as outside the law and, unlike 'nice refugees', as violent and criminal, with links to terrorism and drug trafficking, as unfair to others, and as a threat to the Australian nation. The encouragement of fear and hatred is based on two 'moral principles': The first is the schoolmaster principle – if they don't behave themselves, they have to be punished – leave the room or stand in the corner. The second is the schoolchild principle – 'It ain't fair; they pushed in'. Here the supposed Australian cultural value of fairness is turned on its head with the claim that it is the asylum seekers who are being unfair.

At the same time, asylum seekers are depicted as not being in the national interest. In 2001, such discourse centred around 'border protection' and moral values. But the national interest as a criterion of rejection of asylum seekers came to the fore in a different way in April 2006, with regard to relations with a neighbouring country. The granting of Temporary Protection Visas to 42 West Papuan separatists was condemned by the Indonesian government. Consequently the Australian government agreed to give Indonesia the opportunity to 'respond, in future claims of persecution before decisions on asylum are made'.[20] This was coupled with a plan to process asylum seekers only outside Australia, thus denying them humane conditions. These plans were subsequently defeated in the Senate, with some government senators crossing the floor. However, the government had made the point that the human rights of asylum seekers were subordinate to good relations with a neighbouring country if the two were in conflict.

Is this racist discourse?

The question can be posed – are the above instances from the discourse on asylum seekers racist? Broadly we can differentiate between overt and covert racist discourse. The former 'is intended for a homogeneous, sympathetic audience and makes no attempt to conceal its message or the ideology that lies behind it'.[21] An us/them dichotomy creates two worlds by the use of different vocabulary for the in-group and the out-group, members of which are seen only in terms of their ethnicity, often associated with physical attributes. Covert racist discourse is indistinguishable linguistically from any other discourse as it makes the pretence of being reasoned, objective, and reasonable and is 'addressed to heterogeneous groups who are not necessarily supporters of the point of view'.[22] Clearly the quotations which we have discussed are not of the first category. However, language is skillfully employed to represent a group of people in the worst possible light and persuade the hearer (reader) that they need the protection of the speaker (writer) to face the threat of the group. But the group is not defined in terms of ethnic group affiliation or physical attributes. The fact that the asylum seekers are from countries such as Iraq, Iran, Afghanistan, the Palestinian Territories, and Sri Lanka and therefore not of European origin may be a factor in the positions expressed but it is not mentioned explicitly. The asylum seekers are derided because of alleged personal traits which distinguish them from 'genuine refugees'. Thus it is their behaviour which is contrasted with the desirable behaviour of Australians. It is not possible to conclude whether there is a cultural component.

Relation to multiculturalism and the Australian values debate

I believe that the discourse on asylum seekers is an important landmark in the xenophobic debate on Australian values which has been propagated particularly strongly by the federal government in 2005-2006. Part of the debate has been explicitly directed towards Muslims. This is done by generalising the public statements of a small number of extremist imams to the entire Islamic community in Australia. But the attitudes have been extended to undermine the entire policy of multiculturalism. One example of this has been Treasurer Peter Costello's outburst against what he describes as 'mushy multiculturalism' and his suggestion that those who do not share 'Australian values' should be stripped of citizenship and leave the country.[23] Another was the decision to introduce a controversial test, encompassing 'Australian values' and English language, for all candidates for Australian citizenship. A third has been the attempts of the Prime Minister and the Parliamentary Secretary for Citizenship and Multicultural Affairs, Andrew Robb, to replace the term 'multiculturalism',[24] culminating in its being dropped from the name of the Immigration Department in the ministerial reshuffle of January 2007. A much discussed substitute is 'integration', which, while not incompatible with multiculturalism, is currently employed in Europe and Australia as a synonym for assimilation. Another alternative, favoured by Robb, is 'shared values', which expresses only part of the reality of the Australian nation, together with tolerance of and understanding of different values. In other words, it is the policy, not the term that they wish to replace. Interestingly, in the shadow ministry established by the new Opposition Leader, Kevin Rudd in December 2006, Tony Burke became shadow minister for immigration, citizenship, and *integration*.[25] Multicultural affairs reappeared in a subordinate role, along with urban development and consumer affairs, removing it from issues of Australian identity. It appears that once again the Federal Labor Party is simply reacting to the discourse created by the government. In an address to the Fabian Society of Victoria on 13 December, Tony Burke did emphasise the complementarity of integration and multiculturalism.

Historical tradition?

As I have already mentioned, Prime Minister Howard has consistently stressed his strong attachment to 'traditional Australian values'. These he contrasts with 'political correctness':

> Our national character springs not from particular ideologies but from mainstream egalitarian values … There is a school of 'history' which ignores or trivialises all those parts of the past which can't be conscripted into glorifying a politically correct version of the present.[26]

Is the recent treatment of asylum seekers consistent with our 'traditional values'? Keeping some people out has been part of Australia's discourse for most of its history as a federated State. We only have to think of the 'White Australia' policy and the dictation test. Recurrent themes in the British colonial history of Australia were the threat of hordes of unwanted people invading Australia from the north, also known as the 'yellow peril'. (These were the days before Islamophobia!).

The recent past has been characterised by the use of inclusive language. This is symbolised in the current wording of the national anthem *Advance Australia Fair*:

For *those who've come* across the seas
We've boundless plains to share.

However, among the issues about the time of Federation, which was celebrated with the singing of *Advance Australia Fair*, were a boatload of Chinese from Hong Kong wanting to land on Australian shores, the annexation of New Guinea by Germany, the annexation of New Caledonia by France, and Russian ships seen in the region. The same passage in Peter Dodd McCormick/Amicus' original 'politically incorrect' and jingoistic version of *Advance Australia Fair* ran:

For *loyal sons* across the seas
We've boundless plains to share.

'Loyal sons' are defined in another verse as those 'from England, Scotia, Erin's isle'. ('Daughters' were apparently appendages of 'loyal sons'.)

Early paranoia about border protection is abundantly evident in a lesser known verse:

Should foreign foe e'er sight our coast
Or dare a foot to land,
We'll rouse to arms like siers of yore
To guard our native strand;
Britannia then shall surely know,
Beyond wide oceans roll
Her sons in fair Australia's land
Still keep a British soul,
In joyful strains then let us sing
Advance Australia Fair.

The contrast between the different versions underlines the historical tension between open cosmopolitan and narrow isolationist strands in our history. It also demonstrates the manipulation of language and choice of vocabulary to emphasise and generate fear. In these days of wedge politics, we need to be aware and make the community more aware of the abuse and power of language.

Notes

1 This is based on a talk: 'Words Excusing Exclusion' given at the conference on Seeking Asylum, Monash University, November 2005.

2 26 July 2005.

3 *The Age*, 9 January 2007.

4 *Herald Sun*, 8 October 2001.

5 *The Age*, 8 October 2001.

6 Jones, L, 'Immigration and parliamentary discourse in Great Britain: an analysis of the debates related to the 1996 Asylum and Immigration Act', in R Wodak and T van Dijk (eds) *Racism at the Top: Parliamentary Discourses on Ethnic Issues in Six European States*, Klagenfurt, Drava, 2002, pp 79-106; Sedlak, M, 'You really do make an unrespectable foreigner policy: discourse on ethnic issues in the Austrian Parliament', in Wodak and van Dijk, ibid, pp 107-168; Van der Valk, I, 'Parliamentary discourse on illegal immigrants, asylum and integration: the case of Holland', in Wodak and van Dijk, ibid, pp 261-282.

7 Vetter, E, '*Rassismus – ein internationaler Vergleich*', *Wiener Linguistische Gazette* vol 51/52, 1994, pp 40-63.

8 *Herald Sun*, 8 October 2001, emphasis added by author.

9 Hansard, 29 August 2001, Senate and House of Representatives.

10 Hansard, 30 August 2001, House of Representatives, p 30703.

11 Australian Press Council, Guideline 262: 'Status of unauthorised arrivals', June 2004, <www.presscouncil.org.au/pcsite/activities/guides/guide262.html>.

12 ABC radio program, 'AM', 8 October 2001.

13 *The Age*, 8 October 2001.

14 Prime Minister's Action Plan for the Future – Election campaign, November 2001.

15 Hansard, 29 August 2001, House of Representatives, p 30586.

16 Cf Clyne, M, 'Cultural differences in the organization of academic discourse', *Journal of Pragmatics*, vol 11, 1987, pp 211-247.

17 PM's letter to voters, November 2001.

18 Ros Clowes, Liberal candidate for Chisholm, November 2001.

19 Anna Burke, sitting Labor member for Chisholm, November 2001.

20 *The Age*, 8 April 2006.

21 Clyne, M, 'Establishing linguistic markers of racist discourse', in C Schäffner and A Wenden (eds), *Language and Peace*, Dartmouth, Aldershot, 1995, pp 111-119; Clyne, M, 'The use of exclusionary language to manipulate opinion – John Howard, asylum seekers and the re-emergence of political incorrectness in Australia', *Journal of Language and Politics*, Vol 4, 2004, pp 173-196.

22 Clyne, 'Establishing linguistic markers', ibid.

23 *The Age*, 24 February 2006.

24 *The Age*, eg, 13 December 2006; 5 January 2007.

25 The State Labor governments still have ministries for multicultural affairs, often headed by the Premier, emphasis added by author.

26 John Howard, cited in Markus, A, 'John Howard and the naturalization of bigotry', in G Gray and C Winter (eds), *The Resurgence of Racism,* Melbourne, Monash University Department of History (Monash Publications in History), 1995, pp 79-86.

17

NICK HASLAM • ANNE PEDERSEN

Attitudes towards asylum seekers: the psychology of exclusion

There can be little doubt that the attitudes of the Australian public towards asylum seekers have been unsympathetic and often hostile in the past decade. Surveys conducted around the time of the *Tampa* incident and since have shown that clear majorities supported the federal government's policies of border protection and mandatory detention.[1] People seeking asylum in Australia have encountered a relentless and punitive policy regime, and most citizens have agreed with it.

For those who disagree, there have been several vocal responses. One is to indict the federal government for its attempts to manipulate public opinion with fear-mongering rhetoric. Another is to indict the public for its deeply-rooted racism or xenophobia. Although these responses contain germs of truth, and satisfy our moral instincts to apportion blame, they are unsatisfactory on their own. The rhetoric of 'illegals', 'queuejumpers' and 'children overboard' did not simply implant fear and loathing in a credulous public, nor did it simply mirror the public's natural hostility. The truth is more complicated: rhetoric appeals to and inflames people's existing apprehensions, and the public mood influences the manner in which it is expressed. Most people do not accept media images of asylum seekers uncritically, but actively make their own sense of them. To understand attitudes to asylum seekers we need to understand the psychology of public opinion.

Any attempt to understand prejudice towards asylum seekers faces a significant challenge. The phenomenon has many dimensions, and can be examined from many angles. Most asylum seekers are ethnically different from Australia's white majority, so antipathy towards them might be expected to have an ethnic component.

They are often presumed to be Muslim, making anti-Islamic sentiment another possible aspect of public opinion. Attitudes towards asylum seekers may reflect suspicions about foreigners that attach to immigrant groups in general rather than refugee claimants in particular. These attitudes may have an element of moral condemnation as well, if asylum seekers are judged to have acted illegally or deceitfully, and by so doing offended people's values. In short, attitudes towards asylum seekers are many-layered and multiply determined, and they resist any simple analysis.

Our aim in this chapter is to disentangle the factors that contribute to unfavourable attitudes towards asylum seekers. Throughout our chapter we rely on a body of psychological research, most of it conducted in Australia, which has shed light on the forms of thought and feeling on which this kind of prejudice rests. In particular, the work that we review clarifies the ways in which people who are antagonistic towards asylum seekers differ from those who are not. We organise these pivotal differences under several headings, most of them focusing on the beliefs associated with greater prejudice and the different emotional colorations that it may assume. We conclude with a discussion of the dehumanisation of asylum seekers, and with some reasons for hope for the future.

Social background

Before commencing our examination of the psychology of attitudes to asylum seekers, it is important to recognise that these attitudes are associated with people's social positions. Several studies have shown that men tend to have less sympathetic attitudes than women,[2] as do people with lower levels of formal education.[3] There is evidence that Australians who are suffering financial hardship and those living in rural and outer-metropolitan regions are more antagonistic to immigrants and, most likely, to asylum seekers in particular.[4] However, to understand how these social positions are linked to attitudes, we must turn to the beliefs and perceptions that accompany them.

Beliefs

A variety of beliefs and ideologies appear to underlie unsympathetic attitudes towards asylum seekers. Unsurprisingly, people with more conservative, right wing or authoritarian political beliefs tend to have more negative attitudes.[5] One ideological stance that has special relevance is 'social dominance orientation', the tendency to endorse hierarchical rather than equal relations between social groups, and to see social life as a competitive struggle. Social dominance has been linked to prejudice against a variety of low power groups, and is strongly associated with antagonism to asylum seekers and refugees in Australia and Canada.[6] More specific beliefs about asylum seekers also play a role in public attitudes. To a considerable degree, antagonism towards asylum seekers rests on acceptance of several inaccurate beliefs or myths. Anne Pedersen's research[7] has repeatedly shown that attitudes are least favourable among people who believe that asylum seekers are 'queuejumpers', that they are 'illegal', that they are not genuine refugees, that they are financially well off, and that they receive generous financial handouts from the government. All of these beliefs are demonstrably false on empirical or legal grounds, and many of them can be traced to the public statements of politicians. Although the origin of some of these myths in political rhetoric implies that prejudice has been directly promoted by political leaders, they do not bear all of the responsibility. It is entirely possible that people who are more inclined to prejudice are more accepting of claims that cast asylum seekers in a negative light, and more receptive to the sources of these claims.

Nationalism

Another set of beliefs that deserve particular attention are those that concern national attachment. Many people feel strong bonds of identification with their country, and hold firm beliefs about the nature of national identity. These bonds and beliefs play a variety of roles in attitudes towards asylum seekers. Several studies have shown that people who identify more strongly with Australia, or see their Australian identity as highly important, tend to hold less favourable attitudes towards asylum seekers, and similar findings have been obtained in the Netherlands.[8] Interestingly, though, this link between nationalist beliefs and antagonistic attitudes may depend on the specific quality of people's ties to their nation. National pride – esteeming Australia's political influence in the world and our sporting and other achievements – is not associated with hostility to immigrants, for example. Much more telling in this regard are beliefs about what qualifies someone as 'truly Australian', specifically 'nativist' beliefs that the essence of 'Australianness' is rooted in blood and soil. People who believe that true Australianness is a matter of being born here, having ancestors here, and spending most of one's life here, are much more hostile to immigration and immigrants.[9] More sympathetic attitudes are associated with a cosmopolitan sensibility, in which Australianness is defined in more inclusive and less ethnic terms.

Katherine Betts[10] has argued that unsympathetic views of asylum seekers are grounded in a benign desire for a 'common sense of peoplehood' among Australians. Such a desire is certainly understandable, but a 'sense of peoplehood' can take different forms, with different implications for attitudes to outsiders. People who have a stronger sense of national identity tend to be more hostile to asylum seekers, especially if that identity is seen in ethnic terms, but an identity anchored in civic pride is entirely compatible with a more welcoming attitude.

Norms

Beliefs about what is true – about political reality, asylum seekers or national identity – are linked in interesting ways to attitudes towards refugee claimants, but beliefs about what others believe also have important implications. It has recently been shown that people over-estimate the extent to which others share their attitudes towards asylum seekers, and that people who hold more hostile attitudes perceive this 'false consensus' to a greater extent. For example, in one study the 3% of survey respondents who held the most negative attitudes believed that 83% of Australians felt similarly.[11] This finding may partly reflect the way in which unsympathetic views towards asylum seekers have often received louder and wider exposure in the news media and talkback radio.

The perception of false consensus is not simply an amusing cognitive distortion. When people believe that their views are prevalent, they are apt to feel that these views are socially validated. If people with unfavourable attitudes towards asylum seekers are especially likely to perceive a consensus of the hostile, they are also more likely to act on these views. In one recent study,[12] people's belief that there was widespread support for reducing the number of asylum seekers was associated with their level of unsympathetic attitudes towards asylum seekers and their willingness to engage in behaviour against them (eg, speaking out, signing a petition or attending a rally). Social norms, even if they are inaccurately perceived rather than actual, are extremely powerful.

Fear and threat

One basis for unfavourable attitudes towards asylum seekers is the belief that they represent a threat of some kind. This belief is associated with fear and anxiety, emotions that promote vigilance, apprehension and a desire to avoid and repel the threat. There is ample evidence that asylum seekers have often been seen as threatening. The Middle Eastern and Islamic background of many asylum seekers has led some people to equate them with terrorists, one of the most common false beliefs mentioned spontaneously by respondents in one study,[13] or to suppose that terrorists may be entering the country hidden among other 'boat people'. Attitudes towards immigrants hardened immediately following the 11 September or '9/11' terrorist attacks on the United States in 2001,[14] and people with greater fears of terrorism tend to hold more negative attitudes towards asylum seekers.[15]

What is the nature of the threats that asylum seekers are seen to pose? Conceivably these might vary from the concrete (bombings, crime, competition for jobs or economic resources) to the more abstract (threats to the 'social fabric', values or morals). Both forms of threat appear to be implicated in public attitudes. One study found that people who perceived high levels of threats posed by asylum seekers to Australians' physical and material welfare held less favourable attitudes towards them.[16] There was also a weak tendency for people holding unfavourable attitudes to see asylum seekers as posing a symbolic threat to Australian culture, beliefs and moral and religious values, suggesting that the apprehension that underlies anti-asylum seeker sentiment primarily concerns more concrete threats. Similar findings have been obtained by Winnifred Louis and colleagues,[17] who showed that the perception that asylum seekers pose a threat to Australians' economic and social standing was associated with unfavourable attitudes towards them. In addition, more prejudiced study participants believed that reducing the numbers of asylum seekers would have large benefits for Australia's employment and crime rates, national security and unity, health, reputation, and way of life, implying a belief that the presence of asylum seekers imperils these goals. Surveys of attitudes to immigration tell a similar story: people who are most ill-disposed towards immigrants are especially likely to see them as responsible for crime, taking jobs from Australians, and harming our economy.[18] In sum, threat and fear play key roles in hostility to asylum seekers, and the perceived threats concern material welfare more than cultural worldview.

Anger and illegitimacy

Fear derives from the belief that we are facing a threat, but it is not the only emotional register of unfavourable attitudes towards asylum seekers. These attitudes are frequently coloured by anger, derived from the perception that asylum seekers are illegitimate, immoral or in violation of principles of justice and fairness rather than perceived threat. The primary role that moral values such as these play in both positive and negative attitudes towards asylum seekers has been shown in a recent community survey: people who accept and reject asylum seekers rely on values to the same degree, but draw different conclusions about who deserves blame.[19] Themes of illegitimacy and illegality feature prominently in the public's views of asylum seekers, exemplified by popular labels such as 'illegal immigrants', 'queuejumpers', 'so-called refugees' and 'opportunists'.[20] These terms carry a charge of moral condemnation, making accusations of criminal behaviour, violation of rules of fairness, deception and selfishness. These linguistic labels have real consequences. In one study,[21] simply substituting 'illegal immigrant' for 'asylum seeker' or 'refugee' in a bogus newspaper article led readers to endorse more negative views of asylum seekers.

The psychology of these moralistic perceptions seems to turn on judgments of responsibility and unfairness. Dutch research[22] reveals that members of the public make a sharp distinction between 'real refugees', who had no choice but to seek asylum and whose neediness is beyond their control, and 'economic refugees' or 'fortune seekers' who are seen as having deliberately chosen to seek asylum and as personally responsible for being in need. The former elicit sympathy, whereas the latter elicit anger and resentment. Levels of anger towards asylum seekers were associated with lack of support for pro-immigrant policies, especially in the case of 'economic refugees'. Judgments of deservingness as well as responsibility are implicated here. In an Australian study, the belief that asylum seekers receive more benefits and better treatment than they deserve was associated with more negative attitudes towards them.[23] In this case, hostility to asylum seekers derives from the perceived unfairness of what they receive rather than the perceived immorality or illegitimacy of what they do.

Disgust and avoidance

Although anger and fear may be two of the primary emotional dimensions of prejudice towards asylum seekers, some recent evidence indicates that disgust also has a part to play. Disgust involves a perception that something is offensive, repulsive or contaminating, and a desire to protect the integrity of the self by rejecting it. Beginning as a simple rejecting response to oral distaste, disgust has evolved to serve other kinds of self-protection. In particular, it has come to have a moral dimension, as when behaviour that violates basic values is judged to be disgusting and contact with its perpetrators is urgently avoided as if it were in some way contaminating. Interpersonal forms of disgust can be experienced towards people who are rejected because they are judged to be morally offensive, invasive threats to the social order, or carriers of contagious disease.

One recent Canadian study[24] has shown that people who are especially prone to this kind of interpersonal or moral disgust have more rejecting attitudes towards immigrants, as well as having ideological orientations that are authoritarian and socially dominant. This finding is consistent with evidence that disgust reactions are strongest towards social groups that are stereotyped as lacking warmth and competence, such as welfare recipients and homeless people.[25] Asylum seekers, who arrive destitute, helpless and needy, are likely to be perceived in precisely this disgust-promoting manner. This may be especially the case because asylum seekers symbolically threaten to violate the nation's borders in the same way that disgusting matter – rotten food, dirt, germs – threatens to infiltrate the boundaries of the body.[26] The possibility that 'boat people' might be carriers of contagious disease has been explicitly raised by public officials,[27] increasing the likelihood that some members of the public view asylum seekers not only as sources of dread and moral indignation, but also as objects of disgust.

Dehumanisation

A final observation about the psychology of attitudes towards asylum seekers is that they are often seen as less than fully human. In the media they are rarely shown as unique and suffering individuals, and more often represented as a faceless collective or as an impersonal invading force. Verbal labels sometimes objectify them as 'cargo' or 'flotsam'.[28] People with unfavourable attitudes sometimes view them as callous cheats, or as perpetrators of wild and barbaric acts.

Dehumanisation can serve a number of psychological functions, such as legitimating harsh policies and distancing the self from other people's misery. By perceiving asylum seekers as lacking human qualities, morally questionable behaviour towards them can be seen as justified and appropriate. If they are less human than us, then normal moral restraints do not apply and the sorts of punitive and coercive treatment that we usually reserve for animals can be meted out without compunction. In addition to rationalising harsh treatment, by dehumanising asylum seekers we can protect ourselves from the full empathic comprehension of their suffering.

Psychological research has confirmed the central role of dehumanisation in public sentiment regarding asylum seekers. People who are disgust-prone view immigrants unfavourably largely because they perceive them as lacking traits that distinguish humans from other animals.[29] Moreover, Canadians with negative attitudes towards refugees are especially likely to deny them socially positive values, such as caring for their children and raising them to be humane, and to perceive them as crude and unsophisticated barbarians.[30] Such perceptions are especially common among people who favour social inequality, and are associated with feelings of contempt towards refugees. In Australia, people who identify more strongly with humanity as a whole endorse more welcoming attitudes towards asylum seekers, perhaps in part because they are more likely to appreciate their shared humanness.[31]

Dehumanisation of the downtrodden may be a widespread psychological phenomenon that needs little external encouragement,[32] but in the context of asylum seekers in Australia three real-world factors have played a crucial role. First, the policies of mandatory detention and 'offshore' processing, and the restriction of public and media access to asylum seekers, have inevitably made efforts to humanise them difficult. Secondly, the extreme behaviour that appeared in detention centres, including violent riots and graphic forms of self-mutilation, is likely to have been perceived by many Australians as wild and bestial, and falsely attributed to the barbarism of the detainees rather than the extreme and untenable conditions prevailing in the centres. Finally, if having humane and child-nurturing values is taken to be an index of someone's humanness,[33] then it would be difficult to imagine a claim more likely to dehumanise people than the 'children overboard' myth, according to which 'boat people' deliberately threw their children into the sea in a bid to be rescued. If members of the public dehumanise asylum seekers, they have often done so in response to government policy and rhetoric.

Reasons for hope

In this chapter we have tried to unravel the strands from which unfavourable attitudes towards asylum seekers are woven. However, the situation is not as bleak as our discussion may have made it appear. Unsympathetic views have been far from universal in the population, and there are encouraging signs that public opinion is softening. Many of the false beliefs about asylum seekers on which negative attitudes rest have been thoroughly challenged in the news media, and public acceptance of them is likely to have waned. Many voices that are critical of Australia's record on the treatment of asylum seekers have been raised, challenging less critical people's beliefs that their hostile attitudes reflect a social consensus.[34] Communities have demonstrated strong backlashes against the rejection of refugees, as in the recent case of Sudanese refugees who were initially barred from settling in Tamworth. Awareness of their positive contributions, and in some cases direct personal contact, has humanised asylum seekers and defused the perception that they threaten Australia's values and material welfare. Survey research reveals significant improvement in attitudes towards immigration over the past decade.[35] We can only hope that the tide has truly turned, and that governments can no longer rely on the general public to join a chorus of exclusion when people seek asylum here in future.

Notes

1 Betts, K, 'Boatpeople and public opinion in Australia', *People and Place,* vol 9, 2001, pp 34-48.

2 Pedersen, A, Attwell, J, and Heveli, D (2005), 'Prediction of negative attitudes towards Australian asylum seekers: false beliefs, nationalism, and self-esteem', *Australian Journal of Psychology,* vol 57, pp 148-160; Schweitzer, R, Perkoulidis, S, Krome, S, Ludlow, C, and Ryan, M, Attitudes towards refugees: the dark side of prejudice, *Australian Journal of Psychology,* vol 57, 2005, pp 170-179.

3 Betts, above, n 1; Pedersen et al, above, n 2; Goot, M and Watson, I, 'Immigration, multiculturalism and national identity', in S Wilson, G Meagher, R Gibson, D Denemark and M Western (eds), *Australian social attitudes: the first report,* University of New South Wales Press, Sydney, 2005, pp 182-203.

4 Goot and Watson, above, n 3.

5 Pedersen et al, above, n 2; Goot and Watson, above, n 3; Hodson, G and Costello, K, 'Interpersonal disgust, ideological orientations, and dehumanization as predictors of intergroup attitudes', *Psychological Science,* vol 18, 2007, pp 691-698.

6 Hodson and Costello, above, n 5; Louis, WR, Duck, JM, Terry, DJ, Schuller, RA and Lalonde, RN, 'Why do citizens want to keep refugees out? Threats, fairness and hostile norms in the treatment of asylum seekers', *European Journal of Social Psychology,* vol 37, 2007, pp 535-573.

7 Pedersen, A, Attwell, J and Heveli, D, above, n 2; Pedersen, A, Watt, S and Hansen, S, 'The role of false beliefs in the community's and the federal government's attitudes toward Australian asylum seekers', *Australian Journal of Social Issues,* vol 41, 2006, pp 105-124.

8 Pedersen et al, above, n 2; Nickerson, AM and Louis, WR, 'Nationality versus humanity? Personality, identity and norms in relation to attitudes towards asylum seekers', *Journal of Applied Social Psychology,* (in press); Verkuyten, M, 'Emotional reactions to and support for immigrant policies: Attributed responsibilities to categories of asylum seekers', *Social Justice Research,* vol 17, 2004, pp 293-314.

9 Goot and Watson, above, n 3.

10 Betts, above, n 1, p 45.

11 Pedersen, A, Griffiths, B, & Watt, SE, 'Attitudes toward outgroups and the perception of consensus: all feet do *not* wear one shoe', *Journal of Community and Applied Social Psychology,* (in press).

12 Louis, et al, above, n 6.

13 Pedersen et al, 'The role of false beliefs', above, n 7.

14 Betts, above, n 1.

15 Pedersen, A, Watt, SE and Griffiths, B, *Prejudice against asylum seekers and the fear of terrorism: the importance of context*, Murdoch University, Perth, 2007.

16 Schweitzer et al, above, n 2.

17 Louis, et al, above, n 6.

18 Goot and Watson, above, n 3.

19 Pedersen, A and Griffiths, B, *Attitudes toward Australian asylum seekers: The function of attitudes*. Unpublished manuscript, Murdoch University, 2007.

20 Saxton, A, 'I certainly don't want people like that here: the discursive construction of asylum seekers', *Media International Australia*, vol 109, 2003, pp 109-120.

21 Augoustinos, M and Quinn, C, 'Social categorization and attitudinal evaluations: Illegal immigrants, refugees, or asylum seekers?', *New Review of Social Psychology*, vol 2, 2003, pp 29-37.

22 Verkuyten, above, n 8.

23 Louis et al, above, n 6.

24 Hodson and Costello, above, n 5

25 Fiske, ST, Cuddy, AJ, Glick, P, Xu, J, 'A model of (often mixed) stereotype content: Competence and warmth respectively follow from perceived status and competition', *Journal of Personality and Social Psychology*, vol 82, 2002, pp 878-902.

26 O'Brien, GV, 'Indigestible food, conquering hordes, and waste materials: metaphors of immigrants and the early immigration restriction debate in the United States', *Metaphor and Symbol*, vol 18, 2003, pp 33-47.

27 Mares, P, *Borderline: Australia's treatment of refugees and asylum seekers*, University of New South Wales Press, Sydney, 2002.

28 Saxton, above, n 20.

29 Hodson and Costello, above, n 5.

30 Esses, VM, Veenvliet, S, Hodson, G and Mihic, L, 'Justice, morality, and the dehumanization of refugees', *Social Justice Research*, (in press).

31 Nickerson and Louis, above, n 8.

32 Haslam, N, 'Dehumanization: an integrative review', *Personality and Social Psychology Review*, vol 10, 2006, pp 252-264.

33 Schwartz, SH and Struch, N, 'Values, stereotypes, and intergroup antagonism', in D Bar-Tal, CF Grauman, AW Kruglanski and W Stroebe (eds), *Stereotypes and Prejudice: Changing Conceptions*, Springer-Verlag, New York, 1989, pp 151-167.

34 Mares, S and Newman, L, *Acting from the heart: Australian advocates for asylum seekers tell their stories*, Finch Publishing, Sydney, 2007.

35 Goot and Watson, above, n 3.

PART VI

The future of asylum seeker policies

LINDSAY TANNER

Part VI Introduction

The 2001 election campaign has left a dark stain on Australian public life that will take a long time to fade. The appalling vilification of desperate asylum seekers by the Howard government, and Labor's inability to combat it, still cloud public discussion of immigration issues.

Many Australians are acutely conscious of our nation's origins in the seizure of Aboriginal lands. This subconscious sense of deficient title makes them extremely sensitive to the prospect of others doing the same thing to us. The outcome is deep-seated fear of Asians, ingrained hostility to immigration, and endemic racism.

Many other Australians have very different views. While our government vilified asylum seekers in pursuit of cheap votes, thousands of decent Australians rallied to help them. Across the country are countless individuals who are ashamed of our government's stance, and who've committed themselves to acting to change it.

We don't know how history will interpret these events. Perhaps they'll be regarded as the last twitch of the tail in the long, slow death of the White Australia policy. Maybe they're a portent of things to come, a future dominated by Cronulla riots and Pauline Hansons.

There is cause for optimism. Step by step, Labor has strengthened its position. We have long since abandoned our earlier support for indefinite mandatory detention, and we're about to commit to abolishing Temporary Protection Visas.

Liberal and National moderates have also found their voice. The collapse of the government's recent proposed changes to immigration laws was a triumph for decency. It couldn't have happened without Labor, the Democrats and the Greens but by ourselves we weren't sufficient. Whatever else they look back on over their careers, conservative MPs like Petro Georgiou, Judi Moylan, Russell Broadbent, Bruce Baird, John Forrest and Judith

Troeth should take great pride in stopping this legislation. It's easy for some to take a hard line on these issues. It's much harder for dissident conservatives.

I'd like to think the tide has turned, decent Australia has found its voice, and the ugly voices of bigotry and prejudice are in retreat. Pauline Hanson has become a parody of a parody. Her comment in 2007 that she didn't object to Christian Muslims says it all. Ignorance is the core ingredient of bigotry.

Time will tell, but in the meantime, important contributions like this book help to turn the tide even further. In amongst the fog of emotionally charged politics there are serious and complex issues surrounding asylum seekers. The more considered debate about these issues, the better our country will be.

18

DAVID MANNE

Post-Palmer reform of the Immigration Department: progress and pitfalls

This chapter focuses on the so-called 'post-Palmer reform process' and on how the Immigration Department ('Department'[1]) is progressing with it, rather than focusing on government policy. Since the Mick Palmer and Neil Comrie reports,[2] to what extent has there been significant reform within the Department in areas identified by them, and are there areas in the reform process which have been deficient? While it was government policy to accept, comprehensively, the recommendations made by Palmer and Comrie,[3] reform of government policy itself was clearly outside their briefs. Nevertheless, these policies, which continue to amount to one of the toughest, most legally controversial, hostile and extensive anti-asylum seeker systems in the Western world – including mandatory detention; temporary protection and humanitarian visas; 'excision' of Australian territory; naval repulsion of asylum seekers arriving by boat; and the 'Pacific solution' – provide crucial context for the reform process.

First, let us take stock, and recall where we have come from in recent times. During 2005, the shocking and tragic circumstances of the Cornelia Rau and Vivian Alvarez cases awakened in Australians a recognition of the scandalous abuse and cruel indifference which the Immigration system was perpetrating on innocent and vulnerable people, including asylum seekers. A number of significant developments flowed from this. The government rejected credible calls for a Royal Commission and instead established the Palmer Inquiry, amidst much scepticism as to whether Mick Palmer could and would do the job required. Mick Palmer's report surprised many sceptics – it ultimately made findings constituting one of the most devastating indictments of a major government department in Australia's history.

The key problem areas of Departmental practice which Palmer identified centred on two things: a 'culture that is overly self-protective and defensive, a culture largely unwilling to challenge norms or to engage in genuine self-criticism or analysis';[4] and a systemic approach and 'entrenched culture' described as 'fixed on process and apparently oblivious to the outcomes being achieved'.[5] It was largely in response to the Palmer Report – and the Petro Georgiou MP-sponsored-and-proposed Private Members Bills and the compromise deal subsequently struck with the Prime Minister[6] – that a process of 'wide-ranging, systemic reform' of the Department was promised and commenced in the first half of 2005.

So what has been achieved since then? To what extent has there been significant reform within the Department in the areas identified by Palmer; and are there areas where the reform process has been deficient? In addressing these issues, I want to give an impressionistic – rather than systematic – sketch of some key areas and themes from the viewpoint of a legal practitioner and advocate heading a leading agency whose daily work includes dealing directly with some of the most complex and difficult interactions with the Department for clients and stakeholders. I think a useful way to address the question of progress is to compare some examples of problem areas in Departmental operation before and after the Palmer Report under two broad categories: treatment of clients, that is, *people*, who must always matter most in the administration of the Immigration system; and treatment of stakeholders.

Treatment of clients

Processing of boat arrivals

The Refugee and Immigration Legal Centre Inc is somewhat uniquely placed in comparing the Department's approach to processing of the claims of asylum seekers arriving by boat informally during, say, 2001, and then in 2006. During 2001, for example, we provided independent legal representation to groups of mainly Afghan and Iraqi Protection Visa applicants held in remote detention centres such as Curtin Immigration Reception and Processing

Centre ('IRPC') and Port Hedland IRPC. The Department named these processing regimes in remote detention 'Taskforces'. Taskforces essentially involved very short periods of approximately one to three weeks in which a team of legal advisers advised and prepared full written, individual applications for refugee status[7] for asylum seekers in large groups, which were then lodged and assessed by Departmental officers in client interviews.

As coordinator of legal teams which performed some of this work, our overwhelming experience was that the Department brought a 'siege' mentality to much of the work under this process, in which there were serious deficiencies in procedural fairness. There were significant delays in clients being able to access legal assistance, with some clients being held in 'separation'[8] or incommunicado detention for many months before ultimately being allowed to access legal help. Treatment of clients was often confusing, hostile and at times intimidating from the outset, framed by an institutional suspicion which started with the assumption that these people may *not* be, or probably *were not,* refugees, but rather, cynical opportunists. Unrealistic and overly onerous conditions were often imposed by the Department on the advice and preparation of claims. Clients were interviewed by Departmental officers who were often poorly prepared or equipped, with insufficient understandings of the clients' claims, and cultural and country background. Questioning was regularly irrelevant, disrespectful, and/or aggressive. The role of the legal adviser was commonly severely restricted and not sufficiently appreciated, resulting in a general disinterest or lack of engagement in legal submissions made on behalf of clients. Finally, there was a lack of consistency in approach and decision-making, to the extent that it was often difficult to discern why some cases were approved while others were rejected.

In the words of Palmer, then, the processing regime in place in 2001 was dominated by 'rigid, step-by-step protocols'[9] designed by Senior Immigration officials in Central office and imposed in ways that were inflexible and procedurally unfair.

'Post-Palmer'

Some five or so years later, in late January 2006, a legal team from my organisation, including myself, went to Christmas Island on another Departmental Taskforce, as independent legal advisers. This time, the task was to provide legal assistance to the 43 West Papuan asylum seekers who had arrived some two weeks earlier. Our professional experience was somewhat rare and unique. It is clear that the processing of the West Papuan claims was seen as a significant test case of the new, reforming Department. As I remarked publicly shortly after 42 of our clients were granted Protection Visas in late March 2006, our clients were grateful that justice had been done; that their treatment and the due legal processes provided by the Australian government and the Department had been fair, reasonable, just and decent. What features of the process contributed to this judgment?

The West Papuan refugees were treated with respect and dignity from the time of their arrival. From our observation, they were treated, quite properly, as if they *may well be* refugees and accordingly, may have certain rights and needs. They were promptly provided with experienced, competent legal representatives, who were given sufficient time to both advise and prepare detailed written claims for submission in support of each person's formal application for a Protection Visa. These claims were examined by a Departmental delegate at an interview with the client, legal adviser and qualified interpreter present. Clients were treated with respect and dignity, and given a genuine opportunity to put their case forward. Post-interview, there was reasonable opportunity for lodgement of detailed legal submissions. There was great flexibility and decisions about the functioning of the process were made in a general spirit of cooperation and guided by the aim of achieving fair and reasonable results.

Of course, this is not the full picture. In response to Indonesia's fury and threats over the grant of Protection Visas to the 42, the government presented a radical, rearguard retreat from a commitment to such fair and decent treatment, with the introduction of the Migration Amendment (Designated Unauthorised Arrivals) Bill 2006 ('offshore processing Bill'), which sought to preclude any future refugee applications by people arriving by boat being made in Australia at all, let alone fairly. It represented the sudden ushering in a new era of extreme harshness and potential cruelty – a new policy of 'Radical Rejection'.[10]

Essentially, at the first sign of external political trouble, the Australian government's commitment to a fair and decent process for asylum seekers appeared to be surrendered. This revealed the radical contradictions in government policy and its reform principles, and thus the inherently fragile and tenuous nature of reform in this context. But one legacy, at least, of the Papuan processing is a concrete case study of how processing of asylum claims – albeit illogically, irrationally and at exorbitant expense conducted on Christmas Island under government policy – should and can be done properly. It is an important precedent.

Case management, including vulnerable clients and those with 'complex' circumstances

In the pre-Palmer era, one of the enduring and intractable problems centred on the Department's treatment of people detained, as well as particularly vulnerable people in the community. A number of common concerns arose. There was a lack of 'case coordination' – that is, a lack of a holistic understanding of and approach to clients' often interrelated health, welfare and legal needs – and a lack of a consistent approach to clients' cases within the Compliance and Detention areas of the Department. There were no proper systems for risk assessment regarding a client's needs and rights, so that the Department was routinely responding in a rigid and myopic way to an individual's immigration status. Finally, there were numerous structures and processes which obscured and avoided responsibility for a client's needs, to the extent that it was often difficult to discern to whom such concerns should be addressed.

I briefly refer to a refugee case which provides a graphic illustration of the terrible problems and consequential damage resulting from such an approach. The following was far from an isolated incident. The case involved Ibrahim,[11] a stateless asylum seeker from the Middle East, who had initially arrived in Australia informally. He suffered from a mental impairment which severely diminished his capacity to accurately present his claims for refugee status. Ibrahim applied for protection, the application was refused, and he continued to remain in detention for a number years. Ultimately, he was released from detention by way of a *habeas corpus* order of the Court. Upon his release he underwent, for the first time, a full needs assessment when a non-government agency with expertise in assisting asylum seekers became concerned about signs of potentially serious psychological issues. Expert health assessments revealed that Ibrahim had a serious intellectual disability which directly diminished his memory and capacity to answer questions about his refugee claims accurately, especially when under pressure. Apparently, such disabilities are difficult to detect with a non-expert eye. It became clear to welfare workers that the client had never given an accurate account of his claims, and that it would be necessary to contact family overseas to help with reconstructions is his real history. This had not been identified by the Department when he was in detention. Ibrahim was then able to access intensive, expert legal help to re-state his claims. Upon a Departmental reassessment of his claims, he was found to be a refugee under the United Nations Refugees Convention,[12] and was granted a Protection Visa. Had the Department undertaken a comprehensive, holistic assessment of Ibrahim's needs, it is likely that they would have detected barriers to him properly presenting his claims and could have explored avenues to rectify this situation. Of course, this may have not only resulted in quicker attention to treatment of the client's health and welfare needs, and less damage to him, but also the timely recognition of refugee status and release from incarceration into the community.

'Post-Palmer'

Progress by the Department after the Palmer Report is such that there is now a reduced chance that situations such as the one just described would happen now. This is largely due to one of the reform flagships, Case Management (and the related Community Care Pilot),[13] which have been developed and commenced implementation. These are specifically aimed at the better treatment of, and provision of targeted, coordinated, holistic assistance to those with 'complex' circumstances, and particularly disadvantaged or vulnerable clients.

Although it is too early to fully assess the case management model, some positive and tangible progress has been made. For example, in a number of cases, the Department has quickly ensured that a holistic assessment of a client's needs is undertaken. This innovation has resulted in prompt referral to independent agencies with expertise in legal, health or welfare matters. It has been facilitated by the formalisation and funding of processes which are aimed at a higher and more consistent degree of collaboration and coordination amongst key stakeholders. For example, the Australian Red Cross, International Organisation for Migration, and certain health and welfare services and legal providers with expertise in working with asylum seekers and migrants are now working together with the Department to comprehensively deal with complex cases. We have also witnessed the Department shift from an approach of apprehension about seeking and acting on expert health and welfare advice, to one of readiness, if not, at times, enthusiasm, to do so. One tangible initiative has been the introduction of Departmental Case Managers and Detention Review Managers, tasked with managing not only holistic needs assessment, but also assessment of whether detention is lawful and reasonable.

Despite some substantial improvements, one of the principal concerns of Case Management remains lack of consistency in implementation and service delivery. Some clients have still fallen through the cracks, and have not been properly assessed in relation to health needs and legal rights, resulting in potentially dire consequences. These problems have been particularly, but not exclusively, present for clients in the community. Although the Compliance Section of the Department has vastly improved its practices, with flexible and reasonable treatment of clients now becoming the norm, application of Bridging Visa laws still suffers from unevenness on matters such as work rights and duration of visa grant. There also continue to be incidents involving imminent or actual manifest injustice and harm to clients – including on issues concerning detention and removal from Australia – which have not been properly identified by the Department unless and until there has been active intervention by non-governmental organisations or individuals. Given that one of the hallmarks of fairness in public administration is consistency, these are substantial concerns.

Finally, the tension between imperatives of the reform process and other government policies has also been evident in Case Management and the Community Care Pilot. Whether 'special care' services should continue for a client who seeks judicial review or Ministerial intervention is one of clearest cases in point. More work remains for the Department to ensure that the potential tension between the imperatives of 'removal'[14] and proper treatment of clients is *routinely* resolved in favour of the client's rights, needs and dignity – that is, in a way which is 'fair and reasonable', and with recognition that to achieve this aim, removal may, at times, need to be deferred while the client explores options and is cared for.

Processing of 'offshore' applications

The post-Palmer reform process has rightly developed a fresh framework of values for the Department, which include it being 'an open and accountable organisation', and 'having fair and reasonable dealings with clients'.[15] The Secretary has stressed that it is essential that these values be applied to work done by the Department 'offshore' as well as in Australia.[16] Regrettably, there is no substantial evidence that the post-Palmer reforms are taking hold in the operations of overseas posts, where much of the Department's work on individual visa applications is done. Much 'offshore' processing is nothing short of eccentric in the context of contemporary Western legal systems.

A compelling case in point is the current approach to the processing of applications made by clients under the Refugee and Special Humanitarian Program. Openness, accountability, fairness and transparency continue to be almost *non-existent* in the processing of these claims. For decisions which involve matters that could hardly be more grave – family reunion and protection from persecution – written refusals are issued with a *pro forma* statement which does not disclose any specific reasons for the failure of the particular application. Legal advisers are left with no idea of the basis of the refusal, and applicants and their Australian 'proposers' are commonly left baffled and distraught.

The absence of transparency is so fundamental that copies of Departmental file records obtained under Freedom of Information provisions rarely give any further hint of the specific reasons for refusal. If they do, it is commonly a comment as oblique and incomprehensible as 'claims not current'. In the case of an Afghan widow with five young children, from a persecuted minority ethnic group, stranded illegally in Pakistan and from a family with an adverse political profile in Afghanistan, I am reliably informed that this phrase is code for a judgment that she no longer has a need for human rights protection and can return to Afghanistan. Such judgment is completely at odds with trends in decision-making for Protection Visa applications made and assessed by government officials *in* Australia. When advisers seek explanations for such refusals, it can be left to another Departmental official to read between the lines, if there *are* any lines. In many cases, there are not. In processing of 'offshore' applications under the general migration program, similar systemic problems persist. They include arbitrary use of documentary or expert evidence, and the application of sweeping, unsupported cultural stereotypes on issues crucial to determination of the visa application, such as age, family relationship and identity.

Treatment of stakeholders

It is also important to ask whether there has been post-Palmer progress in the treatment of stakeholders. Why does this issue matter? Principally, if stakeholders are doing their job properly, they should be well-positioned to comment on the things that matter most to clients in their interactions with the Department. They should also be able to help shape the Department's approach to clients and their communities, enriching its understanding of the content of its self-proclaimed duty to have 'fair and reasonable dealings with clients'.[17]

The Secretary and his Department have prioritised stakeholder engagement, so that stakeholders are to be considered 'an asset, rather than a liability or obligation'.[18] However, stakeholder engagement by the Department has historically been very problematic. There has been a lack of genuine dialogue and preparedness to openly discuss operational or client-based issues, including defensiveness and withholding of information about the bases of decisions. There has been a lack of responsiveness to requests for information about clients or systemic issues. In some senior ranks there has been a 'fortress mentality' and inadequate dissemination of key information to less senior departmental officials. Key stakeholder fora have failed to have appropriate representation of those working directly in the fields of relevance. Finally, there has been a reluctance to consult with known critics and an institutional misunderstanding and mistrust of legal practitioners.

'Post-Palmer'

Post-Palmer, there have been some substantial and tangible improvements, both attitudinal and practical. On the attitudinal front, the Department has displayed a far greater openness and interest in engaging in meaningful and respectful dialogue with stakeholders. This has included an increased willingness at both State and national levels to discuss and debate issues of concern on client-specific, as well as more systemic issues. In relation to practical measures, there has been a significant increase in the development of fora for dialogue, such as the establishment of Client Reference Group meetings in some States.

An area of particularly important progress has been the inclusion of key stakeholders on national steering/reference or advisory groups to collaborate on the development and implementation of new reform programs, such as the Community Care Pilot. Stakeholders chosen have been from agencies which directly deal with the issues at stake, including legal practitioners. The establishment of the Detention Health Advisory Group to provide the Department with advice regarding the design, implementation and monitoring of improvements in health care (particularly mental health care) for people in immigration detention,[19] comprising experts from right across the health sector, including some well-known critics of past policies and practices, has been another significant development. There has been increased follow-through and responsiveness from Departmental officials, greater implementation of stakeholder suggestions, and energetic efforts by senior officials to build relationships across a wide range of stakeholder groups.

Nevertheless, some considerable problems remain. Levels of responsiveness have been inconsistent. Consultation processes have sometimes been scattergun, confusing, and poorly coordinated across different fora. Frequent changes of key personnel have produced a lack of continuity. The community legal sector – which provides a substantial proportion of the legal assistance in the relevant areas of the reform process and more generally – has continued to lack representation at peak fora.

Stakeholder engagement is also vulnerable to the dictates of external government policy factors. For instance, in early June 2006, the Department held a day-long debriefing session with key agencies and officials involved with the West Papuan Taskforce and settlement of the clients in Melbourne. It was a commendable idea, but the session was held at the very point when the 'offshore' processing Bill had been introduced into Parliament and looked likely to become law. The effect of the proposed laws would have been to deprive all future boat arrivals of the ability to apply for protection in Australia. We were being debriefed on lessons learnt about something which looked likely to be non-existent in the near future.

Conclusion

The shape and trajectory of the reform process is very fragile and tenuous because it remains ever-vulnerable to the dictates of the external political environment. Only 400 or so asylum seekers arriving by boat in Australia between 1989 and 1992 triggered the introduction of a mandatory detention system. Further asylum seeker boat arrivals that were relatively miniscule by international standards triggered the legislative 'excision' of parts of Australian territory pre-election 2001. Indonesian fury at the grant of protection visas to 42 West Papuans triggered an attempt to legislate that all future boat arrivals be denied the right to apply for protection in Australia, and be 'exiled' to Nauru instead.

The reality is that the fundamental planks of the government's Immigration policy are in many respects at odds with the principles of the Departmental reform process, which is therefore vulnerable. Framed by fair and reasonable treatment of clients, the reforms are potentially limited because, in many areas, we do not have fair and reasonable government policies. Adherence to the reform imperatives depends on the external environment remaining substantially unchanged and benign.

The situation of eight Burmese asylum seekers who arrived by boat in August 2006 is a stark reminder of this tension. The then Immigration Minister, Senator Amanda Vanstone, who had a discretion to allow the men to remain in Australia and apply for protection under Australian law, exercised her discretion *against* them, sending them to possible indefinite exile in Nauru. No reasons were given; no legal review or other redress was available. This decision ran radically counter to the reform process in at least two key respects: first, it deprived the Burmese men of access to the due legal processes and other benefits of the reform process itself; and second, they have become subject to a policy which has, in recent years, produced terrifying human destruction of many, rather than holistic care. Rather than operating on values of openness and accountability, it is a policy which can be characterised as 'out of sight, out of mind, out of rights'. It is also, it would seem, outside the reform process.

Ultimately, the reform process has involved some notable improvements in numerous key areas, while poignant tensions and problem areas remain. The reframed core principles are correct, and much will depend on their effective and extensive implementation, as well as the political environment remaining relatively unchanged and benign. In a broad sense, much will depend on how focused, disciplined and robust the Department can be in ensuring that the principles and programs of the reform process are implemented without fear and *in favour* of the government's policy to comprehensively accept and act on the recommendations of the Palmer and Comrie reports. The Department must do so with as little interference or infection as possible from other key aspects of the government's Immigration policy, which are at fundamental odds with this agenda.

Notes

1 Hereinafter, 'Department' will be used to refer to the Department of Immigration under its various full titles in recent years, such as the Department of Immigration, Multicultural and Indigenous Affairs.

2 Palmer, M, *Inquiry into the circumstances of the Immigration detention of Cornelia Rau: Report*, Commonwealth of Australia, Canberra, July 2005 ['Palmer Report']; Commonwealth Ombudsman, *Inquiry into the circumstances of the Vivian Alvarez matter*, Report by the Commonwealth Ombudsman of an inquiry undertaken by Mr Neil Comrie, AO, APM (Report no 3 of 2005), Canberra, October 2005.

3 Hereinafter, unless expressly stated otherwise, references to the 'Palmer' or the 'Palmer Report' should be read as including the Comrie brief and report referred to above.

4 Palmer Report, above, n 2, p ix.

5 Ibid, p 169.

6 The drafting by Liberal MP, Petro Georgiou, of Private Members Bills sought a serious curtailment of the mandatory, indefinite detention system, and the abolition of Temporary Protection Visas. The compromise deal subsequently struck with the Prime Minister represented a significant, albeit seriously inadequate, set of reforms which had the real potential to limit or end the suffering of many still subjected to the system, if implemented quickly and in good faith. They included: provisions for release of children and their families, as well as others from detention centres; quicker processing of refugee applications; oversight of cases involving over two years of detention by the Commonwealth Ombudsman; and oversight of the reform process by an Inter-Departmental Committee chaired by the head of the Department of Prime Minster and Cabinet.

7 Under Australian migration legislation, an application for refugee status is an application for a Protection Visa (Class XA). See, in particular, *Migration Act* 1958 (Cth) s 36, and Migration Regulations 1994, Schedule 2, clause 866.221 which requires the Minister be 'satisfied that the applicant is a person to whom Australia has protection obligations under the Refugees Convention' (being the 1951 Convention relating to the Status of Refugees as amended by the 1967 Protocol relating to the Status of Refugees).

8 For an explanation of the term 'separation' detention see, for example, *Report of an Own Motion Investigation into the Department of Immigration and Multicultural Affairs' Immigration Detention Centres*, March 2001, p 13, which states, inter alia: 'Separation detention is an administrative arrangement that restricts a person or a group of persons to a particular area of a detention facility on initial arrival at or before removal from a facility. Detainees are kept separate from the main population of the IDC and are not permitted to make telephone calls to, or correspond with, people in the Australian community'.

9 Palmer Report, above, n 2, p 79.

10 See further, speech by David Manne for Castan Centre for Human Rights Law: *Boatloads of Extinguishment?,* 'Forum on the proposed 'offshore' processing of 'Boat People', 5 May 2006, <www.law.monash.edu.au/castan centre/events/2006/manne-paper-5-5-06.pdf>.

11 This man's real name has been changed to preserve confidentiality.

12 He was found by a Departmental delegate to meet the definition of a refugee.

13 See Departmental Fact Sheet: 'Quality Case Management and the Community Care Pilot', <www.immi.gov.au/about/department/perf-progress/dima-improvements/_fact_sheets/Quality_case_management_and_commu nity_care_pilot.pdf>.

14 The term is used to refer to removing a person from Australia, whether voluntarily or involuntarily. See, for example, *Migration Act* 1958 (Cth) s 198. Removal from Australia of unlawful non-citizens.

15 Transcript of Plenary Address, Transformations Conference 2006, Federation of Ethnic Communities' Councils of Australia, Canberra, Mr Andrew Metcalfe, Secretary of the Department of Immigration and Multicultural Affairs, 29 November 2006, p 2.

16 Ibid, p 3.

17 Ibid, p 2.

18 Ibid, p 6.

19 See Departmental Fact Sheet: 'Fact Sheet 82. Immigration Detention', at <www.immi.gov.au/media/fact-sheets/82detention.htm>.

19

GRANT MITCHELL

The need for a uniform community-based reception policy for asylum seekers in Australia

Major disparities exist in Australia's reception and processing of people who seek asylum. Different rights, entitlements and conditions apply to asylum seekers according to their means and place of arrival, when their asylum claim is lodged, and where the claim lies within the determination process. Under current policy, they may be held for the duration of their claim in a detention facility on the Australian mainland, or held in an 'offshore' facility. Alternatively they may be held in a community detention arrangement, or live in the community on a bridging visa. During this period, they may be eligible for essential government-funded welfare support or they may be left destitute in the community with no right to an income or healthcare.

Based on 10 years of experience working with more than 1000 asylum seekers in the community, this chapter by Grant Mitchell of Hotham Mission's Asylum Seeker Project aims to unpack the welfare impact of existing reception policies, arguing for a uniform community-based reception policy for all individuals who have sought Australia's protection and who have completed identity, health and security checks, in line with United Nations High Commissioner for Refugees (UNHCR) reception and detention guidelines.[1]

Introduction

While the concept of settlement is clearly defined and understood in Australia in relation to the integration and support needs of newly arrived and existing migrant and refugee communities, the concept of 'reception' remains little understood. Reception is defined as 'the starting moment a person enters a country and presents his/her claims for asylum to a national authority, lasting through the period during which the application and any appeals are examined until the person either receives a more permanent residence permit, or is expelled, repatriated voluntarily or resettled into a third country'.[2] Reception should thus be viewed in the Australian context as including both the Protection Visa determination process and the request on humanitarian and non-refugee protection grounds to the Immigration Minister under s 417 of the *Migration Act*. The outcome for an asylum seeker may be settlement or return; however, the process they are undergoing is reception. There are legal and administrative elements of the reception and determination process. However, this paper focuses on the welfare component of reception, namely the entitlements and conditions allocated to people seeking asylum in Australia.

The reception needs of asylum seekers

Asylum seekers exhibit a number of inherent vulnerabilities due to the likelihood of multiple stressors, including past trauma in their home country or during flight, family separation, anxiety or fear and uncertainty about the present and future. Because of these vulnerabilities, as well as the fact that asylum seekers may be found to be refugees, certain minimum standards of care should be adhered to. UNHCR guidelines stand as a clear indicator of appropriate care response as well as suitable conditions to be imposed upon asylum seekers. Particular concern is noted for female, minor and elderly asylum seekers, survivors of torture and those with health conditions.

In the first instance, the UNHCR Guidelines on the Detention of Asylum Seekers are quite clear that detention of asylum seekers is 'inherently undesirable', and should only be used where clear identity or security concerns are present.[3] Any decision to detain should be reviewable, either judicially or administratively, with conditions imposed on asylum seekers that are not punitive or arbitrary in nature. While certain restrictions may be placed on freedom of movement in relation to detention or reporting requirements, these should be based on comprehensive assessments of actual risk, and should be fair, reasonable, reviewable and time-limited.

Clear standards are outlined in terms of appropriate welfare, rights and entitlements for those remaining in detention. Other freedoms, such as freedom of information and association, should not be restricted. Asylum seekers should be provided clear and concise translations of information relevant to their rights, entitlements, processing and conditions. Access to legal advice and information about non-governmental organisation (NGO) services available is crucial. Once asylum seekers are assessed as not having any identity, health or security concerns, they should be released under a uniform community-based reception system.

Certain minimum reception standards should be in place for all asylum seekers awaiting a refugee or humanitarian decision in the community, and should continue for the entire duration of their claim.[4] These standards should include work rights, ensuring a degree of self-sufficiency for individuals able to work; access to healthcare; and access to income support[5] and casework for vulnerable asylum seekers.[6]

The provisions for minimum entitlements to work, health care and welfare support for asylum seekers are embedded in Australia's international obligations. The International Covenant on Economic, Social and Cultural Rights highlights appropriate and suitable healthcare, housing, and income support, which does not exclude asylum seekers. These rights are also vital to ensure asylum seeker children have access to essential health services and income support as required in accordance with the Convention on the Rights of the Child (CROC):[7]

> States Parties shall take appropriate measures to ensure that a child who is seeking refugee status … shall, whether unaccompanied or accompanied by his or her parents or by any other person, receive appropriate protection and humanitarian assistance in the enjoyment of applicable rights set forth in the present Convention and in other international human rights or humanitarian instruments to which the said States are Parties (CROC Article 22(1)).

Furthermore, in 2002, Australia endorsed the UNHCR Executive Committee Conclusion which stated:

> Reception arrangements can be mutually beneficial where they are premised on the understanding that many asylum seekers can attain a certain degree of self-reliance, if provided with the requisite opportunities (Recommendation vii).

The Conclusion also states that:

> asylum seekers should have access to the appropriate governmental and non-governmental entities when they require assistance so that their basic support needs, including food, clothing, accommodation, and medical care are met (Recommendation ii).[8]

Return and settlement needs

Hotham Mission believes that an additional obligation of government is the humanitarian responsibility to provide appropriate repatriation assistance for refused asylum seekers who are facing return. This assistance includes ensuring that asylum seekers have the option of making their own departure arrangements, that detention-based removal is only used as a last resort, and that returnees receive reintegration assistance as required. This response is similar to that provided to returnees from the European Union through the assistance of a number of international NGOs, including the International Organisation for Migration (IOM).

Asylum seekers found to have either protection or humanitarian needs and granted residency should receive settlement supports and not be excluded from available mainstream services. This is essential not only for the wellbeing of the individuals but also to ensure that they are provided the supports required to settle effectively into the community.

The welfare impact of Australia's reception policy

There are a number of areas in which Australia does not currently meet the internationally accepted reception conditions for asylum seekers presented here. These conditions are dictated primarily by three pieces of policy:

1 The introduction of non-reviewable mandatory detention in 1992 of all unauthorised arrivals in Australia who are held until approved or removed;

2 The removal of the right to work and Medicare in 1997 for asylum seekers in the community who had not lodged a claim within 45 days, or had approached the Minister under s 417 of the *Migration Act* and been issued a Bridging Visa E; and

3 The introduction of the 'Pacific Solution' in 2001, namely legislation aimed at denying asylum seekers access to Australia's 'onshore' asylum process, through the creation of 'migration zones', the excision of a large number of islands and 'offshore' processing.

1. Detention regime

The devastating impact of indefinite, non-reviewable mandatory detention on the lives of people seeking Australia's protection has been widely reported and researched.[9] In particular, this has included the impact on the mental health and wellbeing of children and long-term detainees, as well as the inflexibility and inability of the regime to provide an adequate welfare response to vulnerable persons for which the State has a duty of care. A number of these concerns have now been acknowledged by the government in relation to the release of families with children from immigration detention centres into community based detention in mid 2005,[10] the role of the Ombudsman in reviewing long-term detention cases, and acceptance of recommendations made in the Palmer Report into the treatment of people in immigration detention centres.[11]

Despite these changes, a number of concerns remain about detention policy and practice in Australia, noted in a March 2006 Senate Inquiry into the Operation and Administration of the Migration Act 1958.[12] Of particular concern is the requirement to detain a person known or reasonably suspected as being an unlawful non-citizen, including the use of detention pending removal for community cases where flight or security risks are low. Coupled with this is the absence of a judicial or administrative review mechanism to determine the requirement/need to detain. Greater flexibility in the detention regime is required to ensure that officers can issue bridging visas in circumstances where a person has become unlawful for reasons outside their control, where insufficient evidence of unlawful status exists, where it is undesirable to detain, such as for age or health reasons, and where there are no identity, health or security risks.

Concerns also exist about the reception conditions for individuals in immigration detention. These include the unnecessary restrictions on detainee freedom of information and association, such as limitations on access to legal advice, NGO assistance, and translated information about rights and processing arrangements. This concern is particularly noted with regard to the Christmas Island Immigration Reception and Processing Centre, which can be utilised as both an 'offshore' and 'onshore' processing facility, with differentiated rights and entitlements for detainees dependent on mode of arrival. Here there are additional logistical concerns about the centre's ability to provide appropriate duty of care and welfare to detainees, particularly health and social services.

2. Bridging visa regime

While there has been much public debate about the detention regime, the impact of the removal of the rights and entitlements of asylum seekers in the community on bridging visas is less well known and understood. While a small number of especially vulnerable asylum seekers may be eligible for the government-funded Asylum Seeker Assistance Scheme (ASAS) through the Australian Red Cross, many are ineligible for this payment as they have had a primary decision within six months of lodging their claim, or have been refused at the Refugee Review Tribunal (RRT).

There are a number of serious welfare and health consequences for asylum seekers denied the right to Medicare and welfare assistance, particularly children and individuals with health concerns and also those unable to or denied the right to work. Hotham Mission has recently completed the largest research of its kind in Australia, analysing the welfare needs of 554 asylum seekers on a Bridging Visa E (BVE) over a five-year period.[13] The research outcomes highlighted extremely high levels of abject poverty and need, including statistics such as:

- 90% of clients currently have no right to work, Medicare or welfare benefit

- 62% presented homeless, with 73% having experienced homelessness while on a BVE
- 66% reported having health issues since being on a BVE, with 18% denied health services due to not having Medicare or funds to pay
- 30% of clients required treatment for mental health conditions while on a BVE
- 27% of clients are children under the age of 15, with 76% defined as children at risk
- 14% are single mothers, plus 23 cases in total of pregnant women with no Medicare
- 30% of clients have been in Australia for six years or more awaiting a decision
- 30% had never had the right to an income or healthcare while in Australia, and 74% of this group is ineligible for ASAS. Over 15% of this group was later found to have a refugee or humanitarian claim.

Our research found that regulatory changes in 1997 have left many asylum seekers destitute in the community, dependent on charities, friends or relatives to survive. Lack of income after the Refugee Review Tribunal decision led to high levels of nutritional and health concerns for children and pregnant mothers. High levels of anxiety and depression were also reported, with asylum seekers denied the right to volunteer and study, and children unable to socialise normally due to lack of funds for extracurricular and recreational activities. These restrictions dramatically affected asylum seekers' sense of wellbeing and contributed to isolation and mental ill health.

3. 'Offshore' processing

A range of concerns exist regarding the use of 'offshore' processing under the 'Pacific Solution'. First, 'offshore' asylum seekers lack access to legal processes available in Australia, such as proper translation, legal advice and the review of determination decisions. Secondly, Australia is not obliged under the policy to provide protection either to individuals declared to be refugees, or to those found not to be refugees for whom return may be unsafe. Thirdly, the policy raises serious concerns in relation to punishing individuals based on mode of arrival and use of interdiction. Fourthly, the policy prevents access to and independent monitoring of the treatment of asylum seekers. Finally, indefinite processing and prolonged isolation have detrimental effects on mental health and general welfare. These concerns were noted in a UNHCR submission to a Senate inquiry into 'offshore' processing, which stated:

> It is the opinion of UNHCR that the experience gained from offshore processing on Nauru, introduced by Australia in October 2001, should not be considered the 'outstanding success' it is characterised as in the Second Reading, but to the contrary has resulted in prolonged detention-like situations of asylum-seekers and refugees alike, as well as extended separation of families. The practice is also known by UNHCR to have contributed to serious mental health problems.[14]

Moving towards a uniform community-based reception model for asylum seekers

As highlighted above, Australia is currently not meeting its asylum seeker reception obligations in a number of areas. Having individuals indefinitely in detention or left destitute in the community is neither in Australia's nor the asylum seeker's best interests.

While the detention and bridging visa regimes have been established as part of a broader deterrence and border protection strategy, there is no evidence that detention deters asylum seekers. Research has in fact shown that current policy is counterproductive to government objectives of implementing the return of refused asylum seekers. Long term indefinite detention has been found in a growing body of work to cause mental health concerns impacting on both general functioning and ability to cope with the immigration process.[15] Hotham Mission research has found that denying asylum seekers on bridging visas the right to an income and healthcare makes individuals isolated and vulnerable in the community, affecting their health, wellbeing and ability to make departure arrangements.[16] In relation to the 'Pacific Solution', it needs to be noted that there has been minimal success in finding third country resettlement solutions for the 1063 people found to be refugees, with only 4.3% resettled in countries outside of Australia and New Zealand.[17]

The three current approaches to reception of asylum seekers – the bridging visa regime and mainland and 'offshore' detention regimes – all have serious shortcomings in their treatment of people seeking Australia's protection and also in their ability to achieve the settlement and return outcomes desired by government. However Australia currently has a unique opportunity to revise and nurture a new way of working with asylum seekers. With the Australian government now moving towards a case management approach for persons within its detention facilities,[18] comprehensive needs and risk assessments can be used as a basis for case-by-case decision making on the necessity to detain unauthorised arrivals. While previously there has been a 'one size fits all' response to security requirements in detention facilities, legislative change in 2005 introduced the new s 197AB, which essentially allows, for the first time, a tailored response to detention based on personal characteristics, such as age, health, behaviour and likelihood to abscond. This change in policy, together with the new case management approach, stands as an important starting point for the government to introduce a new uniform community-based reception model for all persons seeking Australia's protection.

The Justice for Asylum Seeker (JAS) Alliance, an alliance of more than 25 community and religious groups across the country, compiled a comprehensive community-based model of release from detention in 2003, entitled 'The Better Way', which aimed at achieving government objectives of a well-managed program, which was cheaper, more humane and which did not compromise national security.[19]

The Better Way model makes several core recommendations for the government:

1. Those who have been detained and found to have no outstanding identity, health or security concerns, should be released into the Australian community on bridging visas.
2. An early intervention approach should be developed, whereby all asylum seekers are assigned a qualified caseworker, who provides information about the asylum process, undertakes need and risk assessments, determines

special care needs, and provides ongoing assistance throughout the refugee process.[20]

3. Appropriate welfare supports should be ensured for all asylum seekers during the reception process, including the right to work, healthcare and ASAS.[21]
4. Ongoing caseworker involvement should be utilised to ensure that refused asylum seekers are provided the option of returning voluntarily with adequate support, and those granted residency are provided settlement assistance as required.

Much of this integrated model of working with asylum seekers was built on the tested Swedish model where detention is used only as a matter of last resort and where community-based support and case management are provided. This approach has been found to directly impact on higher levels of voluntary repatriation and low levels of absconding of refused asylum seekers.[22] This model has now been tested in the Australian context through the work of Hotham Mission, which has evidenced the positive role appropriate welfare and casework support plays in improving welfare, and in preparing, supporting and empowering asylum seekers throughout the determination process. In researching 554 asylum seekers living in the community surveyed over a five-year period from March 2001 to March 2006, Hotham Mission found that 79% of refused asylum seekers voluntarily departed Australia, 12% were removed by the Department, 3% remained in detention awaiting removal, and less than 1% of clients surveyed absconded.[23]

These outcomes, together with international research, clearly highlight that detention pending removal is not necessary to achieve government objectives of return of refused asylum seekers. In addition, the provision of the right to income and healthcare is arguably in the national interest by ensuring that a stable, managed 'onshore' program is in place. It is also more likely to ensure that asylum seekers are in a position to respond to immigration decisions appropriately. Providing additional supports for vulnerable asylum seekers in the community, such as income support and casework assistance, has been costed and found to be cheaper than current detention costs.[24] In addition, recent research on the skills of asylum seekers denied the right to work has found that the Australian economy could potentially gain hundreds of millions of dollars if they were allowed to work while awaiting a decision, particularly in relation to the skill-shortage crisis.[25]

As outlined in this chapter, Hotham Mission proposes that Australia nurture a new approach and practice in working with people seeking Australia's refugee protection or humanitarian intervention. This response should be based on a fair and uniform reception, ensuring appropriate duty of care, facilitating the humane return of those not in need of protection, and assisting settlement for those found to need protection, while not compromising Australia's security. All asylum seekers who seek Australia's protection and who have completed identity, health and security checks should be released into the community on bridging visas with appropriate welfare supports pending a decision, in line with UNHCR reception and detention guidelines.[26] This uniform community-based reception response will enable the interests of the government, community and the asylum seeker to be upheld, while ensuring Australia meets its international obligations in our tradition of being an inclusive and fair society.

Notes

1 UNHCR, 'Reception standards for asylum seekers in the European Union', Geneva, July 2002; UNHCR, 'Revised guidelines on applicable criteria and the standards relating to the detention of asylum seekers', Geneva, February 1999.

2 PERCO (Platform for European Red Cross Cooperation on Refugees, Asylum Seekers and Migrants), 'Guidelines on the Reception of asylum seekers for National Red Cross and Red Crescent Societies', Geneva, 2001, p 7.

3 UNHCR, 'Revised guidelines', above, n 1.

4 UNHCR, 'Reception standards', above, n 1.

5 Income support denotes sufficient financial assistance to meet housing, food, utilities and other essentials.

6 The various vulnerability categories are outlined in DIMA's existing Asylum Seeker Assistance Scheme Exception Criteria.

7 States Parties shall recognise for every child the right to benefit from social security, including social insurance and shall take the necessary measures to achieve the full realisation of this right in accordance with their national law: CROC article 26.

8 UNHCR Executive Committee (EXCOM) Conclusion on reception of asylum seekers No 93 (LIII) 2002.

9 See <www.mja.com.au/public/issues/175_12_171201/steel/steel.html> and <www.humanrights.gov.au/human_rights/children_detention/psy_review.html>.

10 Individuals released under 'Residence Determination', while still administratively detained, have freedom of movement and receive casework coordination, income support and access to services.

11 See <www.minister.immi.gov.au/media_releases/media05/v05119.htm>.

12 Further concerns and recommendations listed in the Senate Inquiry into administration and operation of the *Migration Act 1958*, 2 March 2006, <www.aph.gov.au/Senate/committee/legcon_ctte/migration/>.

13 Hotham Mission, Submission to Department of Immigration's Bridging Visa Review, May 2006.

14 UNHCR Submission, Senate Legal and Constitutional Committee Inquiry into the provisions of the Migration Amendment (Designated Unauthorised Arrivals) Bill 2006, 22 May 2006.

15 Steel, Z and Silove, D, 'The mental health implications of detaining asylum seekers', *Medical Journal of Australia,* vol 175, 2001, pp 596-599.

16 Hotham Mission, Welfare and Immigration Outcomes for Asylum Seekers on Bridging Visa E, Hotham Mission, November 2003.

17 Refugee Council of Australia submission, Senate Legal and Constitutional Committee Inquiry into the provisions of the Migration Amendment (Designated Unauthorised Arrivals) Bill 2006, 17 May 2006.

18 The new case management approach follows recommendations found in the Palmer Report of July 2005, and includes early and regular assessment, case planning and ongoing oversight of cases within various immigration streams.

19 Reception and Transitional Processing System, Justice for Asylum Seeker (JAS) Alliance, 2002; see also <www.thebetterway.info>.

20 Casework includes the assessment, intervention and support strategies used to assist the welfare situation and to prepare, support and empower individuals awaiting a final decision on their immigration case.

21 Entitlements should be extended until a final immigration outcome, ie, settlement or return, as well as seeing the removal of the 45-day rule

22 Mitchell, G, *Asylum Seekers in Sweden*, 2001, <www.ajustaustralia.com>.

23 Hotham Mission, Bridging Visa E Review, Hotham Mission, May 2006.

24 Improving Outcomes and Reducing Costs for Asylum Seekers, Justice for Asylum Seekers Alliance, August 2003, <www.thebetterway.info>.

25 Croucher, G, *A Chance to Contribute – Forgone Gains to the Australian Economy of Disallowing Asylum Seekers the Right to Work*, February 2006, <www.safetynotcharity.victas.vca.org.au>.

26 UNHCR, 'Reception standards for asylum seekers in the European Union', above, n 1; UNHCR, 'Revised Guidelines on applicable criteria and the standards relating to the detention of asylum seekers', above, n 1.

20

JULIAN BURNSIDE

Australia's refugee policy

Australia has a mixed record in its treatment of refugees. There have been moments of which we can be proud, and others which are less admirable.

For example, in 1938 Australia participated in the Evian Conference called by Franklin Roosevelt to discuss the fate of Jewish refugees. Australia's representative walked out, saying: 'We have no racial problems in Australia and no desire to import any'. The treatment of the Jewish refugees who arrived here on the *Dunera*, in September 1940, was a warning of our capacity for callous indifference to the suffering of others. By contrast, during the 1970s the Fraser Liberal government shepherded into Australia tens of thousands of Vietnamese and Cambodian 'boat people' each year, and helped them become a part of the Australian community.

In 1992 the Labor government introduced a system of mandatory detention for informal arrivals. The 'boat people', who had hitherto been received with compassion, were now to be locked up, without trial, until their claims for asylum could be determined. By contrast, Australia has for years had an offshore resettlement scheme, under which refugees languishing in refugee camps overseas are brought to Australia for resettlement. Not all countries have a resettlement scheme, and Australia's is one of which we should be proud.

In 2001 refugee policy became a hot political issue. The *Tampa* incident focused attention on the arrival of 'boat people' seeking asylum in Australia. At the time (August 2001) the arrival rate of 'boat people' had increased from an average of about 1000 people per year to a peak of 4100 in 2000-2001.

On 26 August 2001, MV *Tampa* rescued 438 people whose boat, the *Palapa*, had sunk. It rescued them at the request of Australia. It acted according to the tradition of sailors the world over. Apart from the five people smugglers on the boat, the people rescued by *Tampa* comprised for the most part, Hazaras from Afghanistan, men, women and children. They were fleeing the Taliban. We knew all this. We also knew that the Taliban were a brutal and repressive regime. We knew that Hazaras, one of the three ethnic groups in Afghanistan, had been persecuted for centuries, but that the persecution had become increasingly harsh under the Taliban who come from the Pashtun ethnic group.

The captain of *Tampa* asked for medical help. Many of the women and children were ill or injured. When *Tampa* entered Australian territorial waters at Christmas Island, Australia sent the SAS and took control of the ship, to prevent the refugees from coming ashore. Ultimately, the people rescued by *Tampa* were sent to the tiny Republic of Nauru in the central Pacific. Australia paid the bankrupt Nauruan government tens of millions of dollars to detain them there on Australia's behalf. During the next two weeks, New Zealand accepted 12 of them as refugees. Over the next four years, Australia accepted many of the others as refugees, but sent many back to Afghanistan after the Taliban had been removed (temporarily as it turned out) from power.

During the *Tampa* episode, the government closed the port and airspace at Christmas Island to ensure that 'no humanising images' of the refuges would be seen. The *Tampa* episode began on 26 August 2001; Justice North in the Federal Court handed down his decision (in favour of the refugees) at 2.15 pm AEST on 11 September 2001: just nine hours before the terrorist attacks on America. The coincidence of events caused many members of the public to blur the two events in their minds, so that terrorism and 'boat people' became part of a single phenomenon. Arguably the blurring was increased by the fact that, after '9/11', policies to deter 'boat people' from seeking asylum in Australia were referred to collectively as 'border protection'.

Mandatory detention

Under section 196 of the Migration Act, refugees are the only group in our community who can be imprisoned indefinitely, by order of parliament, regardless that they have not committed any offence. No court can order that the person should be released merely because the detention is unnecessary, or cruel, or damaging, or pointless.

The Migration Act defines 'unlawful non-citizen' as a non-citizen who does not have a visa. The Act does not make it an offence to be in Australia without a visa, but s 196 provides that an 'unlawful non-citizen' must be kept in immigration detention until he or she is granted a visa or is removed from Australia. Sub-section (3) provides, rather chillingly, that '[t]o avoid doubt, subsection (1) prevents the release, even by a court, of an unlawful non-citizen from detention (otherwise than for removal or deportation) unless the non-citizen has been granted a visa': 'An "unlawful non-citizen" is defined as a person who is not a citizen and who does not hold a visa. It is not an offence to be an unlawful non-citizen'.

In the media, 'boat people' are often referred to as 'illegals': this is the expression used by politicians, journalists and commentators. It may be a gloss on the words 'unlawful non-citizen' in the Migration Act. Unfortunately, it carries the strong implication that 'boat people' have committed an offence by their manner of arrival, or by their presence here. It is not so. Australia's system of mandatory detention provides for the jailing of people who have committed no offence, and regardless of age, sex or state of health.

In November 2003 the High Court heard argument in the case of al Kateb. Mr al Kateb was a stateless Palestinian who had arrived in Australia as a boat-person. He asked for protection. His application for a protection visa was refused. He could not bear conditions in Woomera detention centre, so instead of appealing the visa refusal, he asked to be removed from Australia. The government could not remove him, because there was no country which could be forced to take him back. Because s 196 of the Act says that an 'unlawful non-citizen' must remain in detention until they are given a visa or they are removed from Australia, there was an *impasse*: neither way out of detention was available to him. In principle, it would have been a simple matter to amend the Act to deal with the anomaly exposed by his circumstances. As it was, the Australian government argued that, in these circumstances, it could hold Mr al Kateb in detention for the rest of his life. On 6 August 2004, by a 4:3 majority, the High Court accepted the government's argument.

The right to liberty is generally regarded as one of the most fundamental rights in a democracy. Deprivation of liberty has always been regarded as a matter of grave importance, and something which should not be possible except after due legal process. Article 39 of Magna Carta provides:

> No free man shall be arrested or imprisoned or disseised or outlawed or exiled or in any way victimised, neither will we attack him or send anyone to attack him, except by the lawful judgment of his peers or by the law of the land.

This has been interpreted (perhaps misinterpreted) as the basic promise of liberty in the Common Law system. It is reflected in the United States Bill of Rights 5th amendment which provides (in part): 'No person shall … be deprived of life, liberty, or property, without due process of law … '.

The automatic jailing of people, and for an indeterminate time, without any offence and without any trial is widely regarded in the Common Law world as deeply incompatible with accepted notions of democratic freedoms. However in a parliamentary democracy without a bill of rights, a law prescribing mandatory detention of innocent people is constitutionally valid, as the decision in al Kateb's case shows.

Influencing public opinion

The mandatory detention policy carries a risk: it is possible that middle Australia would be troubled by the idea of locking up innocent people for life. To avoid that risk, the Howard government implemented a multi-faceted strategy. One element of the strategy was to hold about 80% of asylum seekers in the most remote and inhospitable parts of the country. By this simple device, the chance of them being noticed, and thus identified as human beings in distress, was greatly reduced. In the detention centres until recently, refugees were called by their camp numbers, not their names. They suffer a daily round of small humiliations at the hands of guards. The camps are run by a private prison operator. The effects are very damaging.

The second element was to ban the press from detention centres on grounds of privacy. The government argued that it was upholding the refugees' right to privacy, but at the same time couldn't see the hypocrisy in ignoring their right to liberty. Indeed, the government's concern for the detainees' privacy was so great that, when the Port Hedland detainees asked, in writing, that members of the press be allowed in, the government still refused. But the press, in general, saw no irony in this, and barely complained.

The third element was to neutralise any comment that contradicted the government's views. Anyone who raised a dissenting voice was disparaged by the media and government, and branded 'elitists' or 'intellectuals'. Those who proposed less draconian measures than indefinite mandatory detention were disregarded. It is fair to say that, at least until late 2004, the policy of indefinite mandatory detention was electorally popular, perhaps because it was not fully understood by the general public. Certainly, it was promoted by the government as an aspect of a policy of deterrence for the purpose of 'border protection'.

'Illegals', 'queuejumpers', 'children overboard'

The most important element – the key to the entire strategy – was to demonise asylum seekers: to portray them as sub-human, so as to make it possible to do to them what would otherwise be abhorrent. However it is inaccurate to portray asylum seekers as 'illegals', or 'queuejumpers' or as people who would throw their 'children overboard'. As explained above, they are not 'illegal'. Every person has a right under international conventions to seek asylum in any place they can reach. They commit no offence by arriving without papers, without an invitation, seeking our protection. They are not charged with any offence: they are simply locked up.

In this fact lies the fundamental distinction between immigration policy and refugee policy.

Immigration policy is a reflection of demographic, social and economic considerations which cause a country to say they would like this many people, of this or that skill base, this or that ethnic origin. And it is perfectly reasonable, when referring to immigration policy, to say 'we will decide who comes to this country and the circumstances in which they come here'. As an expression of immigration policy, that is impeccable. People may debate the policy settings, but the principle is perfectly good as a statement of immigration policy.

Refugees have a quite different claim on our hospitality. Refugees are fleeing persecution, torture or death in a place which is unsafe, and they seek protection. If they manage to get to Australia, we have an obligation under international conventions to offer them the protection they are seeking.

The tag 'queuejumpers' was used to suggest some kind of over-reaching by 'boat people', coupled with the threat of the country being swamped if we did not protect ourselves. They are not 'queuejumpers' in any meaningful sense. In the principal trouble spots from which they came (Afghanistan, Iran and Iraq) there was no Australian diplomatic presence, and thus nowhere to queue.

The Howard government regularly emphasised the risk that Australia would be overrun if we did not take firm measures against unauthorised arrivals. For example, in an interview on the '7.30 Report' on 15 November 1999, the following exchange occurred:

> *Kerry O'Brien:* Philip Ruddock, 700 illegal Middle East refugees last week, thousands more potentially on the way. What's behind the surge?
>
> *Philip Ruddock, Minister for Immigration:* Well, I think we need to understand that it's not a new phenomena.
>
> Australia is, in fact, newly targeted in a sense, because something like 33,000 Iraqis entered Europe last year.
>
> The situation is that something like 700,000 people from Iraq have been displaced … they are electing to move to Australia.
>
> And because we're a signatory to the refugees convention, they have a greater prospect under our system of being accepted as a refugee here …
>
> *Kerry O'Brien:* You say you've been forewarned by reliable intelligence that there could be as many as another 10,000 preparing to leave Iraq …
>
> *Philip Ruddock:* Information that has come to the department and obviously to me is that significant numbers of people are now on the move.
>
> I mean, what they see is a situation in which refugee status having been granted, access to Australian benefits that we pro-

> vide generously to people who are refugees, are being utilised by people who have come this way unlawfully … I've been told that large numbers of people are packing up in preparation for this sort of travel to Australia. [1]

The truth is quite different. It is useful to put the number of unauthorised arrivals in context. Every year almost 5 million people visit Australia on short term visits, for holidays or business. Every year 110,000 people migrate permanently to live in this country. Every year – until the time of *Tampa* at least – there were on average 1000 people who arrived without authority and sought asylum; of them, approximately 90% were found to have proper claims to refugee status. The highest number of unauthorised arrivals in one year[2] was just over 4100: most of them fleeing the Taliban or Saddam Hussein.

On any view, 'boat people' are not a demographic threat to Australia.

One of the reasons we do not have a crisis in terms of numbers is that our geography insulates us from most of the world's refugee problems. It is quite difficult to get here in a small leaking boat. By contrast, countries adjacent to the trouble spots in the world have millions of refugees coming across their borders. For us to complain about 4000 is somewhat petty when you consider that Africa has a total of 5.5 million refugees, and Asia has about 8.5 million.

'We will decide who comes to this country and the circumstances in which they come here'. During the November 2001 election campaign, Mr Howard used that slogan to convey the essence of the government's refugee policy. He maximised its effect by falsely suggesting that some refugees had thrown their children overboard whilst seeking entry to Australia. By so doing he not only misled the electorate about what a hapless group of terrified asylum seekers had done: he obliterated the crucial distinction between migration policy and refugee policy.

The Howard government ran the November 2001 election on a platform of border protection. After '9/11', the informal arrival of asylum seekers by boat was elevated to a crisis of border protection. This proved very popular in the electorate. For two centuries Australians have lived in dread that we will be swamped by uninvited visitors arriving in small boats, and we love to have our fears stirred.

Despite the horrors of the terrorist attacks on America, it is not rational to regard 'boat people' as a terrorist risk. Dennis Richardson, the former Director-General of ASIO, stated that not one person among the 5986 asylum seekers arriving in 2001 and 2002 'had received an adverse security assessment in terms of posing a direct or indirect threat to Australia's security'.

In 2001 just 11 people who sought asylum in Australia were rejected on 'character grounds'. Only one was regarded as a security risk because of suspected terrorist links. He came by air, not boat. The terrorists who carried out the 11 September attacks arrived in the United States flying first class, not as asylum seekers but using valid papers.

The 'Pacific Solution'

In the wake of *Tampa* episode, the Howard government introduced the 'Pacific Solution'. The 'Pacific Solution' involves intercepting people before they manage to get to the mainland and taking them against their will to either Manus Island (to the north of Port Moresby) or to Nauru in the central Pacific. They are then forbidden by law to apply for an Australian protection visa except with the consent of the Minister for Immigration. They are 'processed' but what is examined is their claim to be refugees within the meaning of the Refugees Convention.[3] If they are found not to be refugees, they have no rights of appeal of any sort. If mistakes are made, those mistakes go undetected. If they are found to be refugees, the Australian government offers them to other countries. Perhaps unsurprisingly, other countries have not shown much interest in this approach. After all, the arrival rate of asylum seekers in Australia is extremely low by world standards. Ultimately, many of the asylum seekers housed on Manus Island and Nauru have been brought to Australia.

A significant number of refugees caught up in the 'Pacific Solution' were from Afghanistan. When the Taliban fell, the Australian government took the view that it was now safe to send Afghan asylum seekers back to Afghanistan. They were offered $2000 per head for 'resettlement'. Letters from many of them suggest that they were placed under considerable pressure to accept the package and agree to return. Here are extracts from letters written in early 2002 by Afghans held on Nauru:

> You have written your letter asking "Why you return back because Afghanistan is winter now?" You right, but we are obliged to. The Australian Government make oblige us to return back, we do not have enough food or water. We are in a very bad situation in the camp.
>
> As I wrote before, the situation is very hard here, so many people got mental problem, especially after [asylum application] result announcement.
>
> Unfortunately, the Australian authority has a very bad manner; they think that we are slave and they are slave owners. We do not have any freedom; we are in jail, but we do not know our fault and sin. Jail is for those people who make crime and break the law. We are just refugee … After one month I return home because of my wife and son who I love. I decide to die there beside my family.

The interviews between asylum seekers and Immigration officials were all taped. In one of them, the asylum seeker – a boy aged nine – is offered the resettlement package. It is difficult to understand what the official is saying, because the child is sobbing so loudly.

Between 2001 and 2006, approximately 1600 people were held pursuant to the 'Pacific Solution'. By the start of 2006, only two asylum seekers remained there: Muhammad Faisal and Mohammad Sagar. They are both from Iraq; they have both been accepted by Australian officials as refugees. However ASIO assessed each of them adversely on security grounds. The factual basis for the assessment has never been disclosed to them or to anyone else. It is puzzling, since they had both been held on Nauru for five years, and had won the favourable opinion of Ministers in the Nauruan government.

In early 2007, eight Rohingyan Burmese refugees were taken to Nauru by the Australian government. Later 83 Sri Lankan refugees were taken there from Christmas Island. They are still being 'processed' as this book goes to print.

Solitary confinement

Officially, solitary confinement is not used in Australia's detention system. Officially, recalcitrant detainees are placed in the Management Unit for their own safety or the safety of others. The truth is that the Management Unit at Baxter (and the Red One compound) are both places of solitary confinement. A video tape of one of the Management Unit cells shows something of the way Australia now treats asylum seekers. It shows a cell about three-and-a-half metres square, with a mattress on the floor. There is no other furniture; the walls are bare. A doorway, with no door, leads into a tiny bathroom. The cell has no view outside; it is never dark. The occupant has nothing to read, no writing materials, no TV or radio; no company yet no privacy because a video camera observes and records everything, 24 hours a day. The detainee is kept in the cell 23.5 hours a day. For half an hour a day he is allowed into a small exercise area where he can see the sky.

Most disturbing is the behaviour of the person in the cell: he sleeps a lot of the time, typically in the foetal position; he paces around the cell; and – most disturbing of all – he sits on the floor, knees drawn up to his chest, and rocks back and forwards for hours.

No court has found him guilty of any offence; no court has ordered that he be held this way.

The solitary confinement regime involves the withdrawal of all basic privileges and their gradual restoration as a reward for good behaviour. Since isolation is a very real torment for most people, isolation is of itself punitive. However if isolation is necessary for the good order of the camp, its miseries should be compensated for by providing radio, TV or other forms of distraction or entertainment. The solitary confinement regime does not compensate for the torment of isolation: on the contrary, the most minimal comforts are withdrawn and are then gradually restored. If they are restored for good behaviour, their withdrawal can only be seen as punishment. Nevertheless, the government and GSL (the private prison operator which runs detention centres for the government) insists that detention and 'isolation detention' are not punitive.

Amin arrived in Australia in March 2001 with his daughter Massoumeh. She was then five years old. They were held in Curtin, then in Baxter.

On 14 July 2003, three ACM[4] guards entered Amin's room and ordered him to strip. He refused, because, apart from it being deeply humiliating for a Muslim man to be naked in front of others, his seven-year-old daughter was in the room. When he refused to strip, the guards beat him up, handcuffed him, and took him to the 'Management Unit'.

There he stayed from 14 July until 23 July. Each day he was allowed a half-hour visit from his daughter. But on 23 July she did not come. The manager of the centre explained to him that Massoumeh had been taken shopping in Port Augusta. He was assured that she would visit Amin the next day.

The next day, 24 July, she did not arrive for her visit: the manager came and explained that Massoumeh was back in Tehran. She had been removed from the camp and from Australia without giving Amin the chance to say goodbye to her.

Amin collapsed when he heard the news, and remained in detention for another eight weeks. It took three applications in court to get him released. The government did not contradict the facts, or try to explain why they had removed Massoumeh from the country: they argued simply that the court had no power to dictate how a person would be treated in detention.

The judge found otherwise and ordered that Amin be removed from solitary confinement and be moved to a different detention centre. The government appealed that ruling, but failed.

Consequences of detention

Refugees held in detention have not committed any crime. People who commit crimes are held in jails where conditions are significantly better, and their period of detention is fixed. Refugees cannot count the days until their detention ends. Even if they ask to be removed from Australia, they may be held indefinitely until another country agrees to take them.

The detention centres themselves are a shock to the senses. The Baxter detention centre, four hours north-west of Adelaide, opened in August 2002. If you stand outside, facing east, the view is a perfect Fred Williams landscape of dull grey-green scrub on red sand, stretching away undimmed for miles to a rim of hills.

Then turn and face west: a six-metre high electric fence stretches away into the distance; 20 metres of no-man's land, then another tall and glittering line of wire and mesh; inside the second fence, a series of compounds made of uncompromising corrugated iron. The compounds are so designed that the inmates have no view except of the sky; more importantly, no-one outside can see those locked inside.

Getting into Baxter is a long process: you must give one week's notice; fill out a form, show appropriate ID. You are then escorted to an electronically controlled gate. Through the gate and into a metal cage. After a time – five, 10, 20 minutes – the gate at the other end of the cage opens and you can enter a small demountable cabin; there you are searched and scanned; another security air-lock and you are escorted across to the visitors' compound where you find the real tragedy, our hidden shame. Asylum seekers walk around as if still alive; they talk as if they still have a hold on rational thinking. They press hospitality on you: an irrepressible cultural instinct, like the unwilled twitching of a dying animal. But they are not wholly there: they are hollowed out, dried, lifeless things, washed up and stranded beyond the high-water mark. Their minds are gone: shredded, destroyed by hopelessness and despair. Children are incontinent from stress; many inmates are afflicted with blindness or lameness which has no organic origin: the bewildered mind's final, mute protest.

Mr Ruddock announced Baxter as Australia's 'family-friendly' detention centre. It is an ultra high-tech prison. It is surrounded by a vast perimeter fence which is described on the ground plan as a 'courtesy fence'. The 'courtesy fence' is a 9000 volt electric fence. However in the jargon of the department it is ' … not "an electric fence", it is "an energised fence"'.

The consequences of indefinite detention are utterly predictable. Detainees languish and lose hope. Some are driven to self-harm – hunger strikes, sewing their lips together, throwing themselves on the razor wire, hanging, swallowing poison – an entire catalogue of self-destruction. Suicide among pre-adolescent children is almost unheard of – except in Australia's detention centres.

At Easter, in 2002, a number of people broke out of Woomera. A large number of Australians staged a protest there and some of the protestors tore a hole in the fence. About 50 detainees climbed out through the hole in the fence, into the arms of 50 or 60 federal police who were surrounding the breach. The refugees were charged with escaping from immigration detention.

An interesting defence was available to them: the immigration detention centre, as gazetted, extended another 800 metres beyond the fence. The detainees who stepped through the hole in the fence were still inside the detention centre. But in order to run the defence, it was necessary to have evidence about what exactly had happened. In July 2005 I was in Adelaide defending one of the refugees who had been charged with escaping from immigration detention. I went down to the cells (he was still in detention after five years) in order to take him through his evidence and make sure he knew what the case was about, and what he was going to have to talk about. I asked him a few questions, and it quickly became apparent that he had no real recollection of what was going on. He had a powerful interest in remembering, because if he could remember exactly what had happened it would help establish a good defence.

I came at it in several different ways. Soon I began to think there was a problem. I thought perhaps he was not understanding my words, so I asked him what his name was. He told me his name. I asked him my name, and he told me.

I asked him 'What's your mother's name?'.

He stared into the distance for about half a minute and said 'I don't know. I can't remember'.

I asked him what his brothers' and sisters' names were. He stared into the distance again and said, 'It's too long ago; I can't remember'.

I asked him about his childhood, about his growing up. He could remember nothing. His entire past has disappeared. After five years in immigration detention, his mind is so distracted it has torn up all recollection of his past. He did not even know what detention centre he was being held in.

A family arrived in this country from Iran in early 2001. They were members of a religious minority who have been traditionally oppressed, much in the same way as the Jews were oppressed in Europe historically. This group is regarded as 'unclean' by the religious majority. The family – mother, father and two daughters – arrived in Australia and were detained in Woomera. There, over the next 14 months, the condition of the family deteriorated inexorably.

The condition of the 11-year-old daughter was a particular cause of concern. The Child and Adolescent Mental Health Service became aware of the problem. They sent a psychologist to speak to the family and wrote an astounding report in which, amongst other things, they say of this child:

> She refuses to engage in self-care activities such as brushing her teeth. She has problems with sleeping; tosses and turns at night; grinds her teeth; suffers from nightmares. She has been scratching herself constantly. She doesn't eat her breakfast and other meals and throws her food in the bin. She is preoccupied constantly with death, saying "do not bury me here in the camp. Bury me back in Iran with grandmother and grandfather".
>
> She carried a cloth doll, the face of which she had coloured in blue pencil. When asked in the interview if she'd like to draw a picture, she drew a picture of a bird in a cage with tears falling and a padlock on the door. She said she was the bird.

After a number of pages to similar effect the psychologist observed:

> It is my professional opinion that to delay action on this matter will only result in further harm to this child and her family. The trauma and personal suffering already endured by them has been beyond the capacity of any human being.

The report urged that the family be transferred from the desert camp to a metropolitan camp where at least they would get proper clinical attention which the 11-year-old desperately needed. No action was taken, and a month later the psychologist wrote another report trenchantly criticising the department for keeping the family in the desert instead of somewhere where they could get appropriate help.

Eventually the family was moved to one of the metropolitan camps. For the next two weeks, no-one came to see the child, despite the psychologist's report. Then, on a Sunday night at about 8.00 pm, when the mother, father and sister were in the mess hall having their dinner, the 11-year-old took a bedsheet and hanged herself. She did not know how to tie the knot properly, and was still strangling when the family found her. When they found her and took her down, she swallowed shampoo: she had seen adults kill themselves in Woomera that way.

She and her mother were taken to the emergency ward of the local hospital where she was put into intensive care straight away.

The lawyer who had been looking after their refugee application heard about this and went to the hospital later that night, to see if he could do anything to help. He did not need to introduce himself to the guards at the door of the intensive care unit, because he is well known at the Detention Centre. He asked to see the child and was told: 'No you may not, because lawyers' visiting hours are nine to five'.

The 2004 HREOC report into Children in Detention concluded that the treatment of children in Australia's detention centres was 'cruel, inhumane and degrading', and that it constituted systematic child abuse. The Minister for Immigration, Senator Vanstone, did not seek to deny the facts or the findings: instead, she said simply that it was 'necessary', that the alternative would 'send a green light to people smugglers'.

Deterrents

Those who have designed Australian asylum policy are unapologetic about 'sending a message' to deter refugees who might contemplate unauthorised secondary movements or people smugglers thinking about opening up a new route to Australia. As Minister for Immigration, Philip Ruddock said that '[d]etention is not punitive nor meant as a deterrent'.[5] That is ultimately a matter of subjective assessment. Most people locked up without a trial would probably not agree with Mr Ruddock's view. At the same time, he applauded the 'Pacific Solution' legislation because '[t]his strategy has been successful in deterring potential illegal immigrants from making their way to Australia'.[6]

The use of detention as a deterrent is not permitted by the Guidelines on Applicable Criteria and Standards relating to the Detention of Asylum Seekers of the United Nations refugee agency, the UNHCR, nor is it permitted by Excom Conclusion No. 44.[7] It is also morally questionable: it involves instrumentalising innocent people as a tool to achieve another objective.

International opinion

Australia's treatment of asylum seekers has been trenchantly criticised by human rights bodies both here and overseas. Amnesty

International has been extremely critical of the policy of mandatory detention.

In May 2002, Human Rights Commissioner Mary Robinson sent an envoy to inspect Woomera detention centre. The visit had not been easy to organise: initially the Australian government had refused to allow access to Woomera. In preparation for the envoy's visit, ACM management performed massive renovation work at Woomera. If the renovations were calculated to improve the impression conveyed, they failed. The report which followed that visit contained the following paragraph:

> Justice Bhagwati was considerably distressed by what he saw and heard in Woomera IRPC. He met men, women and children who had been in detention for several months, some of them even for one or two years. They were prisoners without having committed any offence. Their only fault was that they had left their native home and sought to find refuge or a better life on the Australian soil. In virtual prison-like conditions in the detention centre, they lived initially in the hope that soon their incarceration will come to an end but with the passage of time, the hope gave way to despair. When Justice Bhagwati met the detainees, some of them broke down. He could see despair on their faces. He felt that he was in front of a great human tragedy ... These children were growing up in an environment, which affected their physical and mental growth and many of them were traumatized and led to harm themselves in utter despair.

Justice Bhagwati found that the conditions he observed at Woomera involved numerous breaches of Australia's obligations under the International Covenant on Civil and Political Rights, the Convention against Torture and the Convention on the Rights of the Child.

In December 2002 a working group of the United Nations Human Rights Committee reported on Australia's detention system. Its report would shock most Australians. The working group, headed by Justice Louis Joinet, said:

> At the end of its visit, the delegation of the Working Group had the clear impression that the conditions of detention are in many ways similar to prison conditions: detention centres are surrounded by impenetrable and closely guarded razor wire; detainees are under permanent supervision; if escorted outside

the centre they are, as a rule, handcuffed; escape from a centre constitutes a criminal offence under the law and the escapee is prosecuted … During talks with government officials it became obvious that one of the goals of the system of mandatory detention and the way it is implemented is to discourage would-be immigrants from entering Australia without a valid visa …

The authorities stressed that these practices have the support of most sectors of public opinion. This is no doubt the case, but with the following reservations:

(a) One could reasonably assume that if public opinion were fully and specifically informed about the conditions to which human beings are being subjected in Australia and the negative consequences for the image of a democratic country, public opinion would change.

(b) Australian public opinion must also know that, to the knowledge of the delegation, a system combining mandatory, automatic, indiscriminate and indefinite detention without real access to court challenge is not practised by any other country in the world.

On Human Rights Day, 10 December 2002, Human Rights Watch also released a report on Australia's treatment of refugees. It said:

> The Australian government penalizes asylum seekers who arrive uninvited … The measures they take to penalize them are also intended to deter future arrivals. They include interception and forcible return to Indonesia; interception and transfer to detention in the Pacific nations of Nauru and Papua New Guinea; mandatory detention within Australia; and temporary protection visas, with restrictions on the rights afforded recipients.

Alternatives

Prolonged detention of innocent people is morally wrong. It is profoundly damaging to the individuals involved. In addition, it blunts the moral sensibility of the community which tolerates it.

This is not to say that informal arrivals should be at once released into the community. But there is a plausible alternative which balances the legitimate, but conflicting, requirements of security, sovereignty and humanity.

Treatment

- Initial mandatory detention of unauthorised arrivals, to enable health and security checks to be carried out;
- Initial detention to continue for no longer than one month, unless a judge is satisfied in a particular case that continued detention is reasonably necessary;
- At end of initial detention, release into the community on an interim visa, pending determination of protection visa application:
    - The interim visa would permit the holder to work, and to be eligible for all relevant benefits;
    - It would be subject to bail-type conditions calculated to ensure that the holder remained available for processing and (if necessary) removal from the country;
    - Conditions would include residence at a notified address and regular reporting;
    - Conditions might, if thought appropriate, include wearing an electronic bracelet to permit the wearer to be tracked.

Processing

- Abolish the Refugee Review Tribunal;
- Establish new, genuinely independent tribunal for merits review of Department visa decisions. Tribunal members should be appointed for a substantial fixed term, rather than the current practice of short-term appointments and re-appointments;
- Person dissatisfied with Tribunal decision to be able to seek leave to appeal to the Federal Court. If the Federal Court gives leave to appeal, that appeal would be a true appeal, rather than judicial review;
- These measures would strike a balance between the competing aims of efficiency and fairness.

How it ends

The federal election of October 2004 was fought on the issue chosen by John Howard: trust. He did not seek to explain away the apparent discrepancies in his various statements on such matters as GST, ethanol, 'children overboard' or family values: rather, it meant 'Trust us to keep interest rates down'. With a large percentage of the population over-mortgaged, this was a seductive message even though many people had become concerned about our treatment of refugees. In the event, Mr Howard won and interest rates rose five times over the next three years. But the way was clear for Petro Georgiou and a few other Liberal backbenchers to take a stand, and aspects of the mandatory detention policy were modified. Later, after a group of 42 West Papuans arrived in Australia and sought protection from Indonesia, the Howard government tried to enlarge the operation of the 'Pacific Solution'. Labor resisted, and with a small group of Liberal dissidents it became clear that the legislation would fail. It was withdrawn. It seems as though the tide has turned.

On 2 February 2007, Muhammad Faisal was granted permanent protection. On 6 February 2007, Mohammad Sagar left Nauru bound for Sweden. Sagar and Faisal were the last two asylum seekers to have been swept up in the 'Pacific Solution'. They were held captive for five years: first on Manus Island, then on Nauru. They had both been accepted as refugees several years earlier. They both suffered immensely as a result of their years in detention, with no idea whether they had futures worth living for. They are both struggling to rebuild their lives, as are the thousands of refugees in the community whose experience of detention compounded the trauma which led them to embark on a dangerous voyage to safety. Their attempts to integrate are made more difficult by the memory of the hostility with which they were treated. The psychological damage they have to repair is greater because of their months or years in detention.

It is easy to think that refugees come here by choice because after all we see Australia as the best possible place to live. Oddly, they do not see it that way. Although it is only anecdotal, most refugees would prefer to live in their country of birth: they just do not want to return to be persecuted, tortured or killed. In our treatment of them – desperate, defenceless and traumatised – we identify something of ourselves.

Notes

1 ABC Television, 'The 7.30 Report', 'Australia a new target for displaced Iraqis', 15 November 1999, <www.abc.net.au/7.30/stories/s66377.htm>.

2 In 1999-2000.

3 The Convention relating to the Status of Refugees, Article 1, defines a refugee as a person who ' … owing to well-founded fear of being persecuted for reasons of race, religion, nationality, membership of a particular social group or political opinion, is outside the country of his nationality and is unable, or owing to such fear, is unwilling to avail himself of the protection of that country; or who, not having a nationality and being outside the country of his former habitual residence as a result of such events, is unable or, owing to such fear, is unwilling to return to it'.

4 Australasian Correctional Management, the then operator of Australia's detention centres.

5 Australian Minister for Immigration, Philip Ruddock, to the Australian Anglican Synod, 27 July 2001.

6 Australian Minister for Immigration, Philip Ruddock, to the Australian Parliament, 19 February 2002, quoted in Fr Frank Brennan SJ, 'Australia's Refugee Policy – Facts, Needs and Limits,' Refugees, Morality and Public Policy: The Jesuit Lenten Seminars 2002 and 2000; Frank Brennan, Jim Carlton and others; David Lovell Publishing; 2002, pp 9-10.

7 UNHCR Executive Committee (EXCOM) Conclusion No 44 (XXXVII) 1986.

Index